DATE			

JAPANESE NEW RELIGIONS IN THE WEST

Cover kanji: Japanese characters for wa – harmony / peace

Japanese New Religions in the West

Edited by
Peter B. Clarke
&
Jeffrey Somers

JAPAN
LIBRARY
Sandgate, Folkestone, Kent

JAPANESE NEW RELIGIONS IN THE WEST

JAPAN LIBRARY
Knoll House, 35 The Crescent
Sandgate, Folkestone, Kent CT20 3EE

Japan Library is an imprint of Curzon Press Ltd
St John's Studios, Church Road, Richmond, Surrey, TW9 2QA

First published 1994
© Japan Library/Curzon Press 1994

British Library Cataloguing in Publication Data

A CIP catalogue record for this book
is available from the British library

ISBN: 1-873410-24-7 [Cloth edition]

Typeset by Bookman in Goudy Old Style 11 on 12pt
Printed and bound in England by Bookcraft, Midsomer Norton, Avon

Contents

Preface

IT IS today a well-known fact that Japanese influence is considerable in the fields of car manufacturing, electronics and other elements of the 'material' culture of the Western world. Less is known about the influence and impact of Japanese religion and spirituality in Europe, the United States, Latin America and elsewhere. The purpose of this volume is to offer a perspective on the growing strength, variety and dynamism of Japanese religion and culture in Western societies by focusing on the Japanese 'new' and 'new, new' religions that are now established across the United States, Europe and Latin America. These movements are also found increasingly in the countries of Eastern Europe, including Russia.

Aware of such developments and interested in the reasons for the rise, appeal and fortunes of the 'new' and 'new, new' Japanese religions, the Centre for New Religions at King's College, University of London, brought together a group of experts in their particular fields at an international seminar to present their opinions on these and related matters. This volume, therefore, comprises these contributions as well as others which were provided by scholars who were unable to attend the seminar.

The editors are most grateful to them all for the time they freely gave to this project and for the care and attention they gave to their contributions. They would also like to thank King's College for providing the facilities for the seminar, all those who attended and all the support staff for making the occasion a success.

Finally, they would like to thank Japan Library/Curzon Press and in particular Paul Norbury for agreeing to publish the volume and for the courtesy, patience and understanding he has shown throughout.

PETER B. CLARKE and JEFFREY SOMERS
Centre for New Religions,
King's College, University of London, February 1994

CONVENTIONS

TERMINOLOGY OF 'NEW RELIGIONS'

shinkō-shūkyō = New religions (lit. newly-arisen religion)
shin-shūkyō = New religion
shin-shin-shūkyō = New, new religion
in general sense = new religion, new religious movement, etc.

PERSONAL NAMES

Japanese personal names are given in the standard order of family name followed by given name, except where otherwise indicated. Where a Japanese has Westernized his or her name – especially in the case of those Japanese living overseas – the name is given in the Western order of given name first.

List of Contributors

CARMEN BLACKER is former Lecturer in Japanese Studies, the Oriental Institute, University of Cambridge.

BRIAN BOCKING is Senior Lecturer in Religious Studies, Bath College of Higher Education.

PETER B. CLARKE is Senior Lecturer in the history and sociology of religion and Director of the Centre for New Religions, King's College, University of London; he also teaches the sociology of religion at the University of Oxford.

CATHERINE CORNILLE is Lecturer in Theology at the Catholic University of Louvain.

RICHARD GOMBRICH is Professor of Sanskrit, University of Oxford.

J. GORDON MELTON is Director of the Institute for the Study of American Religion at Santa Barbara, CA.

CONSTANCE A. JONES is Associate Professor, Sociology Department, Mills College, Oakland, CA.

J. H. KAMSTRA is Professor at the Centre for Asian Studies, University of Amsterdam.

REVEREND DAISHIN MORGAN, OBE, is Abbot of Throsselhole Priory, Soto Zen Monastery, Northumberland.

MICHAEL PYE is Professor of Religious Studies, University of Lancaster.

JEFFREY SOMERS is a Research Scholar at the Centre for New Religions, King's College, University of London, and is a Fellow of the Royal Asiatic Society.

1

Japanese 'New' and 'New, New' Religions : An Introduction

PETER B. CLARKE & JEFFREY SOMERS

THE BEGINNINGS OF THE JAPANESE NEW RELIGIONS

LONG ISOLATED, Japan for some time now has been expanding its economic, technological and cultural influence abroad and, more recently, its religions – particularly its 'new' religions (*shin-shūkyō*). To date, there has been little by way of scholarly research on the spread, appeal and impact of these new religions beyond the shores of Japan and thus one of the main reasons that the present volume, consisting of contributions from a number of outstanding scholars in this field, has been assembled to fill this gap.

The volume is not exclusively concerned with the Japanese new religious movements outside Japan in the West. There is, of necessity, some discussion of the Japanese context itself in order to ensure that the reader has the background knowledge to understand this new and interesting development in the modern history of Japanese religion. What cannot be ignored is its steady advancement overseas with the aim of transforming people's lives by influencing the major issues of the modern world such as those of peace and war, attitudes to work and the environment, as well as individual health, well-being and prosperity.

The first studies of new religious movements in Japan began to appear in the 1950s. Prior to this, such movements were treated variously: some as quasi-religions – examples being Ōmotokyō and Seichō no Ie, and others as sectarian offshoots of Shinto and Buddhism – Tenrikyō and Konkōkyō being Shinto-linked examples, while Risshōkōseikai is linked to Buddhism.[1]

The terms *shinkō-shūkyō* (newly-arisen religion) and *shin-shūkyō* (new religion) came into use among journalists and scholars in the 1950s, and since the 1960s the latter term has been the more widely used of the two, with the former having a somewhat pejorative nuance. There is also a third label in use and that is the controversial term 'new, new religions' (*shin-shin-shūkyō*) which is intended to indicate a more recent stage in the development of the 'new' religions and is applied in particular to those movements such as Mahikari, Shinnyoen and Agonshū that rapidly increased their membership in the 1970s and 1980s while others such as Sōka Gakkai were considered to have peaked.

Controversy likewise surrounds the terms 'newly arisen' and 'new' religions. Depending on the angle from which they are observed many of the movements referred to by scholars as 'new' religions can be interpreted as either 'old' or 'new' or 'new, new'. If seen from the perspective of their content, for example, certain Japanese new religions, as will be seen shortly below, share much in common with the established Shinto and Buddhist traditions. This withstanding the fact that there is a sense in which the movements under discussion in this volume and others of a similar kind are 'new' or 'new, new' religions from the perspective of their organization, methods of evangelization and response to tradition and modernity, among other things.

There is, however, the additional problem of establishing a chronological framework of 'new' and 'new, new' religions. Four suggestions have been made regarding periodization, the first of which looks to the beginning of the nineteenth century as the starting point. Those who take this position point to the rise and popular appeal at this point in time of new religions based on mountain worship such as Fuji-kō. The second proposed starting date is the middle years of the nineteenth century when Kurozumikyō, Tenrikyō and Konkōkyō began to attract followers. The principal reason for this choice of starting point is that all three movements were to have a great influence on later Japanese new religious movements. For similar reasons others look to the beginning of the twentieth century as the most appropriate starting point stressing the importance of the influence of Ōmotokyō and Reiyūkai on 'new' religions in Japan. The fourth position on the starting date suggests the beginning of the post-World War II era when the many new movements began to flourish with the introduction of the principles of religious freedom and the separation of 'Church' and State.

There are problems with all four starting points. For example, it could be argued that the 'new' movements of the beginning of the nineteenth century that were to influence later ones were too few to constitute a solid basis for a trend in this direction. The third position which places the starting date at the beginning of the twentieth century overlooks the important influence of those earlier

2

movements mentioned when discussing position two. Against the fourth position it can be said that it pays insufficient attention to the continuity between pre- and post-World War II 'new' movements such as Sóka Gakkai. This leaves position two as the one favoured by many students of Japanese 'new' religions.[2]

Problems do not end with dating; the question of what to include in the category of 'new' religion is also difficult. The point has already been made that the 'new' religions draw heavily on the established religions for their teachings. Also, there are no clear and precise ground rules for distinguishing between a renewal movement within an established religion and a 'new' religion as such. Many observers adopt the position that if the movement in question has a new founder and a new name then it is new although it might serve the same functions as the older movement from which it has emerged.

Moreover, there is the added difficulty of distinguishing a 'new' movement from a folk religion and in this case there is a tendency to make a distinction between the two on the basis of size, organization and degree of novelty in ideals and aims. Very roughly, a movement that is almost entirely traditional in outlook and goals, that is small in size and one in which followers relate to the leader as 'clients' is perhaps more appropriately classified as a folk religion than a 'new' religion. Here we can delineate some of the more general and frequently shared characteristics of the 'new' and 'new, new' religions before outlining their chief distinguishing features.

GENERAL CHARACTERISTICS OF THE 'NEW' AND
'NEW, NEW' RELIGIONS

When considered in the Western context the 'new' and 'new, new' religions appear to parallel more closely the modern Christian revivalist movements than, for example, the new religions of Indian origin or the so-called 'Self-Religions'.[3] Many of them, as already indicated, form part of an ongoing historical process and what is new about them is not to be found in their content so much as in their emergence as socio-religious organizations with the aim of the reworking and revitalizing of traditional beliefs and practices for the purpose of ensuring their relevance to daily life at a time of unprecedented change in all spheres.

Looked at from this perspective the majority of 'new' and 'new, new' Japanese religions fit the category of manipulationist movements as described by Bryan Wilson.[4] That is, their main concern is with the provision of a modern, relevant faith in a society whose

3

traditional belief systems are not easily accommodated within the new conditions created by the rapid process of urbanization and industrialization which Japan has experienced over the past one hundred and fifty years and particularly since World War Two. Moreover, as a result of the war, Japan has had to completely reevaluate how it sees itself and how it presents itself to the wider world, the 'new' and 'new, new' religions often presenting it as peacemaker and protector of the environment.

Other shared features of the 'new' and 'new, new' religions include the emphasis they place on spiritual healing, on miracles and on the importance of ensuring that the ancestors are at rest. Most, moreover, are built around the personality of a charismatic founder usually regarded as an *ikigami*, that is one possessed by a deity. The differences between these religions, a topic that will be touched on below, can often be attributed to the differences in the personality of the founder or leader in question.

With few notable exceptions these religious movements tend to be highly syncretistic holding to a mixture of beliefs and practices derived from a number of Japanese traditional religious sources and in some cases also from outside Japan, for example, from Christianity, from the American New Thought movement of the late nineteenth century and from Western occult sources. Not only do most have a strong faith in the continuing presence and power of the spirits of the dead to cause harm if left unpacified but almost all are convinced of their power to purify and heal. This attention to the spirits of the dead and to the ancestors is also expressive of the view that life and death are not polar opposites and at the same time it can be interpreted as an affirmation of the primacy of life over death. It also has to be understood in the context of the link between shamanism and ancestor worship that is to be found in many 'new' and 'new, new' Japanese religions.

Almost all of the 'new' and the 'new, new' movements are millennarian stressing that the new earthly paradise of peace, harmony, happiness and plenty is near at hand for those who follow its precepts and this creates among followers a spirit of enthusiasm and optimism.

DISTINGUISHING FEATURES OF JAPANESE 'NEW'
AND 'NEW, NEW' RELIGIONS

While the 'new' and 'new, new' religions pursue, albeit with varying degrees of endeavour and emphasis, the most elemental goals of Japanese religion – the attainment of personal well-being, the purification of the souls of the departed and the veneration of

4

ancestors – they also modify the content and reshape the overall style, the form and the approach to recruitment and, to some degree, to the content of this religion. The modern architectural style of their places of worship is but one mark of the distinctiveness of the 'new' and the 'new, new' religions. The emphasis placed on and the energy put into recruitment is another. Although personal contact is the main means of recruitment many movements are very hardworking on university campuses spreading their message.

The message itself though derived as previously noted from old sources does contain 'new' emphases and elements including the stress on pacificism, environmental care and protection and world transformation. These 'new' and 'new, new' movements also make great use of the mass media and modern technology to communicate their message and enlarge their following. But in their pursuit and use of the benefits of modernity for this and other purposes tradition is not neglected. Although rarely valued purely for its own sake, tradition is drawn upon as a spiritual, psychological and emotional resource to cope with the stresses and strains of modernity.

The Japanese 'new' and 'new, new' religions are contemporary expressions of Japanese religiosity that in certain respects constitute a critique of the older, more established traditions. Unlike the latter they have little or no history of involvement with the Establishment and some even experienced banning and persecution by the latter. Furthermore, they are often less hierarchical and less dominated by a priestly class thereby assigning much more importance to the lay members. Indeed, as a leading spokesperson for Seichō no Ie pointed out, they could quite correctly be interpreted as the vanguards of the development of non-establishment, essentially lay spirituality and religion in Japan, a movement which began in the second half of the nineteenth century.[5]

Another dimension of these religions related to the above which gives them the character of 'newness' is their provision of techniques by means of which members can secure the benefits to be derived from the sacred teachings and practices which the founders of the movements have uncovered. The teachings are often presented as entirely new in the sense that they are put forward as the first ever correct interpretation of a particular sacred text or tradition.

Thus, 'new' or 'new, new' movements sometimes see themselves as presenting what can amount to a radical, alternative version of a long-held belief or set of beliefs. Agonshū is another example of this. Although it had been in existence for some time previously, in 1978 its founder Kiriyama claimed he had discovered new, hidden truths by reading early Buddhist texts known as the Āgama sutras, texts which had been given little attention in Japan. Able to discern the hidden, inner meaning of these texts Kiriyama uncovered a direct and rapid road to Buddhahood for the living and just as importantly for the dead. Agonshū places great stress on the pacification of the spirits of the dead and the need to ensure that they attain Buddhahood (*jōbutsu*) if the living are to be at peace and secure well being and prosperity.[6]

The 'new'and 'new, new' religions in discovering new truths in old texts in this way are attacking the older, established religions by pointing out that they have failed to understand the essence of the truth they preach. In other words they constitute reform movements in this as well as in other ways already mentioned.

They also tend to be more international and universalistic in their vision and outreach than the older, more established religions, regarding it as their mission to bring peace and fulfilment to the whole world. This in part explains their missionary endeavour in many countries outside Japan. It is worth noting here that as Japan expands as an economic power so also Japanese religions are moving out to other lands and for reasons not totally dissimilar from those behind the expansion of Christianity that accompanied European economic and political expansion in the late nineteenth century.

Agonshū is regarded as one of the 'new, new' religions and others are Mahikari and Byakkō Shinkōkai. The term 'new, new' does not suggest a radical discontinuity between those movement to which it is applied and the 'new religions'. It is not even chronologically meaningful in every case. Agonshū's roots, for example, can be traced back to the early 1950s in much the same way as the Church of Scientology's roots can be traced back to the mental health concern known as Dianetics. However, Agonshū did begin to flourish in the late 1970s and throughout the 1980s, while movements such as Sōka Gakkai and Seichō no Ie were considered to have peaked. It is chiefly this factor, and their greater emphasis on traditional spiritual explanations of life accompanied by a strong belief in miracles, the greater degree of importance attached by them to ancestors and to tradition in general and their strikingly lively, thrusting, dynamic approach to the dissemination of their message – making for a close resemblance to the Christian televangelist Churches of North America – that has earned them the label 'new, new' religions (*shin-shin-shūkyō*).

THE APPEAL OF THE 'NEW' AND THE 'NEW, NEW' RELIGIONS

Since most of the contributors to this volume spell out the various aspects of the appeal of the 'new' and/or the 'new, new' religion

6

which they are discussing, there will only be the most general outline of this question here.

Although grounded ritually and doctrinally for the most part in older Japanese religions both the 'new' and the 'new, new' religions are much more concerned with the effects on the individual and society of modernity and contemporary change. They are in search of a new way of responding to modernity and offer many Japanese – perhaps as many as forty per cent of them – beliefs and practices that enable them to respond to the rapid economic, political and cultural changes that their country has witnessed during the past one hundred and fifty years and particularly since the end of World War II. At the highest level of generality this is principally why they appeal. And this is one very important reason why they are worth our attention: the 'new' and 'new, new' movements not only provide the observer with a perspective for understanding the response to the rapid cultural, economic, political and social changes that Japan has experienced in recent history but are also indicators of the direction in which Japanese society and culture as a whole are moving at present.

The 'new' and 'new, new' movements also appeal at the more personal, individual and local level for a variety of other reasons including the above. In certain circumstances the individual is offered the means in the form of rituals to control and modify the impact of changes that are shaping and directing her/his life. Movements also provide a community structure and a sense of purpose to those in urban areas without close links with family or friends.

The modern garb in which they present Japanese core values such as the importance of the pacification of the ancestors and the spirits of the dead, notions of spiritual causality of illness, the emphasis on this-worldly success and happiness, also attracts many. And those in the West who join these movements often stress the relevance of the beliefs and practices of the movement concerned with daily life. They are also attracted by the notion of spiritual causality and the control over their life that this explanation of illness offers. The rituals are also said to enable a development of a sense of self-awareness and self-identity in contrast with the rather impersonal nature of the rituals and limited explanations of sickness and failure of the modern world. The concern of movements with peace and environmental issues likewise attract and give members and would-be members the sense that far from being powerless and incapacitated by modernity they can actually control and harness it in ways compatible with personal happiness and the good life here on earth.

7

IMPACT IN THE WEST

As the foregoing suggests, there is variety and difference in the world of Japanese 'new' and 'new, new' religions and this in part explains the diverse nature of their appeal. The movements do not necessarily appeal for the same reasons to Japanese in Japan and those abroad, or to Japanese and non-Japanese wherever they may be. Very broadly speaking, in the Japanese context many of these movements display the main characteristics of revitalization movements: they rework and reshape traditional beliefs, rituals and symbols in such a way as to make them relevant to the social, cultural and spiritual needs and aspirations of the present. Outside Japan their appeal is necessarily different. For the most part, with a few notable exceptions, the 'new' and 'new, new' Japanese religions that have established themselves in countries in the West are confined in terms of membership mostly to Japanese living abroad and their spouses or relatives who are often European or American. This is the case in, for example, the United States where only Zen has found mass appeal outside the American-Japanese community. However, Sōka Gakkai membership in the West as a whole, which continues to increase steadily, is largely non-Japanese and this holds for a number of other movements, at least in certain countries. For example, it is probably true of Mahikari in continental Europe. In Brazil most recruits in the south of the country are Brazilian-Japanese while elsewhere, including the northeast, the majority of members are Brazilians of non-Japanese descent. This is largely due to the fact that there are relatively few Brazilian-Japanese outside the south of the country.

Less steeped in Japanese culture than other Japanese religions Zen has attracted the more intellectual types in the United States and the West as a whole. Other movements while not attracting as large a following as Zen have on the whole a much broader educational and social base. Sōka Gakkai has members from a variety of social, educational and ethnic backgrounds. It also has almost equal numbers of female and male members which is somewhat unusual in that most movements are either majority female or male. The membership of Seichō-no-Ie in northeastern Brazil is largely female and middle-aged. Most recruits to Zen and other Japanese movements in the West are young adults. Zen, as Morgan shows, has considerable appeal in Britain whereas in the United States, the influence of Suzuki, Humphreys and Watts has been considerable. British Zen has close links with Japan and the United States and for some time followed the guidance of Watts who stressed its intellectual side and the direct method to *satori* (enlightenment).

8

This produced what came to be known as 'Beat Zen' which had recourse to hallucinatory drugs to assist in the process of attaining enlightenment. Zen has since shed its quasi-intellectual, hippy, drop-out image and has moved on to attract a much more variable following. There are numerous Zen centres in Britain today and this holds true also for Europe as a whole.

In the Western world and Brazil, which has the largest population of Japanese descent outside Japan, there is much interest in the spiritual explanations and remedies for illness, lack of success and misfortune that the Japanese 'new' and 'new, new' religions provide. The experimental character of these religions also has an attraction because it aligns with developments in the conversion style in the Western world where people are tending increasingly to see religion as a rich resource and to go in search of a faith which they will then test out to discern whether or not it is suited to their needs and interests of a spiritual, psychological, emotional and material kind. Experience has become a major criterion of truth and falsehood in matters of religion and spirituality.

Several of the contributions to this volume point to the inclusivist nature of Japanese religion whether 'old' or 'new' and this is another feature of its appeal in the West where, with the exception of the fundamentalist minorities, rigid, highly systematized, exclusivist belief systems are being passed over in favour of more flexible and open-ended systems which allow the individual to espouse the beliefs and rituals of more than one religion at a time.

With the exception of Zen, the numbers of non-Japanese joining 'new' and 'new, new' Japanese religions in the West and elsewhere have not been vast. Brazil is something of a special case for, as previously noted, it has a large population, estimated at almost one million people, that is either Japanese or of Japanese descent. Of course, attempting to assess the impact of a movement in terms of its numerical strength is of little value. Very few 'new' religions whatever their country of origin have made great numerical gains in the West. Their influence is almost always subtle and indirect. Movements such as Sōka Gakkai reach millions through their conferences, cultural and educational programmes and literature – the central element in a very important form of conversion in modern society known as intellectual conversion. This comes about as an individual develops an interest in and sympathy for a movement through reading its literature and this often leads on to membership. Where membership is not put on a formal basis there sometimes develops an informal relationship with a movement which can involve the performance on a private, individual basis of spiritual practices and the giving of donations.

Although not as yet numerically very large the 'new' and 'new, new' Japanese religions have already begun to influence ideas and attitudes towards work, the environment, peace and health, and different areas of life in the West, and are perceived by growing numbers as offering above all else not only a system of rituals and beliefs for coping with the stresses and strains of contemporary society but also for maximizing the benefits to be derived from living in a post-modern age.

CONTRIBUTIONS

As previously noted, many Japanese new religions are 'syncretistic' in that they are composed of Shinto and Buddhist teachings and practices. Gombrich in his account of three salient features of Japanese Buddhism in comparative perspective looks at the relation of Buddhism in Japan and elsewhere to other 'common' or 'traditional' religions suggesting that it is always 'accretive'. Likewise, Gombrich argues, the Buddhist view of ritual is similar from one Buddhist society to another. Japanese Buddhism, however, is in certain ways very different from other forms of Buddhism and Gombrich singles out as one of its distinctive features the role of its monks who, unlike their counterparts elsewhere, have assumed the functions of ritual specialists. A further interesting and relevant point made by Gombrich is the tendency among Japanese Buddhist sects to focus all their concentration and energies on one particular Buddhist text, an insight which, along with that of the Buddhist monk as ritual specialist, possibly goes some way to accounting for the rise of vast numbers of new religions in Japan.

Other contributors, including Blacker, have ploughed somewhat narrower furrows focusing on one specific 'new' or 'new, new' movement such as the as yet numerically very small 'new, new' Mother Goddess movement of Ryūgū Kazoku, which has formed around Fujita Himiko also known as Ryūgū Otohime, or such relatively very large and well-established 'new' religions like Sōka Gakkai and Seichō-no-Ie while others treat of the establishment of a whole range of 'new' and 'new, new' movements in a particular Western country. Ryūgū Otohime's movement like many of the 'new' and 'new, new' Japanese movements effectively combines tradition and innovation but, as Professor Blacker points out, it is singular and unusual in several of its claims among them the claim that the salvation of the world comes through the Mother Goddess.

Bocking, interestingly, presents the current controversy between Nichiren Shōshū and Sōka Gakkai as a version of a religious reformation along the lines of the Protestant Reformation in Europe in the sixteenth century. But in suggesting this comparative framework he offers numerous caveats including the different conceptions of priest and priest/laity relations in Japan and sixteenth-century Europe. Sóka Gakkai is the largest and internationally most successful of the Japanese lay movements established and legally recognised as it now is in over one hundred and twenty countries and Bocking looks at its future prospects in the West in the light of the 1991 conflict with Nichiren Shóshú, the priestly order that povides members with the *Gohonzon* or object of worship thought by many to be indispensable to attaining Buddhahood.

Bocking sees the conflict as one between traditionalism and modernism, hierarchy and egalitarianism, the priestly and lay class and the means of access to 'salvation', objective knowledge traditions and subjective understanding, collective authority and individualism, the sacred and the secular, in a new religious movement. He also suggests that these tensions reflect tensions in the wider Japanese society and this supports the point made above that the new movements are often useful perspectives for understanding what is happening in the wider world. Implicit in Blacker's contribution also is the suggestion that Ryúgú Otohime's recourse to spiritual explanations reflects a successful Japan more confident in itself and less prepared than previously to bypass its traditional explanations of illness and misfortune in favour of Western, rational, scientific accounts once deemed essential to the process of modernising the country's image abroad and highering its standing and status.

Few 'new' movements whether Japanese or from elsewhere survive for very long before splintering. Indeed, most of the movements discussed in this volume and the several hundred Japanese 'new' and 'new, new' movements known to exist today emerged, as already noted, out of other previously established 'new' movements.

All religions if they are to take root in foreign soil must adapt in terms of beliefs, practices and organizational style. A religion can of course over adapt and as a result fail or under adapt and fail. 'New' and 'new, new' religions from Japan are no exception. Many are initially very Japanese in content and outlook and largely without meaning and somewhat incomprehensible from the angle of another culture. Cornille shows how one 'new, new' movement, Mahikari, has dealt with this problem of particularism by drawing upon Christianity with a view to giving itself universal relevance.

The presence of Christianity in Japan's 'new' religions is discussed again by Kamstra who takes up the perplexing question of the origin and nature of the monotheistic idea in several of the first generation of Japanese 'new' religions which like Tenrikyō, Ōmoto and Konkōkyō which have deities that have monotheistic qualities. Kamstra attempts to trace the emergence through Japanese history of the monotheistic idea showing how Christian monotheistic notions modified by neo-Confucian and Buddhist influences contributed to the development of a Japanese kind of monotheism that the early 'new' movements drew upon. A new religion's appeal will vary from society to society and sometimes even within the same society. Miraculous healing is very frequently an important part of a movement's appeal as noted above. But Clarke suggests that in the case of Seichō-no-Ie which has a large following in Brazil it is the philosophy of positive thinking that has attracted most of its following in the northeast of the country. It is not the miraculous intervention that will turn things round that people seek but a strong belief in and sense of the power of 'self' to effect change at the personal and wider community level that people are seeking. If this interpretation is correct then this is an example of a 'new' religion operating as a secularising force in what is regarded as religious even mystical world.

Peace, as previously indicated, is a major concern of many Japanese 'new' and 'new, new' religions, as is personal, group, national and world identity and Pye's article on Byakkō Shinkōkai shows how a 'new, new' religion attempts to create both a culture of peace and is also a quest for a 'world identity' for Japan, demonstrating that it is not alone but at the very heart of a global peace process. The idea of Japan as the centre from which world peace will come forth to the rest of the globe, is found in other 'new' and 'new, new' religions including the above-mentioned Agonshū.

Somers' contribution covers a whole range of 'new' and 'new, new' Japanese religions in Britain, most of which are also found in the rest of Western Europe. Some movements have more success in one European country than another and this can be due to a variety of reasons including language, the strength or otherwise of the anti-cult lobby, and the structure of the society in question, some being more open and fragmented than others and therefore more easily penetrated. No movement has a large indigenous following in Europe. As Somers shows Sōka Gakkai has the largest following in Britain of about 5,000 members and is growing steadily if slowly. Membership is composed on the whole of local people. Other movements discussed by Somers include the Institute for Research in Human Happiness (Kōfuku no Kagaku) which has been in the West for only a very short time and has few non-Japanese members there. Seichō-no-Ie, present in Britain for considerably longer, has also failed to attract a local membership of non-Japanese but it does recruit a number of Brazilians most of whom made their first contact with the movement in Brazil.

In their detailed and thorough survey of Japanese 'new' and 'new, new' movements in the United States, Melton and Jones trace the first Japanese Buddhist temples there back to the late nineteenth century. The first 'new' religion to be established in the United States was Konkôkyô in 1919 among Japanese-Americans at Seattle and Tacoma, Washington. Of the many that have arrived since few have extended their base beyond the Japanese-American population. Zen, Milton and Jones point out, is the only Japanese religious movement to have become a mass movement in America. Although Macrobiotics which these contributors define as a 'new' religion has deeply penetrated American culture. Others that have moved beyond the Japanese-American base but not as successfully as Zen include Seichô-no-Ie and Sôka Gakkai. Unlike the pre-1991 situation in Japan the last mentioned movement has to all intents and purposes functioned like a lay movement since its arrival in the United States soon after World War Two.

CONCLUSIONS

While this volume would not claim to be exhaustive or in the case of every contribution highly original in terms of the form, content and ideas of 'new' and 'new, new' Japanese movements in the West, it does nevertheless break new ground in providing for the first time both detailed studies of a number of 'new' and 'new, new' movements and overviews of a whole range of such movements in Western countries. Both the researcher and interested observer of Japanese religious and cultural life should be able to find in this volume some exciting and thought-provoking interpretations of the rise, appeal and impact of the 'new' and 'new, new' Japanese religions. By studying these movements the student can acquire invaluable insights into the changing views and attitudes of Japan regarding itself and the wider world.

While certainly not the only or most direct way to understanding contemporary Japan and the role it seeks to play in the modern world it is undoubtedly one very fruitful approach to this question. Furthermore, although not necessarily representative of how the majority think, the new movements do shed light on what many Japanese and non-Japanese believe to be the most appropriate kind of response to the stresses and strains of modernity. Certainly, tradition must not be wiped out nor should faith in science and technology be allowed to displace explanation of a spiritual kind. At the same time modernity is not to be shunned. Tradition is no permanent escape from the modern world. The emphasis has to be on maximising the benefits to be derived from modern life without destroying tradition, whose emotional psychological and spiritual role is indispensable to this enterprise. The 'new', and 'new, new' movements also open a window on the kinds of Japanese thinking on self-development, health and peace and the care and protection of the environment. Perhaps, above all else, the rise of 'new' and 'new, new' religions provides insight into the growing tendency of people in Japan and the West to regard religion (once viewed by evolutionists, positivists and socialist reformers of the Marxian kind as irrelevant to progress) as an invaluable cultural resource in this 'high modern', or as others would prefer to describe it, post-modern age.

FOOTNOTES

1. Blackler, C. 'Millenarian Aspects of the New Religions in Japan', in D.H. Shiveley (ed) *Tradition and Modernization in Japanese Culture*. Princeton. Princeton University Press. 1971. pp. 579ff.

2. Inoue Nobutaka. 'Recent Trends in the Study of Japanese New Movements', in Inoue Nobutaka (ed) *New Religions*. Tokyo. Kokugakuin University. 1991. pp. 4–24.

3. Heelas, P. 'Western Europe: the Self Religions' in S.R. Sutherland and P.B. Clarke (eds) *The Study of Religion, Traditional and New Religion*. London. Routledge. 1991.

4. Wilson, B. *Religious Sects*. London/New York. Weidenfeld and Nicholson and McGraw-Hill. 1971.

5. Pers. comm. Tokyo. 7 July 1993.

6. Reader, I. *Religion in Contemporary Japan*. Basingstoke. Macmillan. 1991.

2

A Buddhologist's Impression of Japanese Buddhism

RICHARD GOMBRICH

THE FEATURES of Japanese Buddhism which strike a Buddhologist who has first learnt about Buddhism elsewhere are rather different from those that strike a Japanologist, even if the latter is an expert on Japanese Buddhism. That may be why I, who know something about the history of Buddhism in general but very little about Japanese Buddhism in particular, was asked to introduce this conference: I could offer a different perspective.

With considerable diffidence – for I am fully aware of my ignorance of all matters Japanese – I accordingly offer brief remarks on three salient features of Japanese Buddhism: its relation to other religions in the same culture; Japanese ritualism; and the role performance of the Buddhist clergy.

The first feature, I believe, is a respect in which Buddhism in Japan is just like Buddhism in every other country where it has a long history: it co-exists with (at least) one other religion in the life of the society and is always accretive.[1] Buddhism has from the outset concerned itself essentially with what theologians call 'ultimate concerns'. In its own vocabulary, it is supramundane, not worldly. It provides explanations of the moral universe and the individual's place in it. By contrast, it is little concerned with helping people through the crises of life in the world, or with providing ritual systems to mark calendrical events or stages in the individual's life-cycle. Thus, in traditionally Buddhist societies Buddhism does not, for example, provide a marriage ceremony, and marriage is defined as a secular matter. The only life crisis which it is normal for Buddhism to solemnise is death, because death is an apt occasion for pondering on ultimate concerns.

The distinction I am trying to draw is not alien to Christianity; it corresponds, for example, to the Christian distinction between spiritual prayer ('Lead us not into temptation') and petitionary prayer ('Give us this day our daily bread'). However, since Christianity is a religious system which answers to both sets of concerns, ordinary Christians do not need to be keenly aware of the distinction. Moreover, Christians naturally take their own religion as a model and assume that all religions will, like theirs, cater to both spiritual and worldly needs. This assumption is valid, on the whole, for monotheistic religions like Islam, but it is quite wrong for Buddhism. At least, it was quite wrong until the Christians came along. In many parts of the world the earlier ideas of what a religion should be have been influenced by contact with the Christian West, and the unthinking assumptions of Christians have too often been adopted unawares by Buddhists – and those who study them. That this marks a watershed in the history of Buddhism is one of the main arguments I have tried to make in a book about religious change among Sinhala Buddhists.[2]

The system which complements Buddhism by dealing with matters of this world varies from country to country. In Japan it is called Shinto. In the Theravadin societies of Sri Lanka and continental Southeast Asia it has no all-embracing indigenous name, and modern anthropologists have used such names as 'the spirit religion' and 'the spirit cults'; in one book[3] I laid a different emphasis by calling it 'communal religion'. Despite the lack of a local name for the system as a whole, it is indeed a system and closely comparable to Shinto. This 'worldly' religious system hinges on interaction with supernatural beings (both gods and lesser spirits) who are normally contacted through officiants (priests, of either gender). The cult is closely tied to local particulars, and states of spirit possession tend to figure in it quite prominently, though whether these are defined as good (giving direct access to the divine) or bad (demonic and to be exorcised) varies with circumstances.

When, therefore, Japanologists say that Japanese Buddhists have two religions, because they hold Shinto weddings but Buddhist funerals, they are pointing to a feature which has been common to Buddhists everywhere. Since Buddhism is a pure soteriology, those Buddhists who live in the world, and to the extent that they live in the world,[4] need another system to supply their worldly needs, notably that orderly continuation of society which marriage is designed to ensure. With such a system, I repeat, Buddhism is complementary; it cannot co-exist in the same way with another soteriology, such as Islam or Christianity. At the same time, however, the complementarity between Buddhism and the local spirit religion is hierarchic: Buddhism, from its own point of view as a soteriology, is superior to the spirit religion and in a way subsumes it, since it sets the cosmological framework and prescribes the overarching values. The Japanese tradition of attaching Buddhist priests to Shinto shrines to bring the gods within the Buddhist fold and thus serve their spiritual needs, a practice which was stopped by the modernism of the Meiji Restoration, exemplifies this hierarchic complementarity, as does the Theravadin system of offering the merit accruing from Buddhist acts of piety to the gods in exchange for their material help and protection.

I indicated above that Buddhism may even share the religious arena with more than one religion. What constitutes 'a religion' is a matter of definition and almost bound to be contentious, both among the participants and among their academic observers; there is no simple 'right answer' to such a question. Often the question is debated in terms of history, of the origins of institutions and ideas. Thus the non-Buddhist part of the religion of Sinhala Buddhists is sometimes divided into 'Hindu' elements of identified Indian origin and a residual 'folk' element, assumed to be indigenous. I assume that the residue is mainly the product of our ignorance; its elements have entered the culture at a distance – distant in terms of time and/or of social space – from foci of literacy and the consequent opportunities for creating permanent records. I harbour similar suspicions towards attempts to sub-divide Shinto, for example, into Chinese and indigenous Japanese elements.[5]

For the next step in my analysis, however, I do wish to make a distinction within Shinto; but it is a distinction in terms of function, not of history. It is the distinction between State Shinto and the system of local cults. State Shinto, I am aware, is a religion officially obsolete since its defeat in World War Two; but there is still a Shinto cult, however muffled, which centres on the Emperor. This court cult occupies an analogous position in Japanese religious life to brahminical court ceremonial which is still practised in Thailand, as it used to be in all the Theravada countries. The brahmins imported from India to service royal cults in Southeast Asia formed a separate priesthood and offered entirely distinct rituals from the practitioners of the rest of the local spirit cults. In Japan, by contrast, the Emperor has stood at the apex of the Shinto cults.

It is therefore not surprising that after the Meiji Restoration (1868), when the cult of the Emperor acquired so much emphasis for political reasons, State Shinto tried to shake off its position of hierarchic subordination to Buddhism and the government even persecuted Buddhism. This may show the precise point at which Japanese religious pluralism is distinctive. From the Buddhist point of view, as I have explained, the complementarity between Buddhism and Shinto is hierarchic. But Shinto has occasionally disputed, as the spirit religions of Theravada countries have not, that hierarchic relationship, so that Shinto and Buddhism have sometimes been rivals. It is indeed possible that the post-Meiji persecution of Buddhism by State Shinto could be seen as but an example of a more diffuse phenomenon: Dr David Gellner has written to me of 'the sheer number of different types or degrees of accommodation between Buddhism and Shintoism, going all the way from hostility and purism at either end to complete amalgamation'. That, however, would require a monograph.

In considering Japanese ritualism one again has to guard against Christian – here particularly Protestant – assumptions. Ever since the Reformation, when Luther championed faith against works as crucial for salvation, those from a Protestant cultural background have assumed that it is the head and the heart – ideas and emotions – which alone count as truly religious. Since Buddha held much the same position, in that he regarded ritual as irrelevant to salvation, it is tempting to see Buddhism in the same way. Not only will the observer from a Protestant culture assume it is natural for there to be a religious monopoly in a given society; he will also assume that all that goes on in the religious sphere must be part of a coherent pattern. When it comes to ritual – if the observer can even bear to focus on something he considers so lowly and uninteresting! – he will assume the ritual to be a kind of primitive technology, performed in the simple belief that a given rite will produce a given result.

These assumptions do not fit the picture of Japanese religious behaviour drawn by Ronald Dore in his fine book, *City Life in Japan*. Dore, who did fieldwork in 1951 in a ward of central Tokyo, reports:

> The question: 'What religion are you in your family?' produces in overwhelming proportions the reply 'Buddhism', which refers to the fact that a family has a family temple on whose services it calls if need be. On the other hand, the question: 'Do you personally have any religious belief?' produces eighty-eight noes out of a hundred.[7]

So, 88% of Dore's respondents claim to have no religious beliefs at all. When Dore asked them to explain their acts of worship at the domestic shrine, many found the very question confusing.

Dore's results have often been replicated since. For example, Ian Reader reports that 75% of Japanese pray to the *kami* (Shinto gods) at New Year, but only 21% believe that they exist, though a further 15% concede that they might.[8]

From these figures we might jump to the conclusion that the only motive these respondents required for their actions was conformity: following precedent. But there is more to it than that. Dore also reports that Confucian scholars in ancient China:

> . . .clearly expressed that the spirits 'have neither substance nor

shadow', but that rites are performed '*as if* the deceased enjoyed the sacrifice' . . . because sacrificial rites represent 'a state of mind in which our thoughts turn with longing (towards Heaven, the Ancestors) . . . It is the climax of all those ritual prescriptions we embody in patterned behaviour.'[9]

As Dore goes on to say, the Confucians thus had 'a conscious "sociological" awareness of the function of rites for society'. And, I would add, for the individuals in that society. Dore attended a lecture on a Shinto shrine:

The only positive statement of any belief was . . . that the object of worshipping at an Inari shrine was to purify one's heart so that one could face the daily task in a true spirit of piety.[10]

This I find reminiscent of what is the only passage in the Buddhist canon, so far as I am aware, in which Buddha discusses the worship of Buddhist sacralia. The passage is specifically directed to the laity. The Buddha is supposed to have said, shortly before his death, that if people offered flowers or incense to a stupa, or gave it a lick of paint, it would make their thoughts serene, and so help them to get to heaven.[11] (Heaven is not the ultimate goal for Buddhists, who must hope to escape from rebirth in *any* condition; but it is better than most of the other possibilities.)

In my fieldwork among monks in Sri Lanka I found the same rationale for acts of worship. This at least suggests that a sophisticated view of ritual as beneficial in itself, regardless of any magical power or metaphysical meaning, may be a widely diffused part of the Buddhist tradition.

To obviate misunderstanding, however, let me add that this is not the only view of ritual held by Buddhists. Far from it. Traditional Japanese Buddhism is full of rites which aim to cancel or modify the results of past bad actions and so evade the law of *karma*.

Concerning the first two of my three selected features of Japanese Buddhism I have argued that they find parallels throughout the Buddhist world. When it comes to the role of performance of the Sangha (Buddhist monks and nuns), on the other hand, I find the differences as striking as the similarities.

The Buddha expected those who took his message seriously to renounce the world and join the Sangha, the monastic community which he founded. Sympathetic laity were necessary if the Sangha was to find material support, but the Indian tradition of supporting all 'holy men' would ensure that. The Buddha certainly considered lay people capable of spiritual progress, even, in exceptional cases, of achieving Enlightenment; but the Theravadin tradition that an enlightened layman would either join the Sangha or die within the day[12] precisely measures the posited degree of incompatibility between lay life and spiritual perfection. The concept of Buddhist Enlightenment is that it combines two achievements: total control of the emotions and a kind of gnosis, the one being held to entail the other. The normal means to this dual accomplishment is meditation. In Mahayana Buddhism the gnosis came to be emphasised, but in the earliest Buddhism, in practice if not in theory, it seems to have been the other way round. Total emotional control is hard to combine with family life and economic activity, while living conditions in ancient Indian homes, as in most or all traditional societies, can hardly have been ideal for practising meditation.

That truly dedicated Buddhists join the Sangha is a norm preserved in most Buddhist traditions and societies. A member of the Sangha traditionally had a dual role. On the one hand it was his or her duty to strive for salvation (Enlightenment); to provide an environment suited to that striving was the Sangha's primary *raison d'être*. On the other hand, the Sangha, through its members, also served to perpetuate Buddhism and give future generations a chance to achieve holiness in their turn. To this end monks and nuns had to learn and teach the sacred texts. (The institution predates the writing of texts in India, so we cannot call them 'scriptures'.) The Sangha thus became, after the introduction of writing, a literate, educated class – the only such class in relatively homogeneous Buddhist societies such as Sri Lanka and Tibet, a sub-group of the literate class in China.

After what has been said above, it should be clear why in this institutional dichotomy between monks and laity, priests would normally be found on the lay side of the divide. Priests, after all, are functionaries who mediate between men and gods. There is perhaps no Buddhist society in which all monks have remained totally devoid of priestly functions. Moreover, one may argue that in societies in which tantric Buddhism has been dominant – Nepal and Tibet – the dichotomy between monk and layman has become less important than that between initiates and non-initiates.[13] In Japan, however, the distinction between monk and layman as traditionally conceived has been blurred, and deliberately so. The main blurring was the work of Shinran, who at the beginning of the thirteenth century, having himself been ordained as a monk, married a nun and had children by her. Shinran described himself as 'neither monk nor layman',[14] a self-description which I would be extremely surprised to find in any other Buddhist society before modern times. In the Jōdo Shinshū (True Sect of the Pure Land), which he founded, the clergy have ever since been married, and indeed practised hereditary succession to temples. Shinran, like other contemporaries (including Nichiren), believed that he was living in the final age of the Doctrine, in which the Buddha's teaching was destined to disappear from the face of the earth; and that in that corrupt age the *mores* of the Sangha would have declined so far that they were in any case laymen in all but show.[15] Like others who believe in historical inevitability (one has only to think of Communists) he saw nothing inconsistent in giving the process of history a shove in its predestined direction. To put it another way, Shinran held that the true tradition of the Sangha was dead already so that it was wrong to maintain a false pretence.

It is important to realise that monks and nuns in the other Buddhist sects of Japan remained celibate until the late nineteenth century, when they were forced to marry in the persecution alluded to above. Some are still celibate today, but marriage and succession on the Jōdo Shinshū pattern have become usual.

In the late nineteenth century, as modern knowledge spread through the population, the Buddhist clergy presumably lost most of their prestige as an educated class. The Sangha's secondary role as preserver of Buddhist texts and values has become rather unimportant under modern conditions. (Printing has been an important factor in democratising culture, but whereas that came very late to Theravadin societies it has been a feature of Japanese Buddhism almost from the beginning.) Its primary role, as a haven for holiness, is not subject to the same obsolescence. However, I believe that the role performance that Japanese now expect of their clergy is to act as a ritual specialist rather than moral exemplar, let alone as religious virtuoso. If I am right, Japan has perhaps departed further from the Buddhist norm in this respect than have other Buddhist societies. I must stress that what I am referring to is not whether individual monks and nuns are in fact virtuous or spiritual – clearly some are, and are revered for it – but what the laity expect of them by way of role performance.

If the Buddhist clergy in Japan are regarded above all as ritual specialists, this has several causes; but I suggest that one of them lies in the kind of sect formation which is specific to Buddhism in Japan. Unlike Buddhist sects elsewhere, Japanese sects regard a particular text or small group of texts as being of such paramount importance that they virtually ignore the rest. For instance, the Tendai sect (predominantly) and the Nichiren sects (exclusively) worship the Lotus Sutra; the Pure Land sects worship the two *Sukhāvatī-vyūha sūtras* (especially the longer one) and one other; the Kegon sect is concerned only with the *Avatamsaka-sūtra* (the Flower Garland Sutra; *Jap. Kegon-kyō*), which is also of great importance for the Sōtō

Zen sect. My point here is not that the texts tend to be more worshipped than understood; that can happen anywhere, especially where the scriptures are in a foreign language (as here the texts are in classical Chinese translations from the original Sanskrit). What concerns me is something more startling to a Buddhologist: that for each sect the content of its own text or texts is virtually coterminus with the range of Buddhist ideas.

In the words of early Buddhism, a Buddhist is to perfect himself in both 'learning and conduct'. Ethics are the foundation of the holy life. The layman has to keep five moral precepts, which are formulated as undertakings; the monk or nun to live by an elaborate code of conduct known (in Sanskrit and Pali) as the *vinaya* and embodied in a long text of that name. The monk or nun also has to learn and understand certain doctrines, which are embodied in other texts, most of them known as *sūtras*. Knowledge of both *vinaya* and *sūtras*, both in their letter and their meaning, is traditionally considered a precondition for the practice of meditation and the attainment of spiritual progress – except in Japan. Elsewhere, even the Buddhist layman is supposed to know by heart and understand certain formulae, of which the most basic are the five moral undertakings, and he knows that he must both recite and try to abide by those undertakings.

In all Buddhist traditions, particular monks and their pupils have specialised in sets of texts; in the days before writing, when large bodies of material had to be preserved orally, this was a practical necessity. However, in those far-off days no Buddhist would have been unaware that the different bodies of texts were complementary, and in particular that the *vinaya* and the *sūtras*, dealing with conduct and doctrine respectively, were both equally essential for all members of the Sangha. Not so, however, in Japan. There the *vinaya* is the exclusive cultural property of one tiny sect (the Ritsu): they learn that text alone and no other sect learns the *vinaya* at all. This makes it rather less surprising that Japanese monks have at times regarded it as right to kill even fellow Buddhists, though any killing at all both violates the first precept and is a *vinaya* offence so grave that it should lead automatically to exclusion from the Sangha.

Obviously, I am not suggesting that the Japanese clergy have no code of conduct; every social role in traditional Japan entailed distinctive behaviour. Among the Sangha, the distinctive code of behaviour inculcated at the Sōtō Zen training centre at Eiheiji has had a wide influence. Nevertheless, even if that (and other examples) could be argued to be analogous to the *vinaya*, it certainly is not the *vinaya*, and contrasts with the *vinaya* in laying far more emphasis on ritual and less on ethics.

My purpose here is to draw attention to this feature of Japanese Buddhism; fully to explain it lies beyond my scope. Let me add, however, that I guess one element of the explanation to lie in the Lotus Sutra. That text was composed in India at some time in the first two centuries CE, or even a little earlier; the *terminus ante quem* is 255, the date of its first translation into Chinese. It was translated into Chinese six times.[16] In the translation by Kumārajīva (early fifth century) it has been of great importance in Chinese and of supreme importance in Japanese Buddhism. The Lotus Sutra proclaims itself as alone sufficient for salvation and even goes so far as to tell its audience to memorise no other text.[17] It was the first, and possibly the only, Buddhist text to take this position, which runs entirely counter to the spirit of mainstream Buddhism.

It would be naïve to ascribe the textual exclusivity of Japanese sects entirely to the Lotus Sutra's polemics; for one thing, it did not produce the same effect in China. The answer must lie elsewhere, too, in the specifics of Japanese history and society.[18] In those areas I am even less competent, if possible, than in those on which I have already trespassed.

FOOTNOTES

1. I first made this point in *Precept and Practice* (Oxford, 1971), p.49. Since then I have discussed this feature of Buddhism from various angles in several publications. For an account of the structure of belief and practice in a traditional Buddhist society (the Sinhala), see Richard Gombrich and Gananath Obeyesekere, *Buddhism Transformed* (Princeton, 1988), pp.15–29. For a discussion of 'Buddhist Identity' see the section so entitled in my *Theravada Buddhism* (London, 1988), pp.23–29. see also in particular my 'Buddhism in the Modern World: Secularization or Protestantization?', pp.55–79 in Eileen Barker *et al.* (eds.), *Secularization, Rationalism and Sectarianism* (Oxford, 1993); section 2 of that article is called 'Buddhism's Dichotomy between Religion and Secularity' and refers to Japan. There I argue that from the traditional Buddhist perspective most of the Japanese 'new religions' with which the present volume deals is a secular affair.
2. *Buddhism Transformed*; see previous note.
3. *Theravada Buddhism*; see note 1.
4. Ideally the Sangha have left the world (see below); but in practice most monks and nuns do feel worldly needs, and many seek religious means to satisfy them.
5. Helpful references and discussion in D.P. Martinez, 'The Dead: Shinto aspects of Buddhist ritual', *Journal of the Anthropological Society of Oxford* XXI, 2, Trinity 1990, pp.199–209.
6. London, 1958. I have already used the following quotations from Dore in my article 'Buddhism in the Modern World' (see note 1).
7. Dore, p.329.
8. Ian Reader, *Religion in Contemporary Japan* (London, 1991), pp.11–12.
9. Dore, p.327.
10. *Ibid.*, pp.349–50.
11. *Mahā Parinibbāna Sutta* V, para.12.
12. *Milindapañho* p.264.
13. Tantric initiation confers the power to act as a priest.
14. Robert K. Heinemann, 'This World and the Other Power: Contrasting Paths of Deliverance in Japan', pp.212–30 in Heinz Bechert and Richard Gombrich (eds.) *The World of Buddhism* (London, 1984), p.224.

15. James C. Dobbins, *Jōdo Shinshū: Shin Buddhism in Medieval Japan* (Bloomington and Indianapolis, 1989), p.37.

16. Leon Hurvitz, *Scripture of the Lotus Blossom of the Fine Dharma* (New York, 1976), p.ix.

17. See especially the closing verses of chapter 3.

18. I am grateful to Galen Amstutz for pressing this point upon me. I am also extremely grateful to David Gellner and James McMullen for saving me from certain errors and unclarities by their helpful comments on a draft.

3

The Goddess Emerges from her Cave: Fujita Himiko and her Dragon Palace Family

CARMEN BLACKER

FUJITA HIMIKO, or Ryūgū Otohime (the Dragon Palace Princess) as she is also called, is the foundress of the religious group known as Ryūgū Kazoku, or the Dragon Palace Family. She founded the group in October 1973, soon after a dramatic initiatory vision revealed to her the task she was destined to perform in life, and the message she was to bring to the world. The Ryūgū Kazoku should, therefore, be counted among the shin-shin-shūkyō, or 'new, new' religions, which made their appearance during the 1970s and 1980s, and which are readily distinguishable from the older 'new' religions which arose after 1945.[1]

Himiko's group is of particular interest today insofar as her message is, unbeknown to herself, curiously consonant with much that is occurring in the West. This message for mankind is clearly centred on the coming Age of the Goddess, megamisama no jidai. This kairos she claims to be close at hand, despite all appearances to the contrary. The goddess is about to come at last into her own. Having been for centuries quenched by hard, war-like, masculine divinities, who are accorded paramount status beyond their deserts in monotheisms throughout the world, the goddess will once more arise and bathe the world in the millennial joys of her light and love.

While proclaiming such a message, Himiko seems for the most part unaware of the recent surge in the West of literature about the goddess. The remarkable spate of books, papers, conferences and workshops on the goddess and her myth, the work of Maria Gimbutas, Robert Graves, Anne Baring, Miranda Green and many others, has so far neither influenced nor interested her. Her own supernatural revelation has taught her all she needs to know.

This dramatic initiation took place at 11.30 a.m. on 7 October 1973. She was standing outside a large cave near Kumamoto, in company with a woman ascetic called Shioyama, when with extraordinary suddenness the goddess Amaterasu Ōmikami appeared to her in the unusual form of a mermaid. With her fish tail, the goddess gave Himiko a slap on the cheek, and announced that now was the moment of her true arrival, her true emergence from the cave. The myth recounted in the *Kojiki* of her *iwatobiraki* (emergence from the cave) some two thousand years ago was a mere rehearsal of what was now to take place. She emerged now from the dark cave to bring the joyful news that the world would soon be suffused with the light and love of the Mother Goddess. Here was *megamisama no yomigaeri*, the resurrection of the goddess; the world was soon to become *nyoi-hōju*, a wish-fulfilling jewel,

Her companion, Shioyama, heard the sound of the slap, and of the goddess's voice, but was not sufficiently advanced to see the mermaid avatar. Only Himiko both saw and heard the full revelation.

From that moment she felt herself imbued with the tremendous supernatural power of the goddess, and lost no time in proclaiming her message to the world. She also lost no time in having a bronze statue of the mermaid erected inside the cave, where it stands even now for all to see, with an inscription recording the event in 1973 as a turning point in history.

Likewise, from the moment of her initiation, Himiko found that her spiritual powers were greatly enhanced. Before this event she had displayed minor psychic powers, experiencing encounters with divinities both in dream and waking vision. Near the Nachi waterfall, for example, in the course of a pilgrimage from Yoshino to Kumano, she had seen the Thirty-six Boys of Fudō Myōō. Now she found that she could both see and converse with all kinds of spiritual beings, both benevolent and troublesome. In consequence, she was now able to heal all types of sickness, both physical and mental, which are caused by invisible spiritual beings. She was able to see the unhappy ghost, or the neglected divinity, who was causing the headaches, the arthritis, the depression, the lethargy, and after listening to its story she could perform the correct ritual for bringing the entity to its due salvation.

At the same time, she realized that it was not only Amaterasu Ōmikami who had chosen her to be the vehicle of revelation. A number of ancient goddesses and queens had at the same time elected to reincarnate themselves in her body and transmit to her their powers. The powerful and mysterious Queen Pimiko, mentioned in the Chinese *Wei Chih* of the third century, was one of those who conferred her name and power upon her. Ryūgū Otohime, the daughter of the Dragon King, was another; hence her spiritual cognomen Otohimesama. Armed with this identity she feels herself in touch with the network of symbolic correspondences, in Japanese myth and legend, which radiate from the feminine figure – water, dragons, fish, the water world in general. Yet another figure with whom she declares a conscious identity is Happyaku Bikuni, the girl from Wasaka who accidentally ate mermaid's flesh and was condemned in consequence to wander mysteriously over the country for 800 years.

Lastly, she claims identity with the great queen of the lost continent of Mu, which sank below the sea not far from Japan many thousands of years ago.[2]

With this powerful combination of ancient and august feminine figures congregating inside her, with her timely message of an imminent golden age, and with her practical ability to heal sickness and solve troubles, she was admirably qualified to found a new religious group.

The Ryūgū Kazoku is now nearly twenty years old. It is not a large group by Japanese standards, its membership totalling not more than 1500. Most of the members come from the Kansai area, where she has established her headquarters in a flat in Higashi Yodogawa near Osaka. But there is also a flourishing branch in Tokyo, and her mailbag every day contains letters and pleas for help from all over Japan. Living with her in her headquarters is Kawami Yoshiharu, a young man who performs many invaluable tasks for her, not least of which is the editing of a monthly journal.

This journal, the *Ryūgū Otohime*, which has now reached its one hundred and thirtieth issue,[3] gives news of Himiko's latest visions, revelations and travels over Japan and the rest of the world; it contains articles interpreting current events in the light of the imminent advent of the goddess age, and examples of her successful cures of cases of melancholy, asthma, paralysis of the legs, insomnia and terrible fears of death and the end of the world. Patients from all over Japan describe their sufferings, and their fervent gratitude to Himiko for removing the spiritual cause of the malaise.

The journal furthermore reminds its readers every month that with Himiko as their guide and leader, the following services are available to them. First, *reisa* or spirit investigation. We are all overshadowed by spiritual beings, who are usually benign and protective, but which can be displaced from time to time by malicious entities which sap our vital energy and cause sickness and misfortune. Or by unhappy entities who are trying by these means to call attention to their plight. By the technique of *reisa*, Himiko will give you a spiritual check-up to investigate the entities overshadowing you, and will deal appropriately with any which need to be cleared or moved on to other destinations. Second, *mitama-matsuri* a rite which will purify, comfort and placate the molesting spirit, so that its aggressive inclinations are removed. Third, *shukufuku* or the blessing of the Mother Goddess, which acts as a spiritual tonic, enabling you to recuperate from the depletion you have suffered.

Members of the Ryūgū Kazoku are further encouraged to apply to Himiko for regular check-ups, whether they feel ill or not. If you cannot get to her Osaka flat in person, you can send a recent photograph with name, sex, date of birth and a clear statement of the trouble. It is also important to have a *reisa* carried out for any old objects in your house; old books, old trees or wells, any antique objects, even an old used car, are all subject to dangerous spiritual infestation which can cause malaise to their owners. A further service of blessing, *petto-kuyō*, is offered for your dogs, cats or birds, which are also vulnerable to spiritual attack.

Her work with photographs is very systematic, and she showed me several large albums in which she has preserved records of former cases. Her method is to inspect the photograph with her psychic eye, which will immediately see the figure of the molesting or overshadowing entity. She then makes a quick sketch of the entity, speaks to it, listens to its story, and performs the necessary rite to purify it and bring it to its proper salvation. The patient thereupon quickly recovers.

The albums contain the photographs, each with its accompanying sketch of the molesting entity, together with notes for further treatment. Many of the unhappy spirits whom she has saved prove to be centuries old. There are many cases of samurai killed in the wars of the sixteenth century who have lingered without proper absolution for three hundred years. Cases, too, are not uncommon of warrior spirits of even older date, remaining unhoused from the Gempei wars at the end of the twelfth century.

An interesting example of her work with photographs is the *reisa* she performed on a newspaper photograph of Saddam Hussein in November 1990. Overshadowing the face of the tyrant were three sinister figures: a bull, a king riding a horse and a terrifying old woman. The bull she knew by her psychic powers to be Apis, and the king to be Nebuchadnezzar, with whom Saddam Hussein had already identified himself. But the old woman eluded her. She therefore addressed the visionary figure, 'Who are you?'

'I am the Old Woman of the Desert', was the reply. Her insight told her that the figure was a depleted, starved, enraged remnant of the ancient goddess Ishtar, once worshipped all over the Middle East but long suppressed and insulted by Islam. She and the other two figures were all *maibotsujin*, buried gods, suppressed by Islam but now reasserting themselves and demanding due nourishment. Many of them dated back to Sumer and Babylon, on the sites of which Iraq now stood, and were accustomed to receiving offerings of blood sacrifices. To obtain their usual fare they therefore possessed a ferocious chieftain like Saddam Hussein and forced him to invade Kuwait. From the slain in the war they could derive the vital nourishment needed for their revival.[4]

Himiko's work of spirit diagnosis and healing thus occupies most of the time she spends at home. There is another and no less important commitment, however, which takes her away from her headquarters on travels of an adventurous and apparently indefatigable kind. She claims first to have visited every nook and cranny of Japan, every mountain, bay, lake, temple and shrine, and to know every prefecture better than people who have lived there all their lives.

But her journeys are by no means confined to Japan. Her travels abroad have taken her to at least fifty foreign countries. She spent six months wandering over India; she has visited Turkey, Greece, Israel, Tibet, and even Easter Island. She has been to almost every State in America. In the summer of 1989 she made one trip to the United States, and another to England and Scotland, during which she spared an afternoon to visit Cambridge.

When I first became acquainted with her, I imagined that her passion for travel was due simply to a powerful kind of natural wanderlust. I soon understood that the reasons were more complex. The journeys were often undertaken, not simply of her own volition, but at the insistent command of various *kami*. They were themselves *kamiwaza*, actions wrought by a *kami*. She would hear a voice in the middle of the night, ordering her to go at once to a certain place. If she did not instantly obey, the *kami* would harry and nag her until she had no alternative but to do its bidding. The funds for these journeys would invariably be provided for her by a miraculous source, *kamisama no o-hakarai*.

There were two reasons why she should receive supernatural commands to travel to certain places. First, because in the places she is ordered to visit there were miserably unhappy ghosts who have been unable to achieve their proper *jōbutsu* or salvation, whom she can bring to a joyous release. And second, because in these places she is able to make contact with the benign tutelary divinity, converse with them and make sure they are doing their job properly. She thus establishes a spiritual network, *reiteki-nettowāku*, with the local *ubusunagami* or genius loci, so that they agree to cooperate in the great work of the goddess.

Of her work in saving unhappy and neglected ghosts she has

many dramatic tales to tell. In 1990, for example, she visited the group of islands off Nagasaki. On Himejima she found a tablet commemorating 130 Japanese Christians who in the seventeenth century had fled to the island for safety, and taken refuge in a cave with only seaweed to eat. They were discovered before long, captured, put to the water torture and eventually killed. Himiko was at once aware that for three hundred years none of these poor souls had been able to attain proper salvation because no one had performed the correct obsequies for them. They rushed towards her, their faces haggard and woebegone, begging her to rescue them. Within a few minutes she had saved them all, and had the satisfaction of seeing them rise upwards, their faces filled with joy and gratitude.[5]

While travelling in Shikoku in 1990, she found many spirits of the defeated Heike family, who had fled there from the battle of Yashima and the battle of Dan-no-ura in 1185. They, too, for eight hundred years, had been unable to find peace, and had been waiting for someone to perform the correct ritual for them. These also Himiko was able to save; a poor Heike lady, who had been waiting eight hundred years, was rapturously grateful.[6]

Again, during her trip to America in May 1989, she visited the Grand Canyon. There she had the strange experience of seeing large numbers of very ancient ghosts, *kodairei*, gazing at her intently. She asked them who they were.

'We are the spirits of people who died in a war long ago, and for centuries have been awaiting your coming. Please release us from this valley.'

At once she performed the necessary rite, and was delighted to see them turn into black butterflies and fly upwards to the sky released from their bondage. She later discovered that they were the ghosts of Hopi Indians who were the original inhabitants of the valley.[7]

Of her work with the spirit network of local divinities there are likewise many examples. When she visited the island of Kinkazan in October 1987, after a rough crossing, she went straight to the shrine. There the goddess Kanayamabime-no-mikoto, wearing a tunic of pale green, scarlet sleeves and a Nō woman's mask of incredible beauty, appeared to her visionary eye. The goddess danced with exquisite grace, holding a golden fan, and Himiko composed a suitable *uta* to confirm the encounter.

On the island of Chikubushima likewise, the goddess Benten, guardian of the island, appeared to her visionary eye and danced. And on 15 January 1991 Himiko led a party of her followers on a pilgrimage to the Ise shrine. There the goddess Amaterasu Ōmikami appeared to her in fiercely embattled array, wearing armour laced with red lacing. This vision, she prophesied to her disciples, was a clear omen of coming war. And sure enough, that very night, the Gulf War broke out.

These friendly contacts with local genii are also carried outside Japan. During her journey to Scotland in July 1989, she was anxious to communicate with the Loch Ness monster, or Nesshi-chan as she called him. She stood for some time on the lakeside, murmuring a secret spell which might summon him, aware that near at hand were tourist buses and souvenir shops which might impede his appearance. She was nevertheless disappointed to see no sign of Nesshi-chan.[8] But that night he appeared to her in a dream and said, 'I must apologise for not coming to see you earlier this afternoon. There were too many people around for me to show myself.'

This greeting was communicated to her by some telepathic means which was neither English nor Japanese. In her dream she patted him on the head and said, 'You're the guardian spirit of Scotland, and so mind you do the job properly.' Nesshi-chan looked very pleased, and with the single word 'Hai' (Yes!), vanished from sight.[9]

From these examples it will be readily seen that Himiko's work is an interesting combination of old and new, of the traditional work of the holy, empowered person, and a message which is new in so far as it has few parallels among the new religions.

Her indefatigable travelling, for example, the salvation she brings to unhappy lost spirits, the friendly relations she establishes with local *kami*, what are these but an updated version of the work of the old *yūgyō-hijiri* – the wandering holy men, or the *tabisō*, the travelling priest who figures in so many of the Nō plays? Their task was precisely to rescue unhappy souls and to celebrate the local *kami*, so that blessings would in consequence pour down on the village or island. Indeed, some of her stories of visits to old battlegrounds are reminiscent of the Nō plays of Zeami. Unhappy warrior ghosts are brought to final peace through her powers and charismatic gifts. The *uta* too, which she composes as a final capping for a successful rescue, are thoroughly traditional in spirit and inspiration.

Traditional also, or at least common to a good many other new religions, is her partnership with a man. In many cases the woman Foundress is able to expand her group thanks to the organising ability of a man. She is the vessel for the divine revelations. He translates them into action. Himiko is aided in this manner by Kawami Yoshiharu, who edits the monthly magazine, writes a good deal of it himself, looks after the headquarters while she is away on her travels, and does a good many household tasks for which the

Great Mother has no time.

Her emphasis on the diagnosis of sickness as spirit possession, and her consequent healing through the divine powers accorded to her at her initiation, is likewise to be found in many of the New Religions. But in other respects her message is remarkably new. She is unusual in the first place in claiming identity exclusively with supernatural feminine figures, with Amaterasu Ōmikami, with Queen Pimiko and the Great Queen of Mu. Also from time to time with the World Mother. Other Foundresses are usually possessed by a male divinity, as was Ōgamisama the Foundress of Tenshō Kōtai Jingukyō, the Dancing Religion.

She is also unusual, if not unique, in claiming that the coming millennium will be brought about by the revival of the Goddess, Megamisama. Millennarianism is not uncommon among the New Religions, but to my knowledge none except the Dragon Palace Family see it as the re-emergence of the goddess from her dark cave.

Like other 'new, new religions', she puts Japan firmly at the epicentre of the coming New Age of the Goddess. Others in the West may write and speak of the goddess and propound her myth, but it is Himiko's revelation in 1973 which will prove to be the turning point in history. The second bronze statue of the mermaid which she erected in 1990 at the north end of Lake Biwa will serve to confirm the accelerating process.

FOOTNOTES

1. Two articles have appeared in *Monumenta Nipponica* describing Himiko and her teachings. Ben-Ami Shillony, 'The Princess of the Dragon Palace: a New Shinto Sect is Born', vol.39, 1984, and Richard Fox Young, 'Little Lad Deity and the Dragon Princess', Vol.44, 1989. Since becoming acquainted with Himiko in 1988 and making several journeys in her company, I have come to feel that neither of these articles adequately describe her work, particularly her work of spirit diagnosis and healing.
2. Personal communications from Himiko herself, and to be found *passim* in *Ryūgū Otohime*.
3. As from July 1993.
4. *Ryūgū Otohime*, No.98, November 1990.
5. *Ibid.*, No.90, March 1990.
6. *Ibid.*, No.95, August 1990.
7. *Ibid.*, No.81, May 1989.
8. *Ibid.*, No.102, March 1991.
9. *Ibid.*, No.84, August 1989.

4

New Japanese Religions in the United States

J. GORDON MELTON & CONSTANCE A. JONES

IN THE LATE 1950s, a decade after the declaration of religious freedom in Japan, a number of what were termed 'new religions' emerged.[1] Observers, upon closer examination of these movements, found that they were not 'new' in the sense of having originated after World War Two, but were older religions which had emerged over the course of the previous century. As a group, these movements had been suppressed during the Meiji Era and especially during World War Two. An example of this phenomenon, Konkôkyô, one of the more prominent new religions, had been founded in 1860 and had spread from its initial centre in Otani to other rural Japanese communities. Following suppression during the Meiji Era and World War Two, Konkôkyô prospered after the war.

Consideration of Japanese religious movements, whether in Japan or in the West, requires an understanding of the broad development of the country's religious history, which includes a long tradition of religious pluralism. During the eighth century, Buddhism won the heart of the Japanese emperor who replaced the old state religion, Shinto, with his new faith. Simultaneously, a variety of competing Buddhist sects were introduced from China, dispersing throughout the country over the next centuries. The Pure Land sect, destined to become the most popular form of Buddhism in Japan, was introduced in the twelfth century, at about the same time that Zen arrived from China. Throughout the ensuing centuries Buddhism and Shinto would vie for favour at the various imperial courts.

Thus, throughout the last millennium, a number of movements have sought the allegiance of the Japanese public and have provided a context for the continual emergence of new varieties of the traditional faiths. In the mid-nineteenth century, Christianity was effectively reintroduced (having been banned under the Tokugawas) and grew slowly, hampered by harsh legal restraints for several decades (1868-1889). The development of the Christian mission further added to Japan's pluralistic religious situation as both Roman Catholic and Protestant churches established centres and Protestantism, in particular, brought many of its divisions from the United States into the country. While never claiming a large percentage of the Japanese public, Christianity had an association with the West, an image which has had a growing fascination for Japanese intellectuals.

Our understanding of Japanese religion must accent its profound difference from Christianity, a religion which has developed a unique emphasis upon theology and doctrine coupled with a strong sense of boundary. As Christianity has drawn boundaries based upon the acceptance and rejection of various doctrinal affirmations, assent to these affirmations has been central to membership in the Christian community. Rejection of specific doctrinal formulations has been definitive for condemnation of individuals as heretics and apostates, and actions, even today, are taken against individuals deemed to be members of these two classes.

The Japanese have paid a relatively small amount of attention to such extreme boundary maintenance defined by allegiance to specific beliefs, and have, instead, placed a much higher degree of importance upon the performance of traditional rituals and celebration of various holidays. In the shifting dominance of Shinto and Buddhism, both religions have claimed a part of the national consciousness, so that it is not unusual for Japanese citizens to attend rituals regularly at both Buddhist temples and Shinto shrines. This manner of structuring and observing religion, so decidedly different from Western modes of expression, has heavily skewed our perceptions of Japanese religious life, especially when inferences are drawn from questionnaires which are based upon Western Christian assumptions about what it means to be religious.

JAPANESE RELIGION IN THE UNITED STATES

Soon after the intrusion of the West into Japanese life, the first Japanese began to immigrate to American territory.[2] Initially, workers arrived in Hawaii in 1868, but immigration to the United States became significant only in the 1880s after the passing of the Chinese Exclusion Act and the replacement of many Chinese with Japanese (and Filipino) labourers. The first Japanese Buddhist temple was constructed in 1889 in Hilo, Hawaii, and several Buddhist sects formally established themselves on the islands throughout the next decade.[3] A Honpa Honganji mission was opened in California in 1898.

Beginning in 1907, Japanese immigration, with the resulting

influx of Japanese religion, decreased significantly from various attempts to limit Asian immigration. By 1924, when the immigration act effectively stopped Japanese entry into the United States, over 100,000 Japanese had settled in Hawaii and along the West Coast, where centres of all the major forms of Japanese Buddhism were opened and the first Shinto temples appeared. These Japanese-American communities created prior to 1924 were the loci for the appearance of the first of what would later be called 'new religions'.

After 1924, with Japanese immigration severely limited, formation of new groups by Japanese was stymied, although European-Americans converted to a few existing groups, chief among which were Jōdo Shinshū in Hawaii, the Buddhist lodges within Theosophy, and Zen organizations in the continental United States. One former Buddhist lodge of the Theosophical Society survives today in Los Angeles as the Buddhist Brotherhood in America. As might be expected, Shinto (and those new religions which draw upon it most heavily) did not spread beyond the Japanese-American community.

The bombing of Pearl Harbor severely disrupted the Japanese-American community; its religious leaders were among the first to be arrested and interned and many of its centres were closed. Of the Shinto centres in Hawaii at the beginning of the war, only one escaped confiscation and destruction. Thus, Japanese religion in America, curtailed for decades by systematic immigration bans and quotas, met its most significant challenge during the war years when not only Japanese religion, but Japanese civil rights as well, were abruptly violated.

After the war, with Japan's new and favourable relationship with the United States, the situation began to change dramatically. Members of the American occupation forces brought Japanese Buddhism, especially Zen, back with them. As Americans became more interested in Japanese religion, Japanese, who had traditionally been wary of sharing their faiths with Americans, became more and more open to teaching the Americans (and Europeans) who flocked to their shores. Groups with American missions began to send priests who spoke and appreciated English to their American centres. Even with this specific infusion of Japanese influence, overall growth of Japanese religious forms remained inhibited by immigration laws until 1965, when an entirely new immigration policy towards Asia was institutionalized in law. Since 1965, thousands of Japanese have been welcomed to the United States annually. With this growth of immigration has come the whole array of Japanese religions, including those movements most open to the conversion of non-Japanese.

As part of the sudden spurt of new religious activity in the late 1960s and early 1970s, Japanese religions were seen for a while as simply one segment of new religions which were appearing and spreading due to the social unrest of the times. However, given the hindsight of a generation of steady growth, coupled with detailed study of the histories of individual groups, the emergence and penetration of American culture by the new religions can be seen as part of the century-long trend of migration by Japanese religions to the West. A new phase of that penetration occurred coincidentally at the same time that America was experiencing a period of social unrest, but had no essential connection to it. While Eastern religious practices have continued to expand in the United States, the period of unrest soon passed into history.

NEW RELIGIONS IN AMERICA

As the movements which were termed 'new religions' in the 1960s are placed in the larger flow of Japanese religious development and have, in turn, been succeeded by a new generation of 'new, new religions', which appeared in the 1980s, terminology has become confusing. For purposes of this discussion, the term 'new religions' will be retained as a working label to designate those groups other than the 55 Buddhist groups and the 13 Shinto groups which were recognized by the Meiji government prior to World War Two and those Christian groups which entered Japan as missions from the West. Over 400 such groups have now been located and include a variety of indigenous groups, including several who consider themselves to be Jews and the Japanese to be descendants of the lost tribes of Israel.[4] The great majority of the new religions, especially those which arose in the 1980s, are limited to Japan and have not yet been exported to the West. On the other hand, new Japanese-based religions have appeared in the West, schisms of groups introduced from Japan, which have no affiliates in Japan. Most of the uniquely Western Japanese new religions have emerged as older groups have attempted to adapt to Western styles and languages.[5]

While most of the new religions draw the major components of their faith and teachings from one of the traditional religions of Shinto, Buddhism or Christianity, they have tended to be syncretistic in combining elements from the other two traditional religions with their unique religious contribution. The centrality of healing, for example, is noticeable in many of the new religions, an emphasis which can, in some cases, be traced to Christian influences.

Scholars of new religions, in addition to locating groups with traditional lineages and belief systems, have sought to characterize movements in structural terms. The early literature on new religions highlighted the prominent role of a charismatic founder/leader. Now, after close observation of religions founded in the West in this century, we are aware of the undue emphasis placed upon this observation. Indeed, a new religion is usually founded by a single person (or a very small group of individuals) and the religion is fruitfully seen as an extension of this initial vision; the *raison d'être* of a new religion is the perpetuation of the leader's teachings and a charismatic leader tends to have a unique role in defining teachings during his/her lifetime. However, observation of the transition of power following the death of religious founders has discounted much of the superlative language used to describe their power and influence in the next generation. A leader's death provides a time of formal transition to more collective leadership, but that process is usually well under way prior to the leader's death. Even the most autocratic prophet speaks to a relatively narrow set of issues and must, as the movement grows, rely upon assistants to apply the leader's teachings. Throughout the West, and in countries such as Japan which have been strongly influenced by the West, the move to collective leadership has been greatly encouraged by the laws governing religious corporate structures.[6]

PRE-WORLD WAR TWO

The first of the new religions to find its way to the United States was Konkôkyô, which draws most strongly on Shinto. Founded in Japan in 1859, Konkôkyô entered the United States in 1919 among Japanese-Americans in Seattle and Tacoma, Washington, from which it has spread along the West Coast. With 13 centres at present, Konkôkyô has not spread beyond the Japanese-American community.[7]

During the first decades of this century, members of another Shinto-based group, Tenrikyó, migrated to Hawaii and the West Coast. Their residence in the United States allowed two missionaries from Tenrikyó headquarters in Japan to pass through the immigration barriers erected in 1924 and to begin, in 1927, the organization of followers in Seattle, Washington and Portland, Oregon. The arrival of the missionaries was part of a coordinated programme developed in Japan to plant Tenrikyó centres in all of the Japanese communities around the world. Although Tenrikyó is among the most evangelical of the new religions, it, like Konkôkyô, has had little success outside the Japanese-American community.[8]

37

In the nineteenth century Zen entered the United States. In the 1880s Zen centres were established to serve the Japanese-American community and later, following the response to Soyen Shaku's talks at the 1893 World Parliament of Religions, various attempts were made to establish Zen groups for non-Japanese. However, a stable community, the First Zen Institute of America, was not founded until 1930. The founder of the Institute, Sokei-an Roshi had arrived in the United States in 1906, but did not find any encouragement for his efforts until he settled in New York during the 1920s. Except for a brief disruption during World War Two, the Institute has prospered, and has attained some special importance in that Sokei-an's wife, Ruth Fuller Sasaki, became the mother-in-law of Episcopal priest Alan Watts, who emerged as one of the great populizers of Zen thought and practice in the 1960s.[9]

SINCE WORLD WAR TWO

During the 1950s, Japanese Zen became something of a fad in America and heralded the influx of Japanese religions which followed the changing of immigration laws in 1965. Possibly the single most important influence in the spread of Zen was the writings of D.T. Suzuki (1870-1966). Orphaned at an early age, he found his way to Engakuji monastery, one of the few religious centres in Japan which, in the late nineteenth century, had a window open to the West. In 1897 he joined Paul Carus of Illinois to translate Buddhist documents into English. (While there he also discovered the writings of Emanuel Swedenborg, which he translated into Japanese.) He and his Western wife, Beatrice Erskine Lane, enjoyed a successful joint career through the 1920s and 1930s at Ōtani University as editors of *The Eastern Buddhist*, an English-language journal.

While primarily a follower of Pure Land Buddhism (Ōtani University takes its name from the main school of the Higashi Honganji) Suzuki was also an accomplished Zen master and he wrote books explaining both traditions to his Western audience. The Zen materials found by far the greater response and were required reading through the 1950s for those attracted to Zen practice.

Zen was the first Japanese import to find mass appeal outside of the Japanese-American community. Because it had few of the trappings of popular religion, for which there has been a certain scholarly disdain, and because it is less embedded in cultural forms than other Japanese religions, Zen had a special attraction for intellectuals. Although Zen has been praised for its emphasis on direct participation and unmediated experience and for the futility of transmitting any understanding of its essence in books, more books have appeared on Zen than any other of the Buddhist traditions imported to the West. The abundance of Zen literature in print and the numerous sitting groups throughout the country contribute to the image that Zen is a very popular movement among young adults in the United States. Yet, these sitting groups are generally quite small. While many come to sample the practice and while Japanese Zen is more popular than Chinese and Korean varieties, very few Americans stay to follow Zen's rather austere path.

Simultaneous with the flowering of Zen in the 1950s, a few new Japanese religious leaders were allowed into the country to meet with followers. Revs. Higuchi Kiyoko and Henry Ajiki settled in Hawaii in the early 1950s and organized the first centres of Sekai Kyūsei Kyō outside of Japan, in Hawaii in 1953 and in Los Angeles the following year.

Sekai Kyūsei Kyō, better known by its anglicized name, the Church of World Messianity, is one of the Japanese healing groups, and, in spite of its reliance upon Shinto, has been able to attract members from outside the Japanese-American community. The Church was founded in 1934 by Okada Mokichi, a businessman driven to religion by bad health. His interest in religion was further strengthened by a series of calamities which wiped him out financially. In the 1920s he joined Ōmoto, one of the nineteenth-century new religions and among the first to emphasize healing. In 1926 he began to receive revelations of his own, in the wake of which he began to see himself as the channel for the Light of God; subsequently, he instituted *johrei* (*jōrei*), the process of purifying the spiritual body.

Okada left Ōmoto in 1931 to found his own independent movement. Meanwhile Ōmoto was becoming increasingly involved in politics. Its leader had a long history of criticism by the government, especially in his assuming prerogatives traditionally preserved for the Emperor. In 1935 he was arrested and sentenced to life imprisonment, and all of Ōmoto's buildings were systematically levelled with dynamite. Okada had not been away from Ōmoto long enough to escape the sweep of people identified with the now outlawed movement, and, under threat of arrest, he had to give up the practice of *johrei*. The movement was further suppressed once World War Two actually began, but, unlike Ōmoto, was never physically destroyed. This suppression probably spurred Okada's increasing interest in Christianity, so evident in the later stages of his life.

After the war, the Church of World Messianity prospered for a few years, but had to overcome a significant problem when it was charged with tax evasion. Okada was arrested and this ordeal sapped his health. He died in 1955 and leadership of the Church passed to his daughter. In 1971 a schismatic group emerged, led by former leaders who complained that the church was departing from Okada's teachings, and formed what is known in the United States as the Society of Johrei.[10]

Ōmoto also gave birth to one of the most interesting of the Japanese new religions, Seichō-no-Ie, founded in 1930 by Taniguchi Masaharu. As a young man, Taniguchi had been an active leader in Ōmoto and the editor of several of its periodicals. Then, in 1921 he left the group and began a period of spiritual search. In his quest to resolve personal problems Taniguchi found a crucial element in his great love of English, the study of which prepared him for his chance encounter with *The Law of Mind in Action* by Fenwicke Holmes, brother of the founder of the Church of Religious Science. In the pages of this book, which he translated into Japanese, he found the answer to his physical and financial problems. Religious Science, one segment of the American New Thought movement, became the key which allowed Taniguchi to put together all of the elements of his religious pilgrimage. In 1950 he founded Seichō no Ie as a Japanese form of Religious Science.

Seichō no Ie was imported to Hawaii in 1938 by three Japanese-Americans who had taken the 15-day training intensive during a visit to their homeland. After World War Two, the Church was formally organized and ministers were sent from Japan. The movement quickly spread to California and other Japanese-American communities. While based upon a Western teaching and potentially open to non-Japanese converts, the church developed in the United States precisely in those areas, along the West Coast, where its parent body had its strongest presence. Thus, Seichō-no-Ie, although a member of the International New Thought Alliance and integrated nationally into the New Thought movement, has been, until recently, contained within the Japanese-American community. Recently, as second and third generation members have been anglicized and have discovered Taniguchi's books in English translation, the movement has expanded beyond a purely Japanese context, although Religious Science continues to attract non-Japanese Americans who might in its absence join Seichō-no-Ie.[11]

MACROBIOTICS

Possibly the first new Japanese religious movement to arrive in

North America after the war, and certainly the single most successful movement in its ability to permeate American culture was Macrobiotics. Ishizuka Sagen (1893-1910) perfected the synthesis which is Macrobiotics from a combination of Western ideas and Chinese wisdom philosophy in a Japanese Zen Buddhist context. Ishizuka introduced his ideas to Nishihata Manabu who in turn passed the synthesis to Sakurazawa Yukikazu, better known by his westernized name, George Ohsawa (1893-1966). Ohsawa's expansive attitude toward Macrobiotics led him to France in 1929. From Paris the teachings spread to England and other European countries. In Japan, the movement developed a significant following on university campuses, but was suppressed as the war began because of its philosophy emphasizing world peace. Ohsawa spent part of the war in prison because of this teaching.

Macrobiotics actually entered the United States in 1929 through a brief visit by Ohsawa, but attained no following until Ohsawa's student Kushi Michio moved here in 1949. Kushi's wife Aveline joined him two years later and they, along with Herman and Cornelia Aihara, gathered a small following in New York City during the 1950s. In 1961 the group was formally organized as the Ohsawa Foundation. The movement spread as the Kushis moved to Boston in 1965 and the following year Aihara moved to California, establishing the East West Foundation (Boston) and the Ohsawa Foundation (California).

Macrobiotics is best known for its teachings on diet. Just as many people never move beyond hatha yoga postures to yoga's religious teachings, so many people appropriate the macrobiotic diet quite apart from the underlying religious teachings. However, for those most deeply involved in the movement, the basic Taoist metaphysics is equally important. The most prominent proponent of the system, Kushi Michio, has written widely on the macrobiotic 'philosophical' perspective and has continued his career as a peace activist.[12]

THE CHILDREN OF NICHIREN

Among the oldest of the new religions is Nichiren Shôshû, which dates to a thirteenth-century split among the immediate disciples of Buddhist prophet/reformer Nichiren (1222-1282). In 1290 one of the six senior disciples of Nichiren, to whom the upkeep of his tomb had been assigned, separated from the other five over the question of responsibility for Nichiren's final resting place. To this issue was added a doctrinal problem over interpretation and use of the Lotus Sutra, the Buddhist writing considered most authentic and sacred by Nichiren. The two groups of Nichiren's followers which resulted from this dispute, the Nichiren Shū and the Nichiren Shōshū, became distinct movements and have existed side by side since the thirteenth century.

Nichiren Shōshū, which has existed on the edge of the Buddhist community over the centuries, is classified as a new religion because of an organizational change which began in the 1930s. In 1930 Sōka Kyōiku Gakkai (Value Creating Education Society) was founded as a lay organization by Tsunesaburo Makiguchi, an anti-Shinto member of Nichiren Shōshū. His refusal to acknowledge the Shinto deities led to his arrest during World War Two and only after the war, under the leadership of his successor Toda Jōsei, did the Society prosper. The success of Sōka Gakkai was phenomenal, so that in 1958 when Toda died, a quarter of a million attended his funeral.

Sōka Gakkai emerged as the militantly evangelistic arm of Nichiren Shōshū, with two discrete doctrines which thrust them into the spotlight. First, they advocated a government aligned to Buddhism and in 1964 founded a political party to that end. Second, support, for both the organization and its politics, was built through a policy called *shakubuku*, literally 'bend and flatten'. *Shakubuku* was embodied in high-pressure recruitment tactics which included personal confrontation and, according to numerous reports, the use of physical violence to instill the allegiance of the extended families of Sōka Gakkai members.

The overwhelming success of Sōka Gakkai led other religious groups, both Buddhist and non-Buddhist, to unite to stop its spread. Throughout the 1970s, these groups were able to make the organization an object of public controversy and to stunt its growth, at least in Japan. Meanwhile, Sōka Gakkai exported Nichiren Shōshū to the Japan-in-diaspora communities around the world. Initial informal organization in the United States began soon after World War Two, with a formal establishment by Sadanaga Masayasu in 1960. After his decision to make the United States his permanent home, Sadanaga changed his name to George Williams and assumed the role of director of Nichiren Shoshu of America.

In the West, Nichiren Shōshū is significantly different than in Japan. In Japan, Sōka Gakkai arose within the context of a well-established organization of Nichiren Shōshū temples and priestly leadership. In the United States, and other countries of diaspora, no such temples and priests existed. Only in 1965, by which time Sōka Gakkai was a national organization, was construction begun on the first temple and the first priest welcomed from Japan. Subsequently, other temples have been built, but, clearly, the lay organization, operating out of its huge worship centre in Santa Monica, California, constitutes the centre of the movement. The majority of American members have no relationship to the temples, which attempt to express a traditional Japanese culture, and have never even visited one of the several temples.

The very success of Sóka Gakkai, now the primary source of Nichiren Shóshú members, has led to intensified self-assertion and the development of what amounts to a form of Buddhism which has little need of temple life. Throughout the 1980s tensions have developed as Sóka Gakkai has assumed prerogatives (performing marriage and burial ceremonies) previously the exclusive right of temples. These tensions are found among Western followers, but have little impact among those groups who regard temples as minor appendages.[13]

The controversy over Sóka Gakkai has overshadowed the emergence and spread of other Nichiren groups. One such movement, Reiyúkai, was founded in Japan in the 1920s by a Nichiren layman, Kubo Kakutaró (1892-1944), who, because of his enthusiasm for the religion, developed his own edited version of the Lotus Sutra, the *Blue Sutra*, and developed a lay practice free of temple structures. The organization was given a boost in 1930 when a prominent Japanese nobleman, Baron Nagayama Taketoshi, identified with the group as its president. His affiliation slowed government suppression of the group throughout World War Two, and thus Reiyúkai came out of the war immediately ready to enjoy the new era of freedom. During the first two post-war decades, Reiyukai spread to all parts of Japan with speed. The movement arrived in the United States in the 1970s and, after an initial spread among the Japanese, has attracted a non-Japanese following who are largely attracted to its strong youth program.[14]

In turn, Reiyúkai spawned another movement, Risshókóseikai, founded by Niwano Nikkyó and his wife Myókó Naganuma. In addition to the Lotus Sutra, Niwano uses its two related, shorter sutras, the *Muryógi* Sutra and the *Kanfugen* Sutra. Integral to Niwano's interpretation of Buddhism is the ability of humans to break the bondage of reincarnation and to escape the consequences of the law of cause and effect by repentance and perfect living. Although Risshókóseikai entered the United States in 1957, it has remained largely confined to the Japanese American community.[15]

SUZUKI ROSHI

Prior to 1965, while few Japanese were allowed to migrate to the United States and while no facilities existed to train priests in the

United States, Japanese-American communities had made provision to replace the leadership of established religious centres by Japanese-trained priests whenever an incumbent died or returned to Japan. Such a turnover in leadership in 1959 brought Suzuki Shunryū Roshi to the Sōkōji Temple, the traditional Sōtō Zen temple which had served San Francisco's Japanese community since the early years of the century. Suzuki differed considerably from previous priests, however, in that he had long had a desire to come to America, he spoke English, and he had an open friendliness to non-Japanese.

Suzuki's arrival in America coincided with the wave of interest in Zen associated with the 'hippie' movement, of which San Francisco was the West Coast centre. His person and his skills of assimilation provided a solution to a major problem faced by hippie Zen enthusiasts in California: their community knew only about Zen what they had learned from a few books and they desperately wanted the real experience of Zen. As the answer to their problem arrived in the guise of Suzuki, young students began to gather around him. Soon, non-Japanese outnumbered Japanese and, in the face of rising tensions between the two cultural groups, the youthful non-Japanese group of Suzuki's followers separated and organized the Zen Centre of San Francisco, destined to become the mother of a number of similar centres initially along the West Coast and later in the Eastern United States.[16]

The San Francisco centre prospered under Suzuki's leadership and, initially, under that of his successor, Richard Baker Roshi. In 1967 Tassajara Hot Springs was purchased and turned into a rural retreat centre, famous for its healthy bread, which is still marketed throughout the Bay Area. Baker acquired leadership in 1971. All appeared well until the early 1980s when, amid charges of sexual improprieties, Baker was forced out of his position. By this time, several of the leaders serving under Baker had received dharma transmission and could operate without Baker's direction. In the wake of Baker's expulsion, centres formerly affiliated with the Zen Centre of San Francisco became autonomous. The successor to Baker, Tenshin Reb Anderson, also had problems and he and the Centre's board separated, with the board moving towards a more collective leadership. Following the Anderson situation, additional local centres became autonomous and are now in a position to nurture a new generation of Zen practitioners and groups, which draw almost exclusively non-Japanese converts.

Suzuki is important, not only for spreading a new Zen lineage in America, but also for introducing Sōtō Zen to the American public. Most Zen practice by Westerners prior to Suzuki's entrance had been Rinzai, primarily from the lineage of Japanese teacher Imakita Kōsen. The major difference between the two groups is the use of the kōan (Rinzai uses it and Sōtō does not). The kōan is a problem presented to a student in the form of a cryptic utterance by the Zen master. It is the student's task, from his/her experience of meditation to respond to the kōan to the master's satisfaction. By introducing a form of Zen which does not rely on the use of kōans, a process not easily adapted from Japanese culture to American students, Suzuki paved the way for the further acculturation of Japanese Zen into an American context.

In the 1960s several other Sōtō lineages were successfully transplanted to the United States from Japan. Students of Yasutani Hakuun, who had visited Los Angeles on several occasions in the early 1960s, formed the Zen Centre of Los Angeles in 1967 under the leadership of Hakuyu Taizan Maezumi Roshi, formerly of the Zenshūji Sōtō Mission, the old Japanese Zen centre in the city's Japanese community. The centre prospered through the 1970s and Maezumi Roshi named four dharma heirs. However, at almost the same time that the San Francisco centre went through its crisis with Baker, the Los Angeles centre experienced a crisis with Maezumi over his alcoholism. In the wake of the problem, two of his leading students, Bernard Tetsugen Roshi and Charlotte Joko Beck, dropped their affiliation and took their centres with them.[17]

In 1969 British born Jiyu-Kennett Roshi moved to San Francisco and began what today is known as the Order of Buddhist Contemplatives. She had completed a long period of study in Japan and had become the head of the Foreign Guest Department of the major Sōtō Zen organization in Japan. In San Francisco, she quickly gathered students around her and organized them into the Zen Mission Society. In 1970 the group moved to Mt Shasta, California, where they have since remained headquartered. Through the 1970s Jiyu-Kennett was very active in writing and establishing centres and training leaders. Besides her American centres, she opened work in Canada and the United Kingdom. In more recent years she has travelled but little and some of the centres she began have become autonomous.[18]

Zen groups have grown to such an extent over the last four decades that the end of the 1980s registered several hundred organized sitting groups, many of which were formally organized around 'zendos' or sitting rooms. Most of these groups have ten to twenty members, comprising a total of 3–5,000 Zen adherents in the country. Although a somewhat miniscule proportion of the larger American Buddhist community, Zen practitioners have nevertheless played an important role in American religion. The Zen community, having emerged as a bastion of male patriarchal structures, has provided a context for the debate over the role of women within Buddhism itself, and subsequently has nurtured a group of prominent women Zen masters, including Charlotte Joko Beck, Jiyu-Kennett Roshi, Toni Packer, and Gesshin Prabhasa Dharma,[19] each of whom has become the leader of her own Zen organization. In addition, the Hawaiian-based Diamond Sangha nurtured the Kahawai Women's Collective, an early voice for women's concerns.

Through the transmission of Zen to North American audiences, Japanese religion experienced its first significant penetration of American culture by escaping the isolation of ethnic enclaves and embracing the larger non-Japanese community. Zen has also served as the source for the development of a number of new religious movements and, while none of these has more than a few hundred adherents, these groups continue to wield an influence over the American culture and consciousness far beyond what their numbers would predict.

SINCE 1965

The Pacific arena of World War Two, the communist assumption of control in China, and the Korean War forced American foreign policy-makers to forge new policies relating to Asia. Seeking to stop the spread of Communism, America sought to implement coalitions of Asian allies. As negotiations were pursued, a fly in the diplomatic ointment appeared. New Asian allies were insulted by American anti-Asian immigration policies and demanded a change in those policies if they were to cooperate with American goals in their part of the world. The end result was the new immigration law of 1965 which placed Asia on a par with Europe in immigration allowances. The results were immediate. By 1967 the annual immigration quotas for all Asian countries, including Japan, were filled as Asians flocked into the United States.

New attitudes towards Asia were reflected in the development of Asian ethnic communities along the West Coast. New Chinese (Taiwanese), Cambodian, Vietnamese, and Korean neighbourhoods emerged in various cities across the country, but were especially prominent in California where the new immigrants tended to alight from Asia and to set up residence. Japanese immigrants, among the most prosperous of the new Asian immigrants, led in the development of Japanese-American cultural centres, tourist attractions, and retail markets, such as Japantown in San Francisco and Little Tokyo in Los Angeles.

Older Japanese Buddhist organizations assumed a certain seniority in the new burgeoning Buddhist communities. For almost a century, apart from a few small Buddhist centres in the several American Chinatowns, the only Buddhists in America were Japanese. Within a few years of the initiation of the new immigration policies, these Japanese Buddhist organizations were the minority as substantial Sri Lankan, Vietnamese, Thai, Korean, Taiwanese, and even Tibetan Buddhist communities developed around them.

Two significant changes have followed the increased immigration begun in 1965. First, as new Asian communities developed, Asian Americans became an important voting block and politicians courted them. During the 1980s in Hawaii, Asians were elected to office at every level of state government and a Japanese Buddhist served as one of the state's senators. In California, Asians were also present throughout the state government and Asian Buddhists held high office, though not yet in a race for governor or senator. At the national level, the US Army appointed its first Buddhist chaplain and educated all chaplains to meet the needs of Buddhists (and other Asian religions) serving in the armed forces.

Second, while Asians and Asian religions were recognized and accepted as a force in the land by many, other Americans were less happy with their growing presence. Many Christians were offended that the very religious groups, among whom they had spent so much time and energy to establish missions, were now colonizing the United States. Less religiously identified Americans watched as their sons and daughters were attracted to, became leaders of, and even evangelized for 'exotic' and 'heathen' faiths. Threatened, these Americans turned on non-indigenous religious groups which had broken out of ethnic enclaves, labelled them 'cults', and began to take action against them. While not supported in most of their efforts, especially in securing governmental and legal backing for persecution, anti-cult groups nevertheless succeeded in creating a significant public sentiment against Asian-based new religions. An anti-cult climate has pervaded the atmosphere in which new religions in general have developed over the last few decades and Asian religions have been particularly targeted for acrimony.

NEW JAPANESE RELIGIONS

As a steady stream of Japanese came to the United States, they slowly brought with them the more successful of the new religions which had emerged in Japan. Among the most prominent were the Perfect Liberty Kyōdan, Mahikari, Reiki, Shinreikyō, Tenshō Kōtai

Jingukyō, and Shinnyoen.

Perfect Liberty Kyōdan originated early in this century through an amalgam of Shingon Buddhism and Shinto. In 1912, Tokumitsu Kanada founded Shinto Tokomitsukyō (literally the divine way as taught by Tokumitsu), initially emphasizing art and nature to which was later added the practice of meditation, brought into the group by a Zen priest, Tokuhara Miki, an early convert. Tokumitsu taught his followers that 'Life is Art' and that they should see their lives as single unified works of art. The artistic life is celebrated with festivals in which visual arts and music surround participants.[20]

Suppressed during the 1930s, Tokuchika's movement rebounded quickly after the war. It emerged as the new religion with the largest window open to the West and the only one to adopt a Western name. Following the immigration of several members to Southern California, Perfect Liberty Kyōdan came to the United States in 1960 and a minister was sent the following year. While based in the Japanese-American community, the organization has made significant efforts to reach out to the larger population. Its lead 'church' is now located in a non-Japanese suburb and approximately a quarter of its current membership is drawn from African-American and Spanish-speaking communities.

Mahikari is a genuinely new religion, founded in 1959 by Okada Kōtama (1901-1974), a former member of the Church of World Messianity. Okada's new message revealed God's divine plan for humanity's creation of a highly evolved civilization and the proper use of the divine light to produce health, harmony, and prosperity. Known in the movement as Sukuinushisama (Saviour), Okada continued World Messianity's emphasis upon spiritual healing through the power of *johrei*, God's healing light and identified Mahikari as a cleansing agent sent by God.

Sekai Mahikari Bunmei Kyōdan (The Church of World True Light Children) was organized in Japan in 1960 and entered the United States in the 1970s. By 1982, a complete English-language edition of the Mahikari scripture, *Goseigen: The Holy Words*, was published. Mahikari has been one of the most successful groups in reaching a non-Japanese constituency and now has centres not only along the West Coast, but throughout the country.[21]

Another Japanese movement which has developed a popular non-Japanese following, to a large extent because it has freed itself from most Japanese cultural trappings, is Reiki, a spiritual healing movement. Reiki was started by Usui Mikao, a Japanese Christian minister in Kyoto during the late nineteenth century. As a minister, he felt challenged by his students in regard to the Bible's healing miracles. Unable to find anyone to answer his students' questions, he came to the United States to work on a Ph.D. at the University of Chicago. He found little help at the university, but in the process of study discovered the Buddha's teachings on healing, an aspect of Buddhist thought neglected by his Buddhist contemporaries. Usui developed Reiki from his own study and meditation upon the Buddhist healing *sutras*.

The Reiki healing practice includes an exacting technique and a study of the nature of the flow of *ki*, the healing power. A set of three degree classes offers progressive growth in the methods of Reiki, from basic to advanced healing techniques, and the conferring of mastership. Reiki masters teach first and second degree classes and are eligible to become grand masters and to convey masterhood.

Reiki was an obscure Japanese movement until the 1970s when Takata Hawayo, who had worked quietly in Hawaii as a Reiki master, was discovered by people interested in effective forms of psychic healing, many of them affiliated with the national organization Spiritual Frontiers Fellowship. Following a lecture tour across the United States by Takata, Reiki quickly became a national movement and Takata appointed her first Reiki master, Barbara Weber Ray, in 1978. Takata had previously initiated her granddaughter Phillis Lei Furomoto. Ray and Furomoto were the only two grand masters created before Takata's death in 1980 and each has become head of her own organization (Ray's Radiance Technique Association International and Furomoto's Reiki Alliance) and lineage of Reiki masters.[22]

Shinreikyó is another Japanese movement emphasizing healing. Based in Shinto, it was founded in post-war Japan by Master Ótsuka Kan'ichi who is considered a saviour by his followers. He combines in his person two great salvific figures, the great sage prophesied to appear when Buddhism is on the wane and the returning messiah of the Christians. He speaks of the Kami-no-michi, the Way of God, which leads to health, happiness, and prosperity. Ótsuka's views on illness and the inhibiting of an individual's life are claimed to attack disease at its root. Shinreikyó has been successful as the number of healing miracles has increased.

Shinreikyó has an intensely nationalistic strain, but has been willing to reach out to Japan-in-diaspora and to anglicized Japanese Americans. An initial mission was opened in Hilo, Hawaii, in 1963 by Kiyoto Kameo and an English language bureau that produced literature for distribution in America was established at the Metaphysical Scientific Institute in Japan. In the United States Shinreikyó has remained small since it entered a fiercely competitive environment and limited itself to the several Japanese communities in Hawaii and the Pacific Coast states.

Tenshō Kōtai Jingukyo is now a worldwide movement founded by a female prophet whom even her critics deem an extraordinary individual. Kitamura Sayo (1900-1967), a nominally religious person in her 40s, had a series of revelations during World War II which transformed her into a prophet and divine embodiment, 'Ōgamisama' (Great God), the name by which she is known among her followers. Tenshō Kōtai Jin, the Absolute God, reportedly ordered her to build the kingdom of God on earth. She proclaimed 1946 as the beginning of the New Era and the following year officially registered the new faith with the Japanese government.

From a basis in Shinto, Ōgamisama presented a picture of the divine which incorporated Buddhist and Christian elements. Thus, Tenshō Kōtai Jin is seen as both the Eternal Buddha and the Heavenly Father. Tenshō Kōtai Jin is also seen as a male-female pair who possessed Ōgamisama, thus establishing a trinity. Ōgamisama presented her message of the divine trinity in extemporaneous sermons which were sung as she appeared in a state of ecstasy. In response, followers would join in an ecstatic dance and the religion became popularly known as the 'dancing religion'.

From its inception Tenshō Kōtai Jingukyo has had an expansive universal outlook and has spread rapidly. Today it is present in more than 75 countries. Ōgamisama travelled widely and first visited Hawaii in 1952, a brief stay which led to the establishment of eight branches of the new movement. Her last visit to followers in Hawaii and California was in 1964 as part of a world tour. In service to an international audience, Ōgamisama's sermons have been transcribed and translated into English and a substantive bi-monthly magazine, *Voice from Heaven*, is published in both English and Spanish editions at Tabuse, Japan, the international headquarters. Leadership has remained in the family and Ōgamisama's granddaughter, Kitamura Kiyokazu, better known as 'Himegamisama', now heads the organization.

THE NEW, NEW RELIGIONS

The explosive visibility and success of new religious movements in post-war Japan were widely documented in the 1960s and the major groups were observed as they progressed through their first generation in a religiously-free situation. More recently, in the 1980s, an entirely new group of religions has been founded, some of which are experiencing success to rival that of the post-war religions. The designation 'new, new religions' has been given to these groups, although this designation is somewhat misleading, even as was the earlier term 'new religions'. Both terms ignore the steady process of religion building which occurs in all cultures, from the daily development of variations in piety to the sporadic emergence of whole movements.

In Japan, from the inception of Christianity to the end of World War Two, new religious movements were founded frequently, although a normal process of development was stymied by the imposition of religious guidelines by the government and, during several periods, new religions were actively suppressed. During the last half of this century in a climate of relative religious freedom, religious culture building in Japan has become more akin to the religious context seen in the United States since the American Revolution. As in America with the introduction of Japanese Buddhism, religious culture building in Japan has been assisted by the introduction of American Christianity which has given potential religious leaders a vast new religious symbology with which to depict their spiritual insight.

Little sign of the arrival of the 'new, new religions' has yet been evidenced in the United States, although there is every reason to believe that some of the more successful and expansive movements are already working in the Japanese communities and will make their appearance to outside observers very shortly.

CONCLUSION

Examination of the development of Japanese religion and its transmission to the West provides a massive set of data from which to theorize about the general development of religion in human society. A broad view suggests that religion is best understood as one continuing aspect of culture, ever growing, ever changing. Although the natural process of religion building is often inhibited by small tradition-oriented cultures, the emergence of new forms of piety spurs change even in conservative contexts. Religious innovation is also inhibited by attempts of secular governments to foster uniformity through the imposition of beliefs in the necessity of religious uniformity for the sake of the health of the state and the identification of religious deviation with treason. States may also oppress religious groups by extracting assets necessary for their survival and by using law enforcement officials to suppress and destroy nonconforming movements. In such contexts, religious movements will often take advantage of periods of social unrest, when the social fabric is temporarily weakened, to present their programs. Such periods do not generate new religions, but rather are used by previously existing dissident movements for their benefit and expansion.

The development of secular democratic governments implicitly undercuts arguments for religious uniformity. The continuation of traditional religious establishments into the modern world thus provided a context which both called for religious liberty and gave rise to anti-religious secularizing philosophies (whose attack on religion in general always attained its power from a primary attack on a particular religious establishment which possessed broad secular powers).

Once religious freedom was established in the modern world, the process of religious development was freed and the world has witnessed, instead of the demise of religion, as some predicted, a flourishing of religion. Throughout Europe and North America, new religious movements arose at an increasing pace.[23] The same process occurred in Japan, the Philippines, sub-Saharan Africa, and Latin America. In fact, new religions grew in all situations where specific state governments did not block them. In the very few years since the opening of Eastern Europe and the countries of the former Soviet Union, a massive growth of new religion has already been noticed and documented.[24]

In the modern world, not only have new religions appeared at a steady rate, but, given the massive movements of peoples internationally, have spread around the world at a rate never possible before the introduction of modern transportation and communication systems. Thus, not only do new religions continually appear, but they insert themselves into unlikely situations as they are carried into new contexts by migrating believers rather than itinerant prophets. By transmission through ethnic groups, such as the Japanese in diaspora, new religions have ready-made bases from which they can more easily penetrate foreign cultures.

The study of new religious movements provides a very optimistic picture for the growth potential of religion in general in the next century. The lead taken by the United States in producing what is arguably the most religious country in history may in fact be the herald of the overall religious trend in the West.

FOOTNOTES

1 Among the early texts on the new religions were: Harry Thomsen, *The New Religions of Japan* (Rutland, VT: Charles E.Tuttle Company, 1963); Clark B. Offner & Henry van Straelen, *Modern Japanese Religions* (New York: Twayne Publishers, 1963); H. Neill McFarland, *The Rush Hour of the Gods* (New York: Mcmillan Company, 1967); and Robert S. Ellwood, Jr., *The Eagle and the Rising Sun* (Philadelphia: Westminster Press, 1974).
2 Concerning Japanese migration to North America, see: Harry H.L. Kitano, *The Japanese*

Americans: The Evolution of a Subculture (Englewood Cliffs, NJ: Prentice-Hall, 1976).
3 Louise H. Hunter, Buddhism in Hawaii (Honolulu, HI: University of Hawaii Press, 1971).
4 The most recent listing of the new religions in Japan can be found in Japanese Religions (Tokyo: Kodansha International, 1972). On the Jewish groups see: Tudor Parfitt, The Thirteenth Gate: Travels Among the Lost Tribes of Israel (Bethesda, MD: Adler & Adler, 1987).
5 The only survey of Japanese religions operating in North America is J. Gordon Melton, Encyclopedia of American Religions (Detroit: Gale Research Company, 4th ed., 1993). Founders/ leaders are profiled in J. Gordon Melton, Biographical Dictionary of American Cult and Sect Leaders (New York: Garland Publishing, 1986).
6 For the most recent work on charismatic leadership see: Timothy Miller, When Prophets Die: The Postcharismatic Fate of New Religious Movements (Albany, NY: State University of New York Press, 1991).
7 On Konkokyo, see: Konko Daijin: A Biography (San Francisco: Konko Churches of America, 1981) and Konko Kyo's 50 Years in America (San Francisco: Konko Churches of America, 1976).
8 Tenrikyo: Its History and Teachings (Tenri, Japan: Tenrikyo Overseas Mission Department, 1966).
9 On the history of American Buddhism, especially its Japanese Zen phase, see: Rick Fields, When the Swans Came to the Lake (Boulder, CO: Shambhala, 1986) and 'Zen in North America', special issue of Spring Wind, Buddhist Cultural Forum 4, 3 (Fall 1984).
10 The Light from the East: Mokichi Okada (Atami, Japan: MOA Productions, 1983).
11 Roy Eugene Davis, Miracle Man of Japan (Lakemont, GA: CSA Press, 1970).
12 Ronald E. Kotzsch, Macrobiotics, Yesterday and Today (Tokyo, Japan: Japan Publications, 1985).
13 George Williams, Freedom and Influence (Santa Monica, CA: World Tribune Press, 1985).
14 The Development of Japanese Lay Buddhism (Tokyo: Reiyukai, 1986).
15 Rissho Kosei-Kai (Tokyo: Kosei Publishing Co., 1966).
16 Shunryu Suzuki, Zen Mind, Beginner's Mind (New York: Weatherhill, 1979).
17 Hakuyu Taizan Maezumi and Bernard Tetsugen Glassman, On Zen Practice (Los Angeles: Zen Center of Los Angeles, 1976): 2 vols.
18 Jiyu-Kennett Roshi's books include: How to Grow a Lotus Blossom (Mt Shasta, CA: Shasta Abbey, 1977); The Wild, Wild Goose (Mt Shasta, CA: Shasta Abbey, 1970, 1978): 2 vols.; and Zen is Eternal Life (Emeryville, CA: Dharma Publishing, 1976).
19 On the work of the women Buddhist leaders, see Lenore Friedman, Meetings with Remarkable Women (Boston, MA: Shambhala, 1987).
20 Marcus Bach, The Power of Perfect Liberty (Englewood Cliffs, NJ: Prentice-Hall, 1971).
21 A study of Mahikari in Japan was made by Winston Davis, Dojo (Stanford, CA: Stanford University Press, 1980). A survey of its history and teaching from inside the movement is A.K. Tebecis, Mahikari, Thank God for the Answers (Tokyo: L.H. Yoko Shuppan, 1982).
22 The most comprehensive survey of Reiki's history and practice is found in the article on Reiki in J. Gordon Melton, The New Age Encyclopedia (Detroit, MI: Gale Research Company, 1990). Because of some rivalry between the two lineages, no study has come from within the movement.
23 Cf. J. Gordon Melton, 'Another Look at New Religions', Annals of the American Academy of Political Science and Sociology 527 (May 1993): 97-112.
24 Cf. Isotta Poggi, 'American New Religious Movements in Eastern Europe in the 1990s', Syzygy 2, 1/2 (1993).

5
Japanese New Religious Movements in Britain

JEFFREY SOMERS

'Shinto is the root and stem of a big robust tree replete with an inexhaustible amount of energy, and Confucianism is its branches and leaves, while Buddhism is its flowers and fruit.'

Prince Shotoku Taishi. (574-622)
(Herbert. 1967. p.47)[1]

THERE ARE at least 200 (so-called) 'new' religions, 'Shinkō shūkyō', in Japan[2]; so far, very few of them have any representation in the West. As far as Great Britain is concerned, the largest, Sōka Gakkai, has only about five thousand registered members. However, the most notable fact about the New Religious Movements (NRMs) is that however small their membership they are continually gaining converts. While we will examine why Japanese NRMs should be taking root in Britain in particular, and the kinds of people who make up their membership, it will also be necessary to examine both the background of the NRMs themselves and their context in Japan. Only the NRMs that have a presence here will be examined: Seichō-no-Ie, Sōka Gakkai, Mitama Kyōkai, Mahikari and Sekai Kyūseikyō. Also examined is one movement, The Institute for Research in Human Happiness, which has been designated in Japan as one of a new category, the new, new religions.[3]

The Japanese have been said to be a people without religion but this is a judgement using Western standards, because when they are asked their religion the majority reply openly that they have none.[4,5] In Jean Stoetzel's book, *Without the Chrysanthemum and the Sword* published in 1955 for UNESCO, 90 per cent of women and 86 per cent of men said they had no religion. None of them said Shinto was their creed. In a survey carried out by the Japanese National Public Opinion Research Institute and quoted in the same book, 11 people out of 2,671 counted religious experiences amongst things that made them happy. The occasion for one of these was when he had a close view of the Emperor. It is not only significant that he should have thought this a religious experience but also that the Institute should have regarded it as such.

It is well known that the Japanese practise two religions, Shinto and Buddhism. Sociologists contend that there is a great deal of practice in Japan but little faith. If you ask any Japanese, especially the middle aged and the young, if they are religious the majority say that they are not. Must we believe them? If we were to ask 'Are you an agnostic?' or 'Are you an atheist?', questions which are not asked in Japan, the suspicion must be that the answers would be 'no' in both cases. The Japanese in common with other orientals have a different attitude to communication than North-West Europeans and Americans.

The cultural heritage of Japan is epitomized in Shinto which is very much alive today. A Japanese may profess that he is indifferent to religion but he is still a Shintoist at heart. 'Shinto is not a doctrine which attempts to define a man's place in the universe and his relationship with God. . . it does not attempt to theorize or standardize; its attitude is emphatically non-intellectual.'[6] Caldarola goes on to say, 'Shinto goes beyond conventional religious practices to express what is essentially Japanese. . . (Shinto) still remains the most outstanding trait of Japanese culture and the very basis of the value orientation that gives meaning and consistency to the modern Japanese.'

Probably the most unusual fact for us is that the Japanese practise two religions and see no conflict in this. In the countryside it is still usual to find in almost every house both a *Butsudan*, (a Buddhist altar) as well as a *Kamidana* (a shelf for the household Shinto gods). But this is in the country and not in the very small dwellings in which most Japanese live in the larger towns. For us this is a critical point. Most of the new religions have grown up and have their followers in the large towns where the extended family and its traditions are no longer the norm.

H. Thompson suggested in his book, *The New Religions of Japan*, that there were a considerable number of farmers that were members of new religions. What is interesting is that he cites the main rural areas for these to be the islands of Kyushu and Hokkaido, the prefectures of Okayama, Hiroshima and Yamaguchi. Each of these areas would contain people who would have special reasons for tending to become interested in new religions. It was in Kyushu and Hiroshima that the atomic bombs were dropped and Okayama and Yamaguchi are neighbouring prefectures to Hiroshima; Hokkaido was the Japanese equivalent of the Wild West and still has a population which could be called 'new' in comparison with the rest of Japan.

In the country, each family would be a member of its local Shinto shrine as well as most probably being a donating member of its nearby Buddhist temple. This is not true for the town-dweller but this is not to say that all or nearly all town-dwellers do not practise one or more religion. Indeed, according to the controlling body for most of Shinto, the Jinja Honsho (The Association of Shinto Shrines), the fastest growing business in Japan is that of providing Inari Shrines for new offices and shops. Most would not wish to be without one.

If we need to search for a reason for the growth of the new religions in Japan we do not need to seek further that the innate need of the Japanese to belong to some sort of group together with the gradual elimination of ancestor worship, a basis of religion in their lives when removed from their country roots. This 'lack of something' has been prominent particularly during the 1930s when Japan had become industrialized but was suffering economically and again after the Second World War when the old religions had lost credit as they were identified with Japan's defeat, and when Japan's economic fortunes were rising.

An example of the fact that the Japanese practise two religions is that Buddhist priests are also followers of Shinto: as long ago as 838 the famous monk Ennin, who went from Japan to T'ang China, called for protection during a storm at sea not on the Buddha or on one of the bodhisattvas but on the important Shinto deity referred to as the Great God of Sumiyoshi.[7]

The early NRMs are the most redolent of Shinto and share the possibility of there being living gods (*ikigami*). It is this belief amongst the Japanese that has given one of the main possibilities for the acceptance of the NRMs and not only those that are based on Shinto. The early NRMs addressed the problems of poverty, illness and peace while the new NRMs deal with the fear of it in the mind. The new NRMs aim to prove that there is a world of the spirit and of mystery. It is not their purpose to address poverty, illness or suffering. They want to prove their miraculous nature to people and this has become more important than the solving of temporal difficulties.

The interest in these religions amongst the affluent youth has possibly come about from their lack of satisfaction with material rewards. There has arisen since the 1970s (the 'Oil Shock' period) a belief that affluence offers no solutions and what is needed is an affluence of the mind or heart. There has been a maxim in Japan that 'high production and high technology is best' which has come to be questioned, it being noted that a high growth economy results in high pollution.[8]

The Japanese Ministry of Education carries out regular surveys of public opinion, and until 1973 the question 'is religion important?' had an ever-reducing score. Since then it has each year been on the increase along with the number of people stating that they are religious. This shows a complete turn-around from the period after World War Two when there appeared to be a turning away from religion.

Japanese children growing up in the 1980s and since are of a generation who do not know poverty and who do not universally subscribe to the extreme Japanese work ethic. These young people have a new purpose, to discover the meaning of life. They come from an affluent background, but at the same time they have a strong perception of the dangers inherent in the world's present situation. To find answers to their questions they have turned to religion or the occult. The new NRMs are perceived by youngsters to have the answers. The IRH, for example, tells them how to live more actively and has an explanation of their purpose in the universe.

Before we look at some of the NRMs and their situation in Britain today, it is useful to consider how we might categorise them. One possibility is chronologically according to either when they were founded in Japan or when they first came to this country. We might classify them according to their religious derivation i.e. Shinto, Buddhist or Christian or by their size here or in Japan. For the purpose of this paper we will use the chronological categorisation since it is the appearance of the IRH, the most recent to be established in Japan, that provides the impetus for a fresh investigation of NRMs.

SEICHO-NO-IE (The House of Growth)

Seichō-no-Ie, the 'House of Growth' was founded by Masaharu Taniguchi (1893-1985) in the early 1930s by a rather unusual method. Taniguchi published a magazine which carried his message into the world. He taught that in the World of Reality (Jisso), man is created in the image of God and is already in possession of the divine attributes of God (Infinite Wisdom, Infinite Love, Infinite Life, Infinite Abundance, Infinite Joy and Infinite Harmony).

When a man comes to the realization that he is a perfect spiritual being his delusions will disappear and he will naturally come to manifest perfect health, harmony and happiness. This can be achieved in our present lifetime. Dr Taniguchi stressed that Seichō-no-Ie embraces all religions, races and creeds. He said that they all emanate from the same God.

Seichó-no-Ie states that the purpose of human life is for man to develop his soul and to awaken to his true nature as a child of God. Obstacles are opportunities to learn to overcome obstacles and develop character. The physical world is said to be a reflection of the mind. To be healthy one should develop the habit of maintaining healthy thoughts and harmonious feelings. It is strongly based on the power of the word, teaching that if one can look beyond phenomena and realize the World of Reality (*Jisso*) this principle will be a living source of salvation.

The movement is now led by Dr Taniguchi's son, the Reverend Seichó Taniguchi, who like his father has written many books. Dr Taniguchi wrote more than four hundred while his son has written about half that number. This is significant because Seichó-no-Ie is propagated through its literature. Dr Taniguchi's major work 'Truth of Life' in forty volumes is the canon of this religion, and it is claimed that it has sold about sixteen million copies. It is in various states of translation in six languages. Seichó-no-Ie now issues six magazines which have a monthly subscription of more than three million copies.

Seichó-no-Ie is divided into three associations, the men's association (Mutual Love Association), the women's association (White Dove Association) and the Youth Association. Each association tries to disseminate the founder's teachings. There are also special groups for educators, businessmen and artists.

Their main activities are carried out in two major shrines and six spiritual training centres in Japan where, in addition to training (*rensei kai*), organizational meetings, study sessions, and religious ceremonies are held. The Grand Shrine is in Nagasaki occupying a site of more than eight hundred acres. Their headquarters is in Tokyo.

Training sessions consist of lectures, study, '*shinsokan*' a form of prayerful meditation, discussion sessions, laughing practice and other practices to encourage and deepen their realization of what they refer to as their 'indwelling divinity'.

Their membership is about four million with one quarter of it outside Japan. It exists in USA, Mexico, Brazil and other parts of Latin America, in Taiwan, Korea and other parts of Asia, and in Europe including Great Britain.[9]

In October 1992 I interviewed the current chairperson for Great Britain who is a Japanese lady married to a Scot. She said that Seichó-no-Ie was first brought to England in the 1980s through another Japanese lady married to an Englishman, and that she had been a member for most of her life as her mother has been a member for forty years. She said that they did not have many members in Britain yet and they did not aggressively recruit. The numbers fluctuated since they had members from the Japanese business community as well as a number of Brazilian members who happened to be in Britain. They have welcomed instructors from both Japan and Brazil.

Some meetings are held in English for British and Brazilian members while others are held in Japanese. The meetings consist of discussions or readings from Taniguchi's works. Members practise *shinsokan* every day alone at home and sometimes with other members for about fifteen to thirty minutes. For beginners to this practice there is a tape recording which helps to instruct them in it.

I was shown her *butsudan* complete with memorial tablets (*ihai*) for dead family members (even her late dog). One could see that her practice was very Buddhist in form and this is true for other members of the movement.

Because of their recent establishment this NRM has not yet made a significant showing in this country. Members are all middle class which reflects the situation in Japan, and the few British members have joined because of some already established connection with Japan.

SŌKA GAKKAI (Value Creating Society)

There are about fifty-five Buddhist denominations in Japan. Until recently, Zen has been the best know in the West but rapidly gaining in fame is Sōka Gakkai (Value Creating Society). It is said to be the fastest growing religion in the world with more than 16 million followers in Japan alone.[10]

The sect is named after Nichiren (1222-1282) a turbulent patriot and priest who based his teaching on the Lotus Sutra. Monks of the orders which stem from him are required to study the sutra but the ordinary believer is only asked to repeat the formula '*Namu-myoho-renge-kyo*' (Glory to the Sutra of the Lotus of Truth). This is chanted in loud tones, often communally, accompanied by much beating of drums.

Makiguchi Tsunesaburo (1871-1944), who was born in Niigata Prefecture,[11] was an elementary school principal and an education-alist. He founded the Sōka Kyoiku Gakkai (Value Creating Education Society) in 1930. This was a difficult period in Japan for any non-orthodox group since the *Kempeitai* (secret police) had their eye on anyone with divergent views. Sōka Kyoiku Gakkai was no exception and consequently grew slowly and by 1937 it had only 60 members. Makiguchi was thrown in gaol with many other followers and died there.

After World War Two Toda Josei (1900-1958), who had shared gaol with Makiguchi and had been second in command, revived the sect as 'Sōka Gakkai'. This reflected Toda's idea that 'Value creating' was not just confined to education and educators but should be directed towards the whole of society. He was a marvellous organizer and by 1955 the sect had over a million followers. His innovation which led to the rapid increase in membership was the aggressive '*shakubuku*' (literally 'break and subdue') policy. To rise in the hierarchy of the organization a member was required to bring in a certain number of other members. This policy was carried out with great vigour. The majority of the membership at that time was from the working and lower middle classes. According to Sōka Gakkai today both the policy and its translation have been much toned down. The new given translation for '*shakubuku*' is 'to teach others the Buddhist view of life and how to chant *Nam-myoho-renge-kyo*'. (See any edition of *UK Express* the monthly magazine of SGI-UK).

It was during the 1950s that Sōka Gakkai began to develop its interest in politics. It was amazingly successful, despite the fact that many of its followers were arrested and accused of, amongst other offences, intimidation. In 1959 all of the 76 candidates put up by Sōka Gakkai in Tokyo were elected as were 261 of the 287 that they had put up in the nation overall. At the same time all the Sōka Gakkai candidates for the Upper House were elected and the party became the third largest in Japan. Called the Komeito or Clean Government Party it has gone from success to success though in the last elections for the National Diet (parliament) it had elected 24 members.

In 1960 Daisaku Ikeda (b.1928) became the organization's third president. He had been a pupil of Toda Josei. It has been Ikeda who has encouraged the worldwide spread of Sōka Gakkai founding in 1975 Sōka Gakkai International which now has approximately 1.26 million members in 115 countries. In 1979 he resigned assuming the role of honorary president (the position he still holds). Hiroshi Hojo became the fourth president of Sōka Gakkai until he died in 1981 when Einosuke Akiya became the fifth president, a post which he still holds.[12]

At the moment Sōka Gakkai is a lay organization independent from the political party, the Komeito and from Nichiren Shōshū, the Buddhist priestly sect, although Sōka Gakkai has links with the priests of one of the original lines descended from Nichiren. The

Nichiren Shóshú sect has its main temple, the Taiseki-ji, at the foot of Mt Fuji, which contains the *Gohonzon* (literally the object of devotion) in the form of a mandala. This mandala is not regarded as existing outside of or separate from one's life.

Sóka Gakkai has adopted many of the practices of Nichiren Shóshú, and members undertake to chant twice daily before a shrine which contains a replica of the Gohonzon. They chant the invocation (*Daimoku*) and two chapters of the Lotus sutra. They believe that chanting (*Gongyo*) can alter one's karma and bring great benefits to both the believer in whatever way he (or she) may wish as well as being of benefit to the whole of mankind. In addition, members have discussion groups (*zadakandai*) which most often are held in their homes where they discuss benefits received from their practice and also expose their current difficulties.[13]

The administration of Sóka Gakkai is carried out by its members and is organized into local, regional and national groupings in countries where the membership is large enough. There are also sections for young men with a separate one for young women and another for children.

Sóka Gakkai has never forgotten its connection with education and it has today its own university, Sóka University which has international links with many universities including London as well as high, junior and primary schools in Japan and kindergartens. It maintains two art museums, the Mid-on Concert Association which in various ways promotes music, and The Institute of Oriental Philosophy founded in 1962 which furthers studies and research in a wide range of disciplines including, of course, Buddhism.[14] It has taken a great interest in the subject of conservation and world peace and circulates exhibitions internationally as well as maintaining various links with the United Nations.

During an interview with two of the leading members, I was told that Sóka Gakkai started in England in the early 1960s, and in 1974 Richard Causten the present Chairman was appointed director, at that time there being about two hundred registered members. It was registered in this country as a charity under the name 'Nichiren Shoshu of the United Kingdom'. It is now applying to have that name changed to 'Soka Gakkai of the United Kingdom'.

Great Britain is divided into twenty areas having more than five thousand registered members. Europe altogether has something like fifty thousand members. Membership now requires six months study, a formal application with recommendations and the approval of one's partner if there is one. They admit to a drop-out rate of between 20 per cent and 30 per cent which they say is about usual for most movements. One of the odd features of the interview was that it was stated that NSUK was a British organization and although there were some Japanese members here and members often visited Japan there was an effort to emphasize the Britishness of the organization here. It was stated that they tried not to use much Japanese terminology. This seems strange taken against the background of constant chanting in Japanese and the use of the terms, 'Daimoku', 'Gongyo', 'Gohonzon' etc., to say nothing of the name of the organization itself.

Membership here is somewhat different to Japan with regard to social class. Most Japanese today believe that they are all middle class, but nevertheless Sóka Gakkai members there are still working and lower middle class in the main while in this country the majority are middle class as is the membership of most 'New Age' movements.

Sóka Gakkai has been called 'Designer Buddhism' and has attracted some Press interest because its membership includes some well-known pop stars and actors. Apart from using the word-of-mouth technique for recruiting membership, many members, especially in London, joined in the 1980s after coming into contact with a very successful Japanese practitioner of Macrobiotics, the late Mr Yoshio Kawahara. Mr Kawahara's funeral in 1989 was remarkable and involved several hundred Só ka Gakkai members in West London who, to the accompaniment of drums and much chanting, bore witness to his body's cremation.

Until recently NSUK had its headquarters in Richmond but although it retains these premises including a retail shop, the new headquarters are at Taplow Court near Maidenhead. This stately house is famous for, amongst other things, being the place where Queen Elizabeth I was kept prisoner when a princess by Queen Mary, and it is now beautifully renovated. It contains not only the administrative headquarters of NSUK but a large hall for communal Gongyo and several large rooms for public exhibitions. Open days for visitors are held regularly.

SEKAI KYÚSEIKYÓ (World Salvation Religion)

Sekai Kyúseikyó (World Salvation Religion) was founded under the name of Kannon-kyo in 1934 by Mokichi Okada. It changed again in 1947 to Nippon Kannon Kyodan and again in 1950 to Sekai Meshiyakyo and shortly after to its present name. Okada was originally a member of Ōmotokyō and the teaching revealed to him is a mixture of Shinto, Buddhism and Christianity but stylistically like Ōmoto.

Okada's main teachings are that the earth is approaching the last judgement and that it will be followed by a paradise on earth, but until this happens man must build model paradises on earth. Two 'miniature paradises' have been created: one in the mountains of Hakone is complete with a museum containing important Chinese and Japanese antiques together with some extremely valuable Western Impressionist paintings. The 'paradise' just above the resort of Atami is the headquarters of Sekai Kyusei Kyo. The opulence of the buildings and collections are redolent of the wealth of this movement.

It was in 1926 that Okada had his revelations from God who asked him to be a messiah and prophet to mankind. He was given at that time, he claimed, 'divine light' (johrei) to heal diseases and perform miracles. He said that people would be cured of anything by applying a piece of paper to their sick part upon which was written the characters for 'hikari' (light). Okada died in 1955, but according to his followers he did not die but merely went ahead to finish purification in the name of all mankind. His wife, Yoshiko, succeeded him as head of the movement until her death in 1962 when Okada's married daughter, Fujieda Itsuki, assumed the leadership.

Okada taught that 'this world consists not only of the visible world, but there is also an invisible, spiritual world. These two worlds are closely connected; indeed, they are like two sides of a sheet of paper, the one not existing without the other. It is the spiritual world which is the main component of this universe because it is eternal and is the source of all energy governing the universe. Everything occurs first in the spiritual world, and is then reflected in the visible world'.

Okada taught that man should live in accord with the spiritual world but that he had turned his back on it for the material world. His idea was that contemporary disasters are caused by God destroying and therefore purifying the old so that a new world can be created. The new paradise that will come will be a work of truth, virtue and beauty. With considerable pride he felt that the Japanese aesthetic sensibility would especially give spiritual nourishment. This latter point added greatly to his success in Japan.

Okada explained that all the evils in the world, spiritual and physical, were explained by a theory which states that everyone and everything gives off a spiritual vibration which is nowadays dense and therefore polluted. Johrei can dissipate the impurities and restore conditions to how they should be, and because of this he made his followers sceptical of medicine, doctors and hospitals. Johrei can be applied to anything and is often applied by Okada's followers to the soil – members avoiding the use of fertilisers. It will come as no surprise to learn, therefore, that many of Okada's followers are farmers.

Sekai Kyūseikyó teaches that the soul is reincarnated after a period of re-education. It is friendly towards other religions, especially Christianity but maintains that it is above any other religion, having a mission to save mankind and the whole world.[15]

Sekai Kyúseikyó has not yet functioned as a religion in Britain where it appears as the MOA Foundation, a charitable organization attempting to be responsive to the needs of the country where it has a presence. In Peru it has funded an elementary school, in Thailand, an agricultural training school and in Mexico a ceramics school. It teaches the Japanese language in Brussels, Paris, Lisbon and Hamburg. It started teaching Japanese and Ikebana in London in 1983 and a year later in Oxford. The principal, Mr Okada, had founded his own school of flower arrangement known as Sangetsu. Since 1984 many seminars have been given on various aspects of Japanese culture. More recently, the MOA Foundation has sponsored festivals and other events to promote social development and trans-cultural cooperation as well as helping Japanese scholars study Japanese objects in British museums.[16]

IESU NO MITAMA KYÓKAI (The Spirit of Jesus Church)

Iesu no Mitama Kyókai (The Spirit of Jesus Church) was officially registered in Japan in 1941 by its self-appointed Bishop Jun Murai who died in 1970. In about 1918, Jun Murai's wife had been converted to Christianity by Mr and Mrs Taylor, who were 'Police Missionaries'. In Victorian times it was not unusual to have attached to police courts missionaries who were primarily concerned with the reform of offenders but some of them did engage in missionary work abroad.

Murai was converted to Christianity by his wife. He later had an inner conflict between what he was being taught and what he came to believe himself. After a period of great despair he attempted to drown himself in the sea but was rescued. He then received the sort of experience that has been described by many Pentecostalists as speaking in tongues. He became convinced that he had received the Holy Spirit and had been instructed to be an apostle and to found his own church. On 23 July 1933 the Holy Spirit descended on Japan and many people had deeply religious experiences.

The new church that he founded is based on The Old and New Testaments which are accepted as God's word. They believe in God and Christ but not the Trinity, and carry out baptism by immersion in water in the name of Christ. The essence of the Church is said to be that it follows the inheritance from the Apostles of the first church. It is neither Catholic nor Protestant but a follower of the Christian church which the Lord initially organized. Its coming to Japan is foretold in the Bible as being due to appear in the last days. It is the true church restored as it existed in primitive Christianity and has the real, the perfect and the exalted mysteries. Bishop Murai may have been chosen as one of the fulfilments of the saying in the Bible that light would come from the East. The members of the church try to reflect the earliest form of the historical church, for example their holy day being Saturday as in the early Christian church.

In September 1992, I visited their church in London called Eikoku Iesu no Mitama Kyokai (The Spirit of Jesus Church in the UK) and attended their service which consisted of prayers, hymns and readings from the Old and New Testaments as well as a sermon given by a young Japanese minister. There were 10 people in the congregation of which two were English and the rest Japanese. All the service except for the hymns (which were sung in Japanese and accompanied on the piano) were given alternately in Japanese and English, using the International edition of the Bible.

Later that day, I interviewed the minister together with his wife who is also a minister. He informed me that a representative of the church first came to this country in 1984, and that there are branches of this church in Brazil, Columbia, Peru, Bolivia, The USA, Canada, Taiwan, Korea, Singapore, The Philippines, Indonesia and France. The organization has 102 churches in Japan and about 40,000 members,[17] and nearly 100 of the people worshipping there are non-Japanese. Twelve years ago a minister from the church in Osaka came regularly to Britain to preach the Gospel. There are about twenty members in London and they do not advertise, new members being recruited through word of mouth.

MAHIKARI

Mahikari originated in Japan in 1959. This was a result of 'revelations' to Yoshikazu Okada who later became known as 'Sukuinushisama' which means 'Master of Salvation' or 'Great

Saviour'. He had been both a soldier and a businessman.

Okada was born on 27 February 1901. He was an Equestrian Flag Bearer in the first Regiment of the Imperial Guards, a great honour in Japan. While on duty in Indochina he fell from his horse and substained injuries which appeared to be incurable. The doctors said that he had only three years to live and he decided to devote these to God. He did not die and subsequently set up several companies but these were destroyed during the Second World War, Okada becoming bankrupt and having several periods of illness. These difficulties seemed to him to bring him nearer to God.

Okada struggled to pay off his debts and then on his birthday, in 1959, he had his first revelation from God. This was that all religions had so far only revealed some of the Divine Truth and that he would receive the innermost depths of the Truth never revealed before. Okada claimed that the Holy Spirit of Divine Truth entered into him and that he was ordered to proclaim what he had been told. He was told at that time to take the name of *Kotama* (Ball of Light) and to prepare the world for very difficult times to come.

From 1959 to 1974 he is said to have ascended to the Divine Spiritual World where he received further revelations from God. Most of these are now contained in two books considered sacred, the Book of Holy Words or Revelations (*Goseigenshu*), and the Book of Prayers (*Norigotoshu*). Other Divine teachings were subsequently revealed from time to time in the monthly Mahikari journal.

In 1961 Okada received the new name of *Seigyoku* (Holy Jewel), which was claimed to be the result of a consultation of a Divine oracle by Shinto priests. In 1965 he received the spiritual name of *Seio* (Holy Bird) and later became generally known as *Sukuinush-isama* (Great Saviour). Okada is said to have been given many missions by 'Almighty God'. These include:

1. To hold up the hand and purify the world.
2. To enable people to channel the power of 'Almighty God'.
3. To build the World Shrine in order to enshrine the Almighty Creator God
4. To awaken all people to the importance of the invisible but real dimensions of existence called spiritual and astral worlds.
5. To change the world from following a back-to-front or illusory path to the righteous path.
6. To give people understanding of the existence of countless souls living in the world of spirit as well as those interfering with people on earth.

These missions are based on the fundamental tenets of Mahikari which are said to be:

1. The origin of the Earth is one.
2. The origin of mankind is one.
3. The religions of the world have the same origin.

Mahikari teaches that faith should be part of everyday life and lead the individual towards happiness which it says has three essential points:

1. Freedom from illness.
2. A state of mind in which antagonistic feelings do not arise.
3. Freedom from poverty.

Sukuinushisama made many prophecies about the future as well as new interpretations of history. These were given, he said, under Divine guidance. Ten days before he died in 1974 he officially handed over his Divine missions to his daughter, Sachiko, whose spiritual name is *Keijusama* (Blessed Jewel). She became the second Great Teacher and Spiritual Leader and is known as *Oshienushisama* (Master of Teaching or Great Teacher).

Followers of Mahikari say that she is the representative of Almighty God on Earth at this time and that her spiritual power is greater than anyone else alive. They say that as contact with her is the closest we can come to contact with God it is most significant to be blessed by her whenever possible.[18]

The full name of the Mahikari organization is 'Sukyo Mahikari'. 'Sukyo' literally means 'reverend teachings' but the implied meaning is that it is Divine teaching that goes beyond ordinary human knowledge or philosophies. 'Mahikari' means True Light. This True Light is said to heal in a way that is more than just the physical removal of toxic material and the rejuvenation of tissues but because it contains Divine wisdom, will and emotion it gives a progressive understanding, removes spiritual impurities and gives protection. Even animals and plants are said to benefit from it. Sukyo Mahikari claims not to be a religion, sect, philosophy or ideology.

Anyone may begin to radiate True Light irrespective of religion or race. This can happen only after attending a three-day seminar called *kenshu* and receiving a Divine pendant called *omitama*. Remarkable claims are made for this *omitama*. It is worn around the neck on a chain and just by raising the hand the person wearing it is said to be able to focus True Light like a channel or lens. The wearer is said to be protected, blessed and continuously purified by wearing it. The first *omitama* one receives looks like a gold-plated locket which is wrapped in a protective cloth and worn around the neck.

The practice of salvation by radiating the light of God through the hands is called *Mahikari no waza* but is also known as *okiyome* (transmission of light). This was given through a special covenant made between God and the founder. The practice of *Mahikari no waza* is said to purify all kinds of evil, negative and poisonous vibrations as well as leading to a healthier life.[19] Sukyo Mahikari is organized into different sizes of training centres. A training centre is known as a *dojo*, which is the usual Japanese term for such a place. A centre for the transmission of the light is called an *okiyomecho* and there are *han* or centres in a home.

The personal hierarchy is:

1. *Shidobucho*. A chief instructor responsible for a region e.g. Europe.
2. *Dōjōcho*. The president of a dōjō.
3. *Doshi*. A minister
4. *Hancho*. The leader of a small section.[20]

In October 1992, I interviewed one of the two resident Japanese responsible for Mahikari in Great Britain, the other one being a Japanese lady. The Doshi came to London in 1989 prior to spending some time some time on Mahikari's behalf in America.

The *dōjō* is in Norwood in South London although some other meetings are held in other parts of London at different times. In the entrance hall is a Te-mizu-ya[21] for washing one's hands and mouth, the same ritual purification required from a person entering the precincts of a Shinto shrine. All visitors are requested to at least wash their hands if they are going into the inner hall which contains a typical Shinto-style shrine called by Mahikari a *goshintai*. This is the usual word *shintai* used in Shinto for an object of worship in which the spirit of a deity is believed to reside, with the honorific *go* placed in front of it.[22] In this case a sacred scroll with the characters for 'Mahikari' is the Goshintai. Also in the shrine is the Chuon, a sort of comma which is the symbol of the god 'Su' rather like the Magatama, the Shinto sacred jewel, together with a statue of Izunome-sama. Izunome-sama is the god who manifests spiritual energy. It is here before the shrine, on mats, that throughout any day it is possible to receive Okiyome which I did from the Doshi. He first of all clapped his hands (*kashiwade*) three times, once more than is normal in Shinto although the number of times is not strictly fixed.[23] He recited a short prayer and administered Okiyome to me. Mahikari practice seems redolent of Shinto though it is true that a major difference is that in Shinto only the priests, shrine maidens and sometimes musicians can officiate.

The Doshi said that Mahikari did not really get established in Britain until 1984. Active membership is currently about 300, whereas in Japan there are about half a million, France about 3,000, Italy 1,000 and about the same number in Belgium and Spain.

The Doshi said he felt that Mahikari was a derivation of Omoto and that some other NRM's were also. The similarity of their symbol to that of Johrei and its practice of healing came about from Mahikari's founder having for a time studied with Mr Okada of Sekai Kyūsei Kyō. He emphasized that Mahikari was not in conflict with any other religion new or old as the individual was free to choose what he followed. He saw his responsibility as being to tell people about Mahikari and to offer them light if they wished to receive it.

A few days later I was invited to a lunch given for some academics who were interested in welcoming Professor Hakan Snellman, Associate Professor of Theoretical Particle Physics at the Royal Institute of Technology in Stockholm who was going to give a lecture later that evening entitled 'Transcending Human Science'. Professor Snellman is a convert to Mahikari and his lecture was sponsored by them. When I interviewed him he stressed, as he did in his lecture, that modern science was not the ultimate approach to knowledge and that there was a way to bring about a relationship between spiritual beliefs and scientific knowledge so that our daily lives would benefit.

KŌFUKU NO KAGAKU (Institute for Research in Human Happiness)

The Kōfuku no Kagaku (Institute for Research in Human Happiness) is often classified in Japan as the predominant new new religion. It was founded by Ryuho Okawa (not his original name) born in 1956 in Tokushima Prefecture. He graduated in Law from Tokyo University and then studied International Finance at New York University while working for a Tokyo-based general trading company.

On 23 March 1981 he received a revelation and realized that his mission was to save all humankind, resigning from his company in July 1986 to establish the IRH to which he devoted thereafter his entire life. He claims to be the reincarnation of the Buddha.[24] He has already published over 100 books which include:

The Laws of the Sun, The Laws of Gold, The Laws of Eternity, The

Rebirth of Buddha, The Essential Messages of Shakyamuni, The Eightfold Path, The Spiritual Messages of Jesus Christ, The Spiritual Messages of Moses, New Prophecies of Nostradamus, The Warnings of Allah.

IRH teaches that happiness starts in the mind. The first step is the study of God's Truth which Mr Okawa states has been the goal of all religions and philosophies throughout the ages. He goes on to say that there are four principles of happiness which are:

1. Love. This is 'the love that gives', attachment is the 'love that deprives'.
2. Knowledge. This includes research into the spirit and the soul and into the universe which is said to be multidimensional.
3. Reflection. This involves looking back and examining one's life. The true causes of our difficulties are usually found to be within us. Only when erroneous thoughts and attachments have been eliminated can we discover our truly free inner selves.
4. Development. This is eternal self-improvement. Whether we are happy or not depends on whether or not we feel we are developing.

The IRH studies the science of the mind, which is research into the study of the mind's characteristics, actions, functions, and mechanisms. The purpose of this study is that it will lead to discovery of the principles of happiness.

The IRH has established a particular view of the universe. There is not, they say, just a physical world and a spiritual world but the universe is multi-dimensional and higher-dimensional. The tenth dimension is where planetary consciousness exists. The ninth dimension is where most developed human spirits dwell. This is also referred to as the 'Cosmic Realm' or the 'Sun Realm'.

In the eighth dimension the spirits dwell who have been supreme leaders in fields such as religion, philosophy and science. This realm is sometimes referred to as the 'Diamond Realm'. The seventh realm contains people as spirits who lived to love and showed mercy when in the physical world. It is also known as the 'Sacred Heavenly Realm'.

The sixth dimension is called the 'Godly Realm' and is inhabited by spirits who lived as scholars, artists, religious leaders and philosophers and other specialists who contributed to the evolution of human kind. People who were very faithful, spiritual and lived good lives when living in the physical world go to the fifth dimension which is also known as the 'Spiritual World'.

The fourth dimension is divided into two and contains the 'Astral

Realm' for spirits who are aware of their death and know of their spiritual existence while the other part is called the 'Hell Realm'. The third dimension is this world or 'Phenomenal World'.

Mr Okawa has given a particular view of history where Japan is said to be the place where in the second half of the twentieth century many Angels of Light have incarnated. Because of this, he says, Japan appears to be one large holy land where the great salvation project will be launched. This is seen against a background where human history is not viewed as something produced by accident or by the trials and errors of people but that history has been watched over by the high spirits of the heavenly world. The Angels of Light have incarnated from time to time in this world to advance culture and civilisation. Mr Okawa gives examples of such Angels of Light as Zeus, Apollo, Moses, certain deities of Shinto such as Ama-terasu-o-mikami, Shakyamuni Buddha, Confucius, Lao-tzu, Chuang-tzu, Socrates, Plato, Aristotle and Martin Luther.

The salvation project has two main parts. The first is the creation of an utopia in the mind of everyone while the second is the creation of the kingdom of heaven on Earth. The Institute is researching the principles that can lead us to happiness.[25]

In September 1992, I interviewed the European representative of the IRH, who is a businessman of about thirty, typical of the young membership. Although interested in religions in general he was originally an active Protestant whose father was a Christian but his mother a Buddhist following Nichiren-shu, (not Sōka Gakkai). He went to a Christian High school and the Jesuit-run university (Sophia) in Tokyo.

Later, he went to work in America and came to London two years ago. A colleague lent him Okawa's book, *Laws of the Sun*, which interested him but its Buddhist flavour slightly put him off. He was interested enough to read other books by Okawa and finally felt that he had found the teaching he was looking for and joined the Institute.

The European representative stressed that although there were original Buddhist elements to the teachings of Okawa the best of everything was included. IRH has two basic goals. The first is the achievement of enlightenment for the individual which is real happiness. No one can give this to you as it has to be achieved by yourself. This is the achievement of utopia in your mind which is like Christ said, 'the Kingdom of God is within you'. The second goal is that of a social utopia. If enough people can achieve utopia in their mind then a social utopia will follow. The second can only be achieved through the first.

71

The path to achieve this is through directed knowledge, and therefore it is very important to read Mr Okawa's books. There is, however, meditation of a basic type, reflecting on oneself. I asked how would one know if one was making progress towards enlightenment? His reply was that the universe is multidimensional and through the study of the book, *The Laws of Eternity*, you could judge at what stage you were. A second way was to judge the level of your love. The higher your enlightenment the greater your love. The different levels of love are described by Mr Okawa.

When Mr Okawa started the IRH he limited its membership, giving people an entrance examination. They were asked to read at least ten of his books and to then write an essay. Mr Okawa would then read all the essays and decided who had succeeded and who had failed. At the beginning only about twenty-five per cent were allowed to join the Institute because he wanted to form a strong base. The people he gathered during this period, which lasted for three years, were of a high standard, being doctors, university lecturers, presidents of companies or even senior people from other religious sects. After joining the Institute study was continued and there were more examinations, to make 'strong instructors' as Mr Okawa called them.

In 1990, the fourth year, the door was opened to more people and although the system of reading books continued a system of recommendation was instituted. Certain members are now eligible to recommend other people. Such a recommended person does not have to write an essay. He said that since the open door policy was instituted the quality of entrants had dropped.

In 1991 IRH claimed 5.6 million members in Japan and Mr Okawa is quoted in *The Times* newspaper as hoping to attract ten million followers by 1994. It is still very small outside Japan, approximate memberships being: 200 in Korea, 200 in Brazil, 400 in the USA and 150 in Europe, which includes 60 in Britain (of which only three are British and one is a German living in this country).

There is a wish to increase the number of British members but the organization here must be on a firm base and this has not yet been achieved as there are only five of Mr Okawa's books published in English at the moment. Mr Okawa's purpose is to educate Japanese members first and it takes time to educate five million members.

As far as practice is concerned the most important thing is practice on one's own and to read the books to gain knowledge, as well as everyday reflection. All over Japan there are local branches formed from what are called 'teams' which have 'team leaders'. Team leaders call team meetings and invite one of the one thousand licensed instructors to come and give a lecture on the teaching. This may be followed by a discussion.

SHINKŌ-KAI

Mr Okawa's teaching continues on from another NRM, 'The God Light Association' (*Shinkō-kai*) founded by Mr Takahashi whose most important contribution was a method for researching and purifying one's self. The self is seen as a third party, and gradually through this process your reincarnated lives are realized. In the process of researching yourself you must not tell yourself lies even if you lie to other people as God is watching you.

Mr Takahashi died in the late 1970s when he was forty-eight years old. Before he died he said that someone would come soon and follow his concept. Many of Mr Takahashi's followers went to join Mr Okawa, as predicted, but not all – some continuing to practise only what Mr Takahashi taught. For a donation of 70,000 yen or more a special symbol is given to wear but it is not essential to the teaching though donation is an important principle.

SUMMARY

The Japanese new religions that have come to Britain have some of the following characteristics:

1. Most of them are syncretic.
2. All of them claim to heal.
3. All of them state that followers will receive their benefits in this life.
4. Most of them have some of the characteristics of a family business.
5. All of them claim miracles.
6. Most claim that Japan is the promised land.

Of the six NRMs we have been considering only two are not syncretic: Nichiren Shōshū is wholly Buddhist and Iesu no Mitama Kyōkai is solely Christian. Sōka Gakkai has had the greatest growth of all NRMs but this is probably not due to its being Buddhist. One suspects that its growth here as in Japan is more due to the clarity of its message and practice together with its ability to organize.

Seichō-no-Ie is a mixture of Buddhism and Christianity in spite of the fact that its founder, Taniguchi, had spent some time in Omoto-kyo, one of the early Shinto-based NRMs.[26] In that it makes a bridge between a Japanese form of Buddhism and non-sectarian Christianity one might suppose that this would appeal in the West as having the best of both worlds.

The founder of Sekai Kyúseikyó was also a former member of Ómotokyó but he made a synthesis of Shinto, Buddhism and Christianity. Its strong emphasis outside Japan on the teaching of the Japanese language, flower arrangement and the sponsorship of artistic and cultural events has brought it in touch with an ever growing number of foreigners.

Mahikari is redolent of Shinto; nevertheless it has some small differences of which the most important are the proclamation of the divinity of its founder and its declaration that it is supra-religious, allowing its members to follow another religion if they so wish. Mahikari's appeal in the West has been largely due to its healing practice.

The IRH is the syncretic religion par excellence. Mr Okawa puts forward the theory that since no religion has completely succeeded none of them possess the whole of the truth, but nevertheless they have some of the truth. Mr Okawa had judged what part of the truth each religion contains and he has brought such truths together to form something that he claims must be superior to any of its parts. All the great religions are included together with some philosophies.

This syncretic approach seems to be particularly appealing to modern youth in the West where the authoritarian and narrow view of most traditional religions is questioned and no longer universally welcome.

All the Japanese NRMs in Britain have healing as either a major or minor element in their teaching. For both Sekai Kyúseikyó and Mahikari physical as well as psychological healing is fundamental. For Seichó-no-Ie, Sóka Gakkai and the IRH it is that psychological well being leads to physical wellbeing and for Iesu no Mitama Kyókai the practice of the true faith will bring a complete life. It is healing that might be said to be the predominant attraction to young people in the West.

All proclaim that their practice is a benefit to followers in this life. Seichó-no-Ie states that when a man comes to the realization that he is a perfect spiritual being his delusions will disappear and he will naturally come to manifest perfect health, harmony and happiness, which can be achieved in one's lifetime.

Members of Sóka Gakkai believe that their practice of chanting can alter one's karma and bring great benefits to both the believer in whatever way he (or she) may wish as well as being of benefit to the whole of mankind.

Sekai Kyúseikyó claims that diseases can be healed and miracles performed by the application of Johrei and that paradise would eventually be established on Earth.

74

Mahikari teaches that faith should be part of everyday life and lead the individual towards happiness which consists of freedom from illness, a state of mind in which antagonistic feelings do not arise, and freedom from poverty.

The IRH teaches that happiness starts in the mind which it studies. The purpose of this study is that it will lead to the discovery of the principles of happiness. Its goal is said to be the initiation of a salvation project with Japan as its centre. This has two main parts. The first is the creation of a utopia in the mind of everyone while the second is the creation of the kingdom of heaven on Earth.

In the case of Iesu no Mitama Kyōkai as in most of Christianity the benefits of followers in this life are less stressed nevertheless part of their teaching is that if you are a good Christian benefits from this will naturally follow. There can be no doubt that the NRMs generate a great deal of money, receiving as they do charitable status both in Japan and in this country. One only has to look at the vast monumental buildings erected by the NRMs in Japan to see that this is true. But what is also true is that Seichō-no-Ie, Sekai Kyūseikyō, Mahikari and Iesu no Mitama Kyōkai are all led by sons or daughters of the founder, and all derive their principal income from being leaders. This is not true for Sōka Gakkai and it is too early to say what will happen in this respect in the case of the IRH.

All the NRMs in their literature and in meetings have members writing or speaking about how they were cured of illness, poverty or emotional difficulties. There can be little doubt that this aspect is one of the main attractions for the NRMs in the West as well as in Japan. In this way the healing benefits and benefits in this life of the NRMs is emphasized.

All the NRMs, except for Iesu no Mitama Kyōkai, stress that Japan is in some way special or is the centre of the world. This is something that, for example, in Mahikari is played down in their teaching in the West, at least until a member has received advanced training. This part of their teaching is unlikely to have much appeal to any but the Japanese.

We have considered the principal new Japanese religions that have come to Britain. Most are still very small but they are growing. But we must ask, why are they growing in Britain? Why should these NRMs which are quintessentially Japanese have an appeal in this country? To begin to answer these questions we must acknowledge that while the Japanese phenomenon of the *shinjinrui*, the new mankind, may not exist here, nevertheless young British people have wider interests and are more internationally aware now than former generations were. There is a spirit abroad of wanting to try things, so we have trial marriages or 'living together'.

The idea of heaven and benefit tomorrow is no longer acceptable to many young people today. Many middle-aged people having a familiarity with Marxism also hold a similar view. Ian Reader has recently written[27] in *Religion in Contemporary Japan* that the Japanese today have a reticence to affirm religious belief and that in a survey of university students 92 per cent said that they would not join any organized religious movement. Would such observations be all that different if we substituted 'British' for 'Japanese'. There is a powerful experiential dimension to religion in Japan today and here too.

A more general familiarity with Eastern religious ideas started perhaps with the founding of the Theosophical Society in 1875. Mysterious Tibet was a subject of discussion in society and interest in Japan was not so far behind. Ten years later, Gilbert and Sullivan's 'Mikado' was staged. If Japan was known to the few before this it quickly became known to everyone. It is not such a great step from being bewitched by Far Eastern art or the martial arts to following an oriental religion. But what is on offer in the Japanese NRMs is not so much a new religion as a reworking of old religions. The Japanese NRMs are, of course, new to this country but they are largely composed of aspects of Shintoism of Buddhism or both. What is fresh is their promise of paradise now. A paradise which is mental, emotional and physical. *Ex Oriente Lux?*

FOOTNOTES

1. Herbert, J. *Shinto.* George Allen & Urwin Ltd. London. 1967.
2. Sutherland, S.R. and Clarke, P.B. (eds) *The Study of Religion, Traditional and New Religion.* RKP. London. 1991.
3. 8. Sukase Masayori. (ed) 'Kofuku no Kagaku' Gensho wo Ou. *Mainichi Shimbun.* Tokyo. 1992.
4. 10. 17. Agency for Cultural Affairs. *Japanese Religion. A Survey.* Kodansha. Tokyo. 1981.
5. 27. Reader, I. *Religion in Contemporary Japan,* Macmillan. London. 1991.
6. Caldarola, C. *Japan. Religious Syncretism in a Secular Society.* Religion and Societies: Asia and the Middle East. Mouton Publishers. Berlin. 1982.
7. Reischauer, E. (trans) *Ennin's Diary.* The Ronald Press Co. New York. 1955.
9. Pamphlet. Seichō-no-Ie Headquarters. Tokyo. n/d but current issue.
11. 15. 26. Thomsen, H. *The Religions of Japan.* Tuttle. Tokyo. 1963.
12. 14. Soka Gakkai International. (booklet) SGI. Tokyo. 1992.
13. Causton, R. *Nichiren Shoshu Buddhism.* Rider. London. 1988.
16. The Japan Society Review. The Japan Society. London. Autumn 1987.
18. Tebecis, Dr A.K. Mahikari. 'Thank God for the Answers at Last'. Yoko Shuppan. Tokyo. 1982.
19. Sukyo Mahikari (booklet). Yoko Shuppan. Tokyo. n/d.
20. Cornille, C. 'The Phoenix Flies West. The Dynamics of Mahikari in Northern Europe.' Paper at 5th International Conference on New Religions. California. 1991.

21. 22. 23. Jinja Honcho. 'Basic Terms of Shinto'. Institute for Japanese Culture and Classics. Tokyo. 1958.
24. Alexander, G. *The Times*. London. 6 September 1991.
25. Okawa, R. Introduction to the Institute for Research in Human Happiness. IRH. Tokyo. 1990.

6
National and International Identity in a Japanese Religion*

MICHAEL PYE

INTRODUCTION

WORLD IDENTITY may be subdivided into two aspects. Firstly, there is what may be called a sense of cosmic identity, well known indeed to the phenomenological tradition in the study of religion. This aspect may be readily combined with the particularist forms of religion, that is, a religion directed primarily towards an ethnic identity, such as Shinto, may convey a strong sense of cosmic rootedness through myths of origin, relation to nature, annual recurrence, and so on. Secondly there is however in some religions an evident attempt to seek a group identity which has a world dimension at human level. Nor is it necessarily just a vague sense of universal goodwill, though in some cases this may be the residue of ebbing religious influence. Much of the interest in the study of major religious traditions lies in the relationship or tension between universalist claims and local, particularist identity-creating forms. Consider Catholicism in Poland and Buddhism in Thailand. Looking at it the other way round, some religions which are strong in local or ethnic identity, such as the Hindu or even more strikingly the Sikh faith, may easily display a universalizing trend when circumstances favour it. Moreover, the various forms of identity creation are often closely interwoven. Cosmic, national and individual identity may be successfully fused in one religious conception.

The search for world identity beyond particularist definitions appears most evidently in the context of the major traditions: Buddhism, Christianity and Islam. Yet it is a theme of some importance in a number of new religious movements, overlooked no doubt because they are so interesting in other ways. This article focuses on one as yet little known modern Japanese movement known in English as the White Light Association. This movement is centred on prayers for world peace in a manner which dramatically emphasizes the search for world identity as a function of religion.

The theme of the article arose out of a fortuitous encounter in Japan, in 1983. On previous occasions I had been intrigued by some vertical stickers seen on doorposts bearing the slogan '*Sekai jinrui ga heiwa de arimasu yō ni*' (May peace be with mankind). Coming across this slogan, prominently displayed in front of a building in Tokyo, apparently open to the public, it became clear to me that this was not a freely floating peace sticker but the mark of an organization of interest to the student of religion, namely the Byakkō Shinkōkai or, in English, the White Light Association. During the month of August 1983 I was able to visit both the above-mentioned branch and the headquarters of this movement and to make observations to which I will return later. First, however, some introductory information will be necessary. I am grateful to the Byakkō Shinkōkai for making various materials available for background study.

The Byakkō Shinkōkai arose as the result of the life-work of Masahisa Goi (name given in Western order) (1916-1980), known to followers as Goi-Sensei which is rendered by the organization into English as Master Goi. His biography will no doubt eventually be the subject of detailed study. His life covered the period of strident Japanese nationalism, defeat, and post-war reflection and reconstruction, a period for the whole of which Japan's relations with its neighbours or with 'the world' (as they say in Japan) have been a crucial determinant of daily life. Thus the question of Japanese identity in the world arises naturally in the movement which he founded. Indeed, as will be seen, the Byakkō Shinkōkai may be taken as a paradigm for the structure of this whole problem. My thesis is that the religious dimension provides both a dramatization and stabilization of this structure in Japanese consciousness.

THE PRAYER FOR WORLD PEACE

The central activity of the White Light Association is a system of prayer for world peace. It is a system in the sense that it takes various predefined forms for use at various levels. Most widely evident are the stickers mentioned above which may be affixed anywhere. Equivalents are available in several other languages, notably English, French, German, Bulgarian, Spanish, Portuguese, Russian and Chinese. (The phrase used for mankind means literally 'world mankind', thus making this dimension of interest quite explicit.)

More substantial is the peace stupa (*heiwatō*), a two-metre high and ten-centimetre-square post which bears exactly the same slogan, without any further indication of the name or the leading ideas of the movement, as is explicitly emphasized in a promotional pamphlet. (These 'stupas', or 'poles' as they are referred to in English-language promotional literature, should not be confused with the much larger 'peace stupas' erected as veritable buildings by a Buddhist movement in the Nichirenite tradition.) The objective is to raise consciousness for peace, starting in Japan, by encouraging people to set up these posts in towns and villages, on mountains, in office and factory grounds, and in shops, temples and shrines.

In a more extended but still general form the 'Prayer for peace of the world' runs as follows:

'May peace prevail on Earth.
May peace be in our homes and countries.
May our missions[1] be accomplished.
We thank thee, Guardian Deities and Guardian Spirits.'[2]

The Japanese text of this prayer, formulated by Goi-Sensei, runs as follows:

'Sekai jinrui ga heiwa de arimasu yó ni
Nihon[3] ga heiwa de arimasu yó ni
Watakushitachi no tenmei ga mattósaremasu yó ni
Shugoreisama arigató gozaimasu
Shugojinsama arigató gozaimasu.'[4]

In another Japanese form of the prayer Goi-Sensei's name is added to the last part, thus:

'. . .Shugoreisama, shugojinsama, Goi-Sensei, arigató gozaimasu' (i.e. 'Guardian Spirits, Guardian Deities, Master Goi, we thank you')[5]

Even in English the prayer may be provided with an interpretative gloss in small print which indicates the spiritual dimension and the mediating function of 'Master Goi' in terms of which the prayer is intended to be understood. This runs:

'Concerning this prayer, an agreement was made between Master Goi and the Divine World. According to this agreement, whenever we pray this prayer, the Great Light of Salvation will definitely shine forth, without fail. Then you yourself will be saved and at the same time an immense power will be manifested, transforming the vibration of world mankind into a Great Harmonious Light Vibration.'[6]

It is clear, therefore, that prayer in this context is more than the mere expression of a political wish. In Goi-Sensei's own words:

'Prayer means opening up one's original mind or buddha-nature, leading the vibrations of light from the world of deities and spirits (the original mind) into the world of flesh.'[7]

There seems to be no doubt, therefore, that the prayer for world peace is more than it may appear to be and that it is understood as leading into religious truth.

It may be recognised in passing that Buddhist themes are drawn upon lightly here. These are immediately balanced by the continuation:

'The sentence in the Lord's Prayer in Christianity "Thy will be done on earth, as it is in heaven" is equivalent to "May peace prevail on earth" and "May peace prevail in Japan".'[7]

In fact Buddhist ideas are adduced quite generously by Goi, but usually he draws away again, in a typically syncretist syndrome, from too close an association with them. An investigation of his work *Hannyashingyō no atarashii kaishaku* ('A New Interpretation of the Heart Sutra')[8] would lead too far afield in this context. It will be noted however that the summary of his teaching entitled 'How man should reveal his inner self' begins with a clear statement running 'Man is originally a spirit from God and not a karmic existence'.[9] A more extensive account of his teaching may be found in the English-language work *God and Man* and here the extensive but un-Buddhist use of the idea of karma and its displacement by the principle of divinity, both within and without man, may be pursued in detail.[10]

The central prayer is also developed into an extended litany which is offered at regular meetings at the headquarters of the movement at Ichikawa near Tokyo.[11] For this a booklet of about 180 pages is used. The litany repeats the second and third lines of the prayer already given, but with the names of as many countries inserted as the Japanese Foreign Ministry lists in its 'table of countries of the world' (*Sekai no kuni ichiranhyō*). To go through all of these by continent at a ritualised pace takes about thirty minutes. After doing this in Japanese the process is then repeated in English, which takes a little longer, to indicate internationalism, the pronunciation of all the English words and names being given in *katakana* (Japanese phonetic script). Thus, to give one example:

'May peace be in the Democratic Republic of Madagascar, May the Democratic Republic of Madagascar's missions be accomplished.'[12]

The whole liturgy is concluded with 'We thank thee, Goi-Sensei, Guardian Deities and Guardian Spirits.'[13]

While the litany is being recited, leaders at the front of the hall place a marker at the position of each country, as it is mentioned, on a huge map of the world hung for all to see. Thus this liturgy of word and action cannot be regarded otherwise than as a sustained effort to identify with the peoples of the whole world, recognising their diversity of destiny (for no attempt is made to define their 'missions' for them) while praying for their peace. As a peace-loving and religious person, as well as being a participant observer engaged in the study of religion, I could not fail to be impressed by this sustained world prayer. Interestingly, however, as has already been suggested, there is more to the White Light Association than the peace prayer, and this means that the nature of the world identity to which aspiration ascends must be understood in a more complex way, as will become clear.

GOI-SENSEI AND THE BELIEVERS

The 'unity meeting' (*tōitsukai*) in the context of which the above described prayer is offered takes place at the headquarters of the movement which is named Hijirigaoka Dōjō. Hijiri is an established term in Japanese religion meaning something like 'holy man with supernatural powers', so that the name Hijirigaoka might be explained, without translating, as 'holy man hill'. *Dōjō* is likewise a standard term meaning 'place of meditation'. The full-length peace prayer in two languages is a central feature of the meeting held here, but it is by no means the only one of interest. For one thing the members enter into a close form of meditative communion while holding up one, two or three fingers, often quivering slightly. Beginners are asked to hold up one finger only because the power of the vibrations would otherwise be too much for them. At another stage in the meeting hands are held firmly against the forehead while communication with Goi-Sensei takes place. Goi-Sensei is present. However, he is not just present in a general or theoretical way. He is present because he is drawn down through upraised hands to participate in the meeting. He speaks through the powerful mediumship of Mrs Masami Saionji (name in Western order).[14] Eventually, hands are slowly raised towards the ceiling and Goi-Sensei returns to the spirit world. Clearly the *hijiri* or 'holy man' of 'Hijiri Hill' is none other than Goi-Sensei himself. The *dōjō* is a place of meditation, but in the sense of meditative unity with the spirit world effected through the link with Goi-Sensei.

The role of Goi-Sensei in the consciousness of believers is central.

The literature says almost nothing about his early life, except that he was born in Tokyo. Nothing is of importance, in the religious consciousness, until he experienced in 1949 his own unity with the divine (*shinga-ittai*) and became an enlightened person (*kakusha*). Thereafter he devoted himself to the life of the White Light Association until he 'returned to the Divine World' in 1980. Publications since 1980 continue to carry writings from his prolific pen as if he were timelessly present. Individually believers may carry, as a protective device, a small photograph of the white light which Goi-Sensei's mind becomes when he 'elevates his consciousness to the Divine Level'.[15] Although doctrinal elaboration about his person might be described as not yet far advanced, he is regarded *de facto* not only as the teacher *par excellence*, but also as pure and bright in his nature and thus unlike other men however wise and splendid they may be.[16]

The Japanese language magazine *Byakkō* carries regular interviews with believers about their experiences, including how they came to be granted a karmic connection with Goi-Sensei. The November issue for 1984, for example, tells of a man in his sixties who, disappointed with various other religions such as Tenrikyō, Ōmotokyō, Tasukaru Michi and Hito no Michi, finally came to a firm faith on reading the autobiography of Goi-Sensei, *Ten to chi o tsunagu mono* ('A man linking heaven and earth').[17] Thereupon his son was healed from an illness and his work-situation improved. Thus he felt 'In my case I have received this-worldly benefits (*genzeriyaku*).'[18]

The direct relationship to Goi-Sensei is also encouraged by means of a letter-writing programme. Even after his return to the spirit world he is regarded as continuing to broadcast the great light of salvation for the happiness and peace of mankind. In addition, the *Byakkō* reader learns, he turns his ear and extends the hand of salvation to those in need of individual assistance. Thus letters may be addressed to Goi-Sensei with messages of anything to be reported, words of gratitude, subjects of grief or requests of any kind. They should be sent to Goi-Sensei's correspondence secretary (if not delivered in person) and will then be placed before him, after which an answer may be expected at any time. After delivery the letters will be offered up in ceremonial flames,[19] and as the envelopes will still be unopened no donations of money should be included.[20]

Less directly linked to Goi-Sensei but nevertheless operative within the religious context which he defined is the principle and practice of purification (*kiyome*). The branch building in Tokyo mentioned earlier had two parts, a Western-style reception area with a small office and stands for the sale of literature and stickers, and a

Japanese-style area consisting of two *tatami* rooms set aside for the practice of *okiyome* (the honorific prefix is usually added). The first of the two *tatami* rooms was used as a simple registration and waiting room, and when a small group of four or five had assembled they were ushered into the smaller inner room to be greeted by the officiant (female). After introductory prayers, each person was free to state particular needs and was then purified by having a series of about twenty hand-claps addressed to them, first facing and then with the back turned. One of those present at the *okiyome* which I observed was a teacher who placed before her on the matting photographs of five children who were experiencing particular difficulties at school, thus enabling them to benefit unknowingly from the *okiyome*. As far as could be ascertained this practice of *okiyome* has no explicit connection (it certainly had none on the occasion observed) with the peace prayer movement. There is an historical question to be explored about the development of the coexistence between these two practices.

INTERPRETATION

As was said at the outset, there is present in much though not all religion a thrust towards universalism which implies a search for identity beyond natural, e.g., clan or national boundaries. This thrust may be regarded as a normal religious motivation which can be observed in Japanese religion just as well as elsewhere. Leaving Buddhism aside, in that its universalizing traits may be held to stem originally from outside Japan, one could take as distinct examples Tenrikyō, Ómotokyō, PL Kyódan, and of course the White Light Association. A transnational or world identity is however not so easily achieved in practice. Much depends on the general level of national consciousness and the extent to which relations beyond the natural group are regarded as a problem in general. The relatively low success rate in universalization (in spite of the theory circulating within the religions) may be regarded as a function of the high importance assigned to the question of Japanese identity. (Zen Buddhism is an exception with exceptional explanations.)

In this context the presentation of the wish for peace by the White Light Association is of great interest. Arising shortly after the end of the Pacific War, it strikes a major chord in the Japanese consciousness of the second half of the twentieth century. The projection of the wish for peace is explicit, sustained and specifically related to all the countries of the world. The message is extremely simple. There is in fact no political peace programme. The definition of the 'missions' of each country is left to the countries concerned (as

I was assured in an interview at the headquarters office). The question of conflicts arising between these 'missions' does not arise. It could only do so on the basis of an inadequate understanding of the 'missions' of each country. But there is no political critique of national self-understanding. Instead there is a ritualised incorporation of all identifiable states into the prayer, even though a great many of these states are in no sense a threat to world peace. To point this out is not to deny possible value in praying for each and any country, or other community, but to make clear that the real purpose of the prayer, or at least its religious function, is to establish an identity. The prayer is the expression of a heartfelt wish, a wish for peace, but at the same time it is a quest for identity, namely a world identity. Japan is to be understood as a respected and indeed a leading member of a chain of nations, extending through all humanity, which are not at war.

The position of Japan is of great importance here. Not only does Japan figure prominently in the short form of the prayer (in the Japanese text only, admittedly, but then most of the members are Japanese); not only does Japan appear first in the long form of the prayer with all the other countries' names following; the writings of Goi-Sensei actually promote and justify beginning with Japan on the basis that this is an acceptable form of patriotism and that if Japan becomes peaceful the peace consciousness will then spread out to other countries.[21] In explaining this Goi-Sensei does refer to political questions in a general way, especially to the conflict between the superpowers and to fear of Communism. Moreover, he urges avoidance of political extremes. This general interest in political questions is maintained today by means of the series of foreign visits being undertaken by Mrs Saionji, as illustrated in the periodical literature and in the brochure *World Peace Through Prayer*.[22] It is clear from all these presentations, however, that quest for world identity has meaning in relation to the question of Japanese identity, which for the majority of Japanese people is an important consciousness issue. This may also be documented by the essay 'Kore kara no Nihon, kore kara no sekai' ('Japan from now on, the world from now on') which is prominently housed in the first volume of Goi-Sensei's collected works.[23] Thus the search for world identity in the form of the prayer for the peace of the world may be understood as a ritualized means of coping with the fact, bitterly experienced, that Japan is not alone in the world.

Naturally this understanding of the matter may be held to be in slight tension with the self-understanding of the believers themselves, of whom at first glance it might simply be said that they are praying for world peace. Of course, so they are. It cannot be overlooked, however, that the prayer for world peace, especially in its longer ritualized form, has deeper functions internal to the White Light Association as a Japanese religion. One major reason for drawing this conclusion has already been made clear above, namely the fact that the peace prayer does not issue in political action of any kind. There is a second reason however, the basis for which has also been laid in the foregoing descriptions, and this is that the White Light Association also solves other religious problems in a manner which may appear to be unrelated to the peace prayer movement (that is, to the casual observer). Thus the branch building had a Western room for solving the world identity problem and a Japanese room for solving personal difficulties through purification. At the large-scale 'unity meeting' the liturgy for world peace is accompanied by the descent of the spirit of Goi-Sensei, which for people of other faiths or none is irrelevant to the solving of political problems. For the believer, what is actually taking place is that the wish for peace as an expression of the need for world identity is being ritually integrated into a context which provides reassuringly Japanese religious features. Thus, for the Japanese participant the various strands do all belong together. They provide identity and succour at family, community, national, and world level. Goi-Sensei has a message for all of these, and hence his presence at the liturgy for world peace is not strange.

One of the basic problems in Japanese consciousnesses, however articulated, is how to deal with outside, abroad, the world. In a period of growing international interaction, this problem is dealt with in many ways to which a large number of religious organizations contribute. There is a wide spectrum to consider, including straightforward missionary outreach through work in foreign languages, the Esperantism of Ōmotokyō, and the public relations for peace carried out by Risshō Kōseikai and Sōka Gakkai leaders. In most cases the function of these activities within Japan, for the benefit of the members of the organizations, is at least as important as any possible effect on the outside world. In this context the *Byakkō Shinkōkai*, because of the prominence given to the peace prayer and the peace liturgy, provides a particularly fine example of the structure of national and international identity in Japan consciousness as articulated by religion.

FOOTNOTES

* This paper first appeared in an IAHR conference volume on the theme of the role of religion in forming and maintaining individual and group identity.

1. Another text has 'our divine missions', seeking a translation element for the *ten* of *tenmei*.

2. Text inside cover of magazine *Heywa* (sic), No. 18, November 1982.
3. Sometimes *sokoku*, 'ancestral country', is added after 'Nihon'.
4. Text frequently reproduced in Goi-Sensei's handwriting.
5. Text in *Sekaikakkoku no sekaiheiwa no inori*, Ichikawa n.d. but 1983.
6. *Heywa*, No. 18, November 1982, inside cover.
7. Goi, Masahisa, *Sekai heiwa no inori*, Ichikawa 1982, p.10.
8. Goi, Masahisa, *Hannyashingyō no atarashii kaishaku*, Ichikawa n.d. but 1983.
9. *Heywa*, No.18, November 1982, inside cover, and many other places. The Japanese text of this summary is worth noting, for it tells us that man is a participatory spirit or a sub-spirit (*wake-mitama*) of the 'original God'. The English version is in general rather free, and it should also be noted that in the last sentence we read 'enlightenment' where the Japanese has 'true salvation' (*makoto no sukui*).
10. Published posthumously by White Light Association, Ichikawa 1983, this work is described as constituting the 'liturgical documents of the Master's White Light Association' (page 1, note). As the selections do not appear to be used liturgically or to be at all suitable for such use, the implication is probably that they represent an authorised core of representative extracts from his otherwise voluminous writings.
11. The address of the headquarters is: Byakkō Shinkōkai, 5-26-27 Nakakokubun, Ichikawa-shi, Chiba-ken 272, Japan.
12. *Sekaikakkoku no sekaiheiwa no inori* (c.f. note 5), p.110.
13. *Ibid.*, p.179.
14. Born in 1941 (and a descendant of the Ryukyuan royal family) Mrs Saionji is the 'Chair Person' of the society (*kaichō*). There is also a president (*rijichō*), Mr Yosuke Seki (name in Western order).
15. Goi, Masahisa, God and Man, page 56 (explained in translator's note).
16. Thus described in a Japanese-language promotional postcard from head-quarters.
17. *Byakkō*, 11, 1984, p.54. The autobiography referred to was first published by the White Light Association at Ichikawa in 1955.
18. *Ibid.*, p.55.
19. This ceremony is thus in principle similar to the *goma* ceremony in Shingon Buddhism, in which simple prayers written by believers on short lengths of wood are burned in the temple by the priests. In the Shingon case the burning symbolises, at least for the priests, the consuming of the this-worldly attachments which are the object of the petitions. It is not clear whether this dialectic is intended in the burning of Goi-Sensei's postbag.
20. *Ibid.*, p.40.
21. Goi, Masahisa, *Sekaiheiwa no inori*, Ichikawa 1982, pp.8ff.
22. Ichikawa, n.d. but 1985.
23. Goi, Masahisa, *Zenshū* (13 Vols.), Ichikawa 1980.

* * *

Appendix 1: Text referred to at note 9

Man is originally split from God, and not a karmic existence.

He lives under the constant guidance and protection provided by his Guardian Deities and Guardian Spirits.

All of man's sufferings are caused when his wrong thoughts conceived during his past lives up to the present manifest in this world in the process of fading away.

Any affliction, once it has taken shape in this phenomenal world, is destined to vanish into nothingness. Therefore, you should be absolutely convinced that your sufferings will fade away and that from now on your life will be happier. Even in any difficulty, you should forgive yourself and forgive others; love yourself and love others. You should always perform the acts of love, sincerity and forgiveness and thank your Guardian Deities and Guardian Spirits for their protection and pray for the peace of the world. This will enable you as well as mankind to realize enlightenment.

Appendix 2: The peace sticker in Japanese

7

Jesus in Japan: Christian Syncretism in Mahikari

CATHERINE CORNILLE

ONE OF THE MOST commonly noted characteristics of Japanese religion in general and of the new Japanese religions in particular, is their tendency towards syncretism. Offner and van Straelen, for example, write:

> The majority of the New Religions are syncretistic to a greater or lesser degree. Teachings and practices from various other religions or philosophical systems are freely incorporated into their scheme. . . From many diverse religions, points of doctrine are quoted with little effort to avoid internal contradictions or to respect their original meanings.[1]

From the tradition of *Ryōbu Shintō* to the present day, the Japanese have attempted to harmonize rather than polarize divergent religious convictions and practices, and to tolerate, if not assimilate different belief systems. Bodhisattvas were regarded as manifestations of Shinto *kami* and vice versa; people worshipped at both Buddhist temples and Shinto shrines, lived according to Confucian ethical principles, and consulted shamans and diviners at times of crisis. The new Japanese religions may then be seen as the institutionalized expression of this age-old tendency towards syncretism.

While the term syncretism has been used and defined in a variety of ways in the history of religions, it refers in the most general terms to 'the mixing of religions'. Where religions and cultures meet, doctrinal or ritual elements belonging to one religious tradition may be taken over by the other through a process of osmosis or in a conscious effort to form a new synthesis. This is usually based on the belief that all religions refer to the same ultimate reality,[2] that other religions are merely manifestations of one true religion,[3] or that all religions find their fulfilment in the new synthesis.[4]

As religions are closed symbolic systems within which one element derives its meaning from its place in the whole, this process of syncretism cannot but lead to internal contradictions or to a shift in meaning in the symbol or ritual which has been taken over within a different religious context. From a confessional point of view, this can only be seen as a violation of the sacred meaning of symbols and rituals and hence as 'illegitimate'. It was from this perspective that syncretism acquired its pejorative meaning as 'the illegitimate mixing of irreconcilable truths'. With the development of the comparative study of religions in the late nineteenth and twentieth century, various scholars have attempted to use the term as a more historical and descriptive category. Gerardus Van der Leeuw, for example, understood syncretism as 'transposition' which he defined as 'the variation of the significance of any phenomenon, occurring in the dynamic of religions, while its form remains quite unaltered'.[5] While this may take place within the development of a single religious tradition, it more often occurs in the transposition of a particular symbol or text from one religious context to another.

Among scholars of Japanese religions, Jacques Kamstra used the term syncretism to describe the encounter of Japan with Buddhism and defined it as 'the coexistence of elements foreign to each other within a specific religion, whether or not these elements originate in other religions or in social structures'.[6] He introduced the distinction between conscious and unconscious forms of syncretism and identified the origins of syncretism in the process of alienation. Of late, however, Kamstra has turned away from the term syncretism (which he believes cannot rid itself from its subjective and pejorative meaning, and from the bias of Western theologians) and instead uses the category of 'religious phenomenalism' to describe Japanese religion.[7] Nonetheless, as Andre Droogers points out, 'the term is so widely used that even a scholarly consensus to do away with it would not lead to a general moratorium on its use'.[8] There are, however, a number of different ways in which the term may be used.[9] While Kamstra defined syncretism as 'the temporary ambiguous coexistence of elements from diverse religious and other contexts within a coherent religious pattern'.[10] Syncretism then leads to the assimilation, fusion, or the dissolution of the two traditions.

While Pye's definition may apply to certain rare forms of religious coexistence,[11] it does not account for the mixing of religions which occurs in the new Japanese religions. Here, teachings and practices of other religious traditions are freely adopted and immediately adapted to the new religion's basic beliefs and interests. Syncretism may thus more broadly be understood as 'the selective adoption and adaptation of elements belonging to one tradition by another'. As a heuristic category, it serves to analyze the process by which a religion attempts to reconcile (seemingly) contradictory or irreconcilable teachings and practices, and to study the semantic shifts which thus take place.

This may be illustrated by the syncretism of Christian elements in one of the 'new, new' religions (*shin-shin-shūkyō*) called Mahikari. According to some scholars, it is precisely the incorporation of Christian elements which constitutes the newness of the new Japanese religions.[12] Mahikari makes use of Christian elements in a variety of ways. It therefore provides an interesting opportunity to study different forms and functions of syncretism. Furthermore, Mahikari has not limited its scope to the Japanese islands alone, finding considerable appeal in the West. This raises the additional question of how the syncretism of elements is received in a predominantly Christian culture.

MAHIKARI

Sūkyō Mahikari, or the 'True Light Supra-Religious Organization', was founded in 1959 by Okada Yoshikazu (later Kōtama), a former imperial guard who after a number of misfortunes and diseases came to discover the way to health, wealth and harmony. Okada had been a member of another new religion called the Sekai Kyūsei Kyō (Church of World Messianity), which itself was an offshoot of one of the earliest new Japanese religions, Ōmoto-kyō. Like its parent- and grandparent-religion, Mahikari is centred on a purification ritual which is said to bring about spiritual and physical healing. In Ōmoto-kyō, the ritual is called *miteshiro* and consists of the transmission of divine energy through an initiate to another person, by means of a rice ladle. In Sekai Kyūsei Kyō, the rice ladle was replaced by the hand and the ritual called *johrei* (*jōrei*). Mahikari continued this same ritual, but called it *okiyome*, which may mean 'purification' or the restoration of energy or *ki*. Okiyome consists of the transmission of the True Light through the palm of the hand of an initiate to the forehead, the neck, the kidneys and any other point of ailment in the recipient. The power of effectiveness of this ritual is believed to generate from the *omitama*, the sacred amulet which members receive at the time of their initiation. This amulet is surrounded by numerous taboos: it is to be wrapped in different layers of paper and attached to one's underwear; it should never drop beneath the waist, and should be kept in a specially reserved and purified box; and in case of defilement, it should be immediately handed over to the leader in order to restore its power. The care for the *omitama* and the practice of *okiyome* constitute the heart of Mahikari. *Okiyome* is often presented as an 'art' which can be practised regardless of the person's beliefs.

But the practice of Mahikari is also based on a particular worldview which members do not necessarily have to subscribe to in order to be initiated, but which is gradually absorbed as the person becomes more deeply involved in the movement. Like Ómotokyó and Sekai Kyúsei Kyó, the worldview of Mahikari is based on a syncretism of Shinto, Buddhist, and Shamanistic elements. The emphasis on purity in Mahikari is distinctly Shinto. It penetrates and dominates the whole life of members. The Light can be used to purify not only people, but also food, rivers, animals, trees, cities, houses, etc. It may serve to prevent calamities as well as recover from them. The transmission of the Light, either explicitly or implicitly, may thus come to occupy every moment of the day.[13] While the understanding of evil as pollution and salvation as purification may be regarded as typically Japanese, it has also found a certain appeal in the West. The materialization and externalization of evil may be felt as a relief from the sense of guilt with which Western consciousness is often imbued.

The Buddhist influence on Mahikari manifests itself in the beliefs in karma and reincarnation. It is the karma carried over from this and previous lives or inherited from ancestors which is considered to be at the root of all diseases and misfortunes. Our present thoughts and actions thus determine not only our own future fate, but also that of our descendants. The normal span of time between incarnation is, according to Mahikari, about 300 years. In the interim period the deceased may continue to interact with the living from within the spirit world.

Here we come to the strong Shamanistic ingredient in Mahikari. More than its parent new religions, but like the other most recent new religions, or 'new, new' religions (*shin-shin-shúkyó*), Mahikari attaches great importance to the spirit world. According to the founder of Mahikari, about eighty per cent of all diseases and misfortunes are immediately caused by spirit possession. An important part of the discourse and practice of Mahikari thus consists of discerning the identity of the possessing spirit and the reason for its possession of the individual. In the first part of the ritual of *okiyome*, when Light is transmitted to the forehead, called 'point 8' in the Mahikari anatomical terminology, the possessing spirits are said to be weakened and may occasionally manifest themselves. This becomes evident in the involuntary movements or speech of the recipient of the Light. At this moment, the spirit may be interrogated by specially trained leaders, the *dóshi* and the *dōjōchō*, or the head of the main training centres (*dōjō*). The person's problem is most often directly and homoeopathically related to that of the possessing spirit: for example, a person who loses a lot of money is said to be possessed by the spirit of a spending ancestor, a person suffering from headaches may be said to be possessed by the spirit of an ancestor who died from a brain tumour, and a woman who cannot find a husband might be possessed by the spirit of the unmarried mistress of an ancestor. Possession may thus be a matter of ignorance or revenge on the spirit's part and, accordingly, may be solved by remorse on the part of the individual, or by the instruction of the spirit. Another important means to satisfy or pacify the spirits and thus protect oneself is the worship of the ancestors. In traditional Japanese (and Chinese) manner, members of Mahikari possess an altar for the ancestor (*butsudan*) where they worship the ancestors of the male side of the family through the offering of food, drinks, flowers, and prayers, and sometimes money and cigars.

This syncretism of Shinto, Buddhist, and Shamanistic elements in Mahikari makes for a typically Japanese religion: the movement manifests certain explicitly nationalistic and ethnocentric traits. The Emperor of Japan plays an important role for the movement and the founder is regarded as an *ikigami*, the traditional Shinto category of 'living god'. Japan is believed to be the place of the origin and the salvation of the world, and the Japanese are regarded as the 'chosen people'. And yet, Mahikari has spread in the West with considerable success. Its appeal lies mainly in the promise of miraculous healing.[14] Many a member in the West turns to Mahikari as a last resort after all other medical and paramedical means have failed. *Okiyome* may initially be regarded as another therapy which may be freely practised without ideological implications. But as the person becomes more involved in the movement, the cognitive side is gradually integrated as theory and practice constantly reinforce one another. The explicit ethnocentric elements are somewhat minimalised in the West, and lines of comparison and continuity are drawn between foreign and familiar beliefs.[15]

Moreover, Christianity forms an important ingredient of the syncretism of Mahikari. While the Shinto, Buddhist and Shamanistic elements are more or less taken over from Sekai Kyūsei Kyō and Ōmotokyō, Mahikari has also borrowed elaborately from Christianity. This becomes evident in the frequent references to Biblical themes and in the importance of the figure of Jesus Christ in the teaching of the movement.

THE LIGHT COMES FROM THE EAST

New religions most often seek a basis of legitimation in old ones. Messianic expectations and apocalyptic predictions of traditional religions are then said to refer to the advent of the new religion. In that way, the figure of Jesus Christ was interpreted in terms of the messianic hopes of the Old Testament, and the New Testament is in turn believed by Muslims to anticipate the coming of the prophet Mohammed, Baha'ullah is understood by his followers to be the manifestation of the *Mahdi*, and various figures have been identified with the Bodhisattva Maitreya, who will come at the end of time. From the point of view of its prehistory, every religious tradition is thus a syncretism, as Joachim Wach pointed out.[16] This form of syncretism serves both a legitimating and a hermeneutical function. Every new religion attempts to place itself within a certain historical continuity and evolution, and is obliged to use existing religious symbols and myths to make itself intelligible. While the form remains the same, the meaning of these traditional symbols and myths changes.

The change often occurs by taking the quotations and symbols out of their original scriptural or symbolic context. In Mahikari, the Light is often associated with 'The true light that enlightens every man was coming into the world,' (John 1:9)[17] and the founder of Mahikari is seen as fulfilling the prophecy of John 16:7-8 and 12-14 concerning the sending of the Paraclete, or the Spirit of Truth.[18] To explain and justify the Japanese origins of Mahikari for Westerners, the Bible is said to have foretold in various places that 'the Light comes from the East'.[19] Biblical quotations are thus taken out of context and made to serve a radically different meaning. But this operation does have a certain efficacy. When asked whether the Japanese origin of Mahikari was of any importance to them, many Western members responded by quoting this expression. Scriptural references thus maintain their legitimating power, even when misquoted or used out of context.

THE POPE AND MAHIKARI

Besides scriptural legitimation, Mahikari has sought institutional justification from Christianity. Christianity is associated with the ideas of 'Westernization' and 'modernization', two of the most important orientations of post-World War Two Japan. While they represent a return to the traditional Japanese worldview and values, the new Japanese religions are also quick to integrate the achievements of modern technological society. They use the most recent high-tech media to propagate their teachings and attempt to convey a sense of their global import.[20] While Japan is believed to be the country of the origin and the restoration of the world in Mahikari, members from abroad are paraded as evidence of the international dimension and the world-wide relevance of the movement.[21]

The importance of the meeting of the founder of Mahikari with the Pope should be seen in the light of this search for international recognition. This meeting occurred during the trip of Okada Kōtama to Europe on the occasion of the opening of the first Mahikari *dōjō* or training centre in the West. On 19 September 1973, he was received in private audience by the Pope, who allegedly said: 'the fact that we meet and that we shake hands has an important significance'.[22] For the members of Mahikari, this 'significance' is taken as the recognition by the Pope of the spiritual authority of the founder, and of the importance of his mission in the West. The picture of this meeting appears prominently in many pamphlets and propaganda books of Mahikari.[23]

The reference to the Pope in Mahikari forms part of the syncretism of Christian elements and symbols in the movement. While Mahikari has no interest in what the Pope stands for doctrinally or in what he teaches, his importance as a worldwide religious figure and the highest authority in what is seen as the Western religion lends the movement a sense of universal institutional relevance. Here again, a Christian symbol is adopted and adapted to the teaching and the interests of Mahikari.[24]

CHRIST IN JAPAN

The life of Jesus has been retold and modified throughout history by numerous movements, each seeking to corroborate the founder of Christianity within their own history or ideology.[25] While some traditions provide a different version of isolated events in the life of Jesus Christ, or a different interpretation of the traditionally accepted events, others develop a completely idiosyncratic account of the life of Jesus of Nazareth. This is the case in Mahikari.

The Mahikari version of the life of Christ is based on the so-called 'Takenouchi documents', a supposedly very ancient collection of texts preserved by a Shinto priestly family of Ibaraki Prefecture. The information preserved in these documents became the basis for a book by Yamane Kiku[26] which in turn became the main source of inspiration for the founder of Mahikari. The account was later 'verified' by Tebecis and consists of the following main storyline: Jesus was born in 37 BC and after travelling through India and China arrived in Japan when he was 18 years old. There he learned mysterious disciplines and acquired magical powers from Shinto priests and mountain ascetics. 'Christ travelled through many countries teaching and performing all kinds of miracles before arriving in Judea to teach the doctrine formulated in Japan. This provoked the Romans who sentenced Jesus to death by crucifixion, but Jesus' brother, Isukiri, voluntarily sacrificed himself on the cross. At the age of 36 Christ went on a four-year journey to northern Europe, Africa, Central Asia, China, Siberia, Alaska, down through both Americas and back to Alaska. He then arrived at Matsugasaki Port in Japan on 26 February in the 33rd year of Suinin, together with many followers from all the countries he had visited on the way. Christ's final years were spent at Herai, where he died at the age of 118.'[27] While there are minor disagreements on details such as whether Jesus died at the age of 106 or 118, or whether or not Jesus married a Japanese woman, Tebecis insists that all historians and archaeologists who have studied the matter agree on these main points.[28]

The life of Jesus is retold to serve the nationalistic and ethnocentric ideology of Mahikari which views Japan as the centre of the original civilization of the world and the Japanese as the chosen people. Every soteriological event or saviour figure must thus originate in, or be somehow related to Japan. While it may strengthen the personal and national pride of the Japanese, the Mahikari version of the life of Jesus has a rather different effect on Westerners. For several, it has been a stumbling block and a reason for breaking with the movement. These ideas, however, are taught only during the advanced course, at a point when the person is already socialised in the movement.[29] Some members then come to regard the belief that Christ died in Japan as an irrelevant point in the whole of the teaching of Mahikari. But this belief may also come to function as an escape from the traditional Christian belief in the redemptive suffering and death of Christ on the cross. For a number of Western members of Mahikari, it becomes merely a confirmation for their inability to believe in this aspect of Christian doctrine. Tebecis, for example, states that 'the doctrine that Jesus Christ was crucified as an act of atonement for people's sins and rose again from the dead. . .was one doctrine that I could never understand, let alone accept, when I was trying my best to be a good Christian in my youth. It was quite a relief to discover later that millions of others were having the same difficulty.'[30] He then goes on to argue: 'If Jesus Christ did not die on the cross, is then the basic message of Christianity invalid? Certainly not. It only means that the doctrine that 'people's sins are washed away by Jesus' blood on the cross can no longer be upheld.'[31]

For Mahikari, the essence of the teaching and the practice of Jesus consisted in the transmission of the Divine Light. It was through the power of this Light that he was able to expel evil spirits and to cure people. In transmitting the Light, Mahikari members are thus believed to emulate Jesus Christ and to become more Christ-like.

WATER AND FIRE

Mahikari claims to be compatible with every religious tradition and ideology. It presents itself not as a religion, but as a 'supra-religious' organization (*Sukyo* Mahikari.) Members are thus told that they can remain Buddhists, Christians, or Moslems while practising the 'art' of Mahikari. But this is only because the movement considers itself to be the fulfilment of all other religions. In the Mahikari conception of the evolution of the world, the traditional world religions belong to the era of the Water-Gods which now (since the foundation of Mahikari) is superseded by the period of the Fire-Gods.[32] Sukuinushisama is believed to have come to prepare the world for the imminent apocalyptic event of the 'baptism by fire,' which will bring about the ultimate purification of the world and the establishment of a new civilisation. Winston Davis points out that 'The sect's emphasis on the coming of the Messiah or Saviour, the Baptism by Fire, the Apocalypse, the Judgement, though modified to fit the Japanese context, are all ultimately of biblical provenance'.[33] Here, however, biblical themes are used to establish the superiority of Mahikari over Christianity. The coming of the new era implies the radical supersession of the traditional religions, which are thus regarded as henceforth worthless. In the sacred scripture of Mahikari, the *Goseigenshū*, the all-pervasive theme of the baptism by fire is closely related to this idea of the superiority of Mahikari and the rejection of all other religions. About Shintoists, Buddhists and Christians, Okada says:

> They began to be absorbed in producing their own selfish manner of religious faith and have completely destroyed the true aspect of the Supra-Religious Teaching and the Divine World. They have no value at all. If religions remain in the present condition, they will only give a hundred harms and no profit for the unity of mankind in the eyes of God. They become much worse than massive, but worthless existences. (p. 149)

While Mahikari uses elements of the Shinto, Buddhist and Christian traditions, it also considers these religions to be inferior to itself and ultimately worthless. The syncretisation of elements belonging to other religions often merely serves to establish the superiority and the uniqueness of the new religion.[34] Christian apocalyptic themes are adopted not so much to express the validity of the Christian tradition, but so as to establish its obsolescence in the face of the advent of Mahikari. This sense of superiority of Mahikari over Christianity resonates with the restoration of the national pride and the revaluation of cultural identity of the Japanese since the seventies.

REVERSE SYNCRETISM

In coming to the West, Mahikari has downplayed its negative attitude towards Christianity. The emphasis has been on orthopraxis rather than orthodoxy. The Japanese ritual forms were taken over, and the Japanese organizational structure copied. A training centre (*dōjō*) in the West looks exactly like the Japanese model, a large empty space with a Shinto-style altar at the front. The main object in the altar is the scroll, called the *goshintai*, on which are inscribed in Japanese characters the word Mahikari, and a comma, called the *chuon*, representing God-Su. On the side of the *goshintai* is the statue of Izonumesama, a god who is worshipped as the fulfiller of material needs. The front part of the altar is reserved for the offerings. The Light is usually exchanged squatting in Japanese fashion, although chairs are provided for Westerners who are too uncomfortable in that posture. The *Amatsu Norigoto* prayer which precedes every session of *okiyome* is incanted in Japanese, or according to the members, in *kotodama*,[35] 'the language of the Gods,' the power of which lies in the vibrations rather than in the meaning of the words. All the other prayers recited at the monthly thanksgiving ceremony are also memorised in their original Japanese form, which adds to the sense of their magical power. Altars for the ancestors are brought over from Japan, and the taboos surrounding the *omitama* are, if possible, even stricter in the West than in Japan. This ritual rigidity illustrates the essentially magical nature of Mahikari. As in traditional magic, it is the exact execution of the ritual acts which guarantees their effectiveness.

While a strict conformity to ritual prescriptions is demanded, Mahikari has shown considerable flexibility and adaptability with regard to doctrine. The explicitly ethnocentric and nationalistic elements in the doctrine have been minimalized, and the similarities with Christianity further elaborated and emphasized. The essence of Jesus' mission is said to be the transmission of Light. It is pointed out that Jesus, too, healed people by casting out evil spirits. The halo on a crucifix in the cathedral of Cologne was identified as the symbol of Mahikari.[36] In the West, the giving of Light is thus understood in continuity with the activity of Jesus Christ. Members are not discouraged from maintaining their Christian affiliation.[37] Mahikari often refers to a Belgian Catholic priest who is also a faithful member of Mahikari. Tebecis quotes him saying:

> Christian followers sometimes ask me, 'Don't you feel guilty practising Mahikari as a Catholic priest?' or 'How can you follow both the teachings of Mahikari and the doctrines of the Catholic Church?' . . . I have lost nothing as a Catholic priest by practising Mahikari no Waza, and there is no turmoil in my life as a Catholic priest because of practising Mahikari. On the contrary, due to Mahikari, I have a better understanding of how I should live as a Catholic priest, and I can achieve my mission even better. I think that Mahikari teachings are not teachings that replace those of Catholicism, but teachings that complement and harmonize with them.[38]

For many Western members like this priest, Mahikari is perceived as an extension of their ability to be helped and to help others. They become members with the hope of resolving a particular problem, usually a severe disease, and while faithfully following the practice, they accept the teachings only in so far as they correspond to their previous beliefs. Some Western members of Mahikari do not believe in reincarnation or in the divinity of the founder of Mahikari. Others deny the theory that Jesus died in Japan and ignore the idea of the impending apocalypse. The practice of Mahikari is understood in continuity with Jesus Christ and the teachings are accepted only in so far as they may be reconciled with the Christian tradition. A reverse form of syncretism thus occurs in which the teachings and practice of Mahikari are themselves selectively adopted and adapted to the Christian tradition by members whose first loyalty is to the Church.[39] Though the mainstream Christian tradition has been unaffected by this adoption of Mahikari elements, it illustrates the infinite propensity of popular religion towards the integration of foreign, most often magical, practices.

CONCLUSION

The selective adoption and adaptation of Christian elements in a new Japanese religion such as Mahikari reveal many of the forms and functions at play in the process of syncretism. Both explicit and implicit, or deliberate and more spontaneous forms of syncretism are operative here. In the teachings of Mahikari frequent references are made to the Bible, and to the figure of Jesus Christ. Biblical verses are quoted so as to corroborate the teachings of Mahikari. One of the basic forms of syncretism consists of taking religious texts out of their original context and thus furnishing them with a radically different meaning. In Mahikari every biblical reference to 'the Light' is seen as pointing to its own understanding of the Divine Light. However, symbols and ideas borrowed from any other religion may serve not only to corroborate particular beliefs, but may themselves contribute to shaping those beliefs. The millennarian conceptions of Mahikari are based on biblical apocalyptic themes. In being used within a different context, the meaning of symbols and myths also deviates from their original meaning. Syncretism is thus necessarily rejected by those entrusted with the preservation of the original tradition in question.

While syncretism may relate to elements which are peripheral to the original tradition, it may also involve the adoption and the adaptation of the very core or essence of a religion. In Mahikari, the traditional Christian belief in the life and death of Jesus Christ is radically transformed in order to fit its own ideology. By claiming that Jesus was taught by Shinto priests during his youth and returned to Japan where he died at an old age, Mahikari interprets the story of Jesus in such a way as to serve its own nationalistic and ethnocentric purposes. Consequently, the traditional soteriological meaning of the death and resurrection of Jesus Christ is denied or ignored, and the emphasis shifted to his healing practices. For Mahikari, the figure of Jesus Christ then becomes a mere forerunner of its own teaching and practices. While the more peripheral forms of syncretism may pass unnoticed, or may even preserve their legitimating function, this transformation of an essential tenet of Christian faith represents a confrontation and a challenge for Christians involved in Mahikari.

The syncretism of Christian elements in Mahikari functions to establish the universal relevance and the international scope of the movement. In this sense, Mahikari can be said to recognise some authority for Christianity. However, as is clearly demonstrated in the belief that biblical prophecies are fulfilled only with the emergence of Mahikari, the superiority of the latter is never in doubt. While Christianity thus possesses a certain legitimating power, it is also regarded as inferior and obsolete. This functional ambivalence of the appropriated tradition is the characteristic of syncretism.

Besides the deliberate adoption and adaptation of Christian elements in the teaching of Mahikari, more spontaneous forms of syncretism take place in the meeting of the movement with the West. Every new religion must use familiar categories and symbols to make itself understood. This points to the essential hermeneutical function of syncretism. Within a predominantly Christian context,

100

Mahikari has spontaneously come to use Christian symbols and to emphasize similarities with the Christian tradition so as to make itself more intelligible and acceptable. This has led to a reverse form of syncretism in which Mahikari teachings and practices have been selectively adopted and adapted to Christianity by Christian initiates who remain loyal to the Church. It is particularly the magical healing ritual which is appropriated and interpreted in Christian terms. This shows how a tendency towards syncretism, especially of magical beliefs and practices, is often at work in religion at a popular level.

FOOTNOTES

1 See Clark Offner and Henry van Straelen, *Modern Japanese Religions*. Leiden: Brill, 1963, pp. 32-33. See also Maurice Bairy, *Japans Neue Religionen in der Nachkriegszeit*. Bonn: Ludwig Rohrscheid Verlag, 1959, p. 59; Raymond Hammer, *Japan's Religious Ferment*. London: SCM Press, 1961, p. 140; Ian Reader, *Religion in Contemporary Japan*. London: Macmillan Press, 1991, p. 197.

2 This presuppositon may be seen at the basis of the syncretism of Theosophy and its derivatives, including the New Age movement.

3 The best example of this is the tradition of Japanese syncretism in which Buddhists came to regard Shinto *kami* as manifestations of Buddhist gods and Bodhisattvas (*honji-suijaku-setsu*, or the 'true nature, trace manifestation theory'), while the Shinto tradition argued the reverse in the theory of *yui-itsu-shintō*, 'one and only Shinto' or *Ryobu Shinto*, 'the Shinto of the two mandalas'.

4 This is characteristic of the new Japanese religions, as of most new religious movements.

5 G. Van der Leeuw, *Religion in Essence and Manifestation* (J.E. Turner, trans.) New York: Harper and Row, 1963, pp. 610-611.

6 In *Op de Grens tussen Theologie en Godsdienstfenomenologie*. Leiden: Brill, 1970, pp. 9-10. The problem with this definition is that the elements may be foreign in origin, but that once they are absorbed in a different religion, they become part of that new symbolic order, and receive a meaning coherent with the elements of that symbolic whole. Syncretism is never an issue for the syncretistic religion itself, but only for the religion from which it has borrowed symbols, beliefs, or practices, or for historians or phenomenologists of religion.

7 Kamstra discusses his shift from the use of the term syncretism to religious phenomenalism in 'The Religion of Japan: Syncretism or Religious Phenomenalism?' In *Dialogue and Syncretism*. (J. Gort, H. Vroom, a.o. eds.) Grand Rapids: Eerdmans, 1989. This term is supposed to be more consonant with the holistic religious experience of the Japanese people, in which no distinction is made between Shinto, Buddhism, Confucianism and Taoism. However, in his article, Kamstra himself continues to refer to these religions as separate entities constituting the whole of Japanese religion.

8 Andre Droogers, 'Syncretism: The Problem of Definition, the Definition of the Problem' in J. Gort, H. Vroom, a.o., *Dialogue and Syncretism*. Grand Rapids: Eerdmans, 1989, p. 7.

9 Droogers delineates the options which may be taken in defining the term syncretism: it may be used as an objective, or as a subjective category; understood as a process or as the result of that process; focusing only on the mixing of religions or also on the mixing of cultures; relating to the origin of a religion, or only to later developments; and a conscious or an unconscious phenomenon. *Ibid.*, pp. 13-14.

10 In 'Syncretism and Ambiguity', in *Numen* 18 (1971), p. 93.

11 Pye's theory is based mainly on the relationship between Buddhism and Shinto expressed in the *honji-suijaku* theory, and may possibly be applied to the relationship between Nichiren Shoshu and Sōka Gakkai, which according to his categories would have led to a 'dissolution'.

12 See Harry Thomsen, *The New Religions of Japan*. Rutland: Charles E. Tuttle Company, 1963, p. 29. Shintoism, Buddhism and Shamanism have been part of Japanese religiosity for centuries.

13 While explicit practice of *okiyome* consists of the chanting of the Amatsu Norigoto prayer before the session and raising the hand, the Light is implicitly transmitted by merely opening the palm of the hand in a certain direction. This is done so as not to appear too conspicuous in public places.

14 For more fieldwork data on Mahikari in the West, see Catherine Cornille 'The Phoenix Flies West' in *Japanese Journal of Religious Studies* 18 (1991) 265-285.

15 For example, ancestor worship is compared to the building of chapels on the gravesites, or with the celebration of All Souls.

16 Every religion, therefore, has its own previous history and is to a certain extent a 'syncretism'. Then comes the time when, from being a summation, it becomes a whole and obeys its own laws. In *Religionswissenschaft: Prolegomena zu ihrer wissenschaft lichen Grundlegung.* Leipzig, 1924, p. 86. Quoted by Gerardus Van der Leeuw in his *Religion in Essence and Manifestation* (J.E. Turner, trans.) New York, Harper and Row, 1963 (original 1933), p. 609.

17 Cfr. A.K. Tebecis, *Mahikari, Thank God for the Answers at Last.* Tokyo: Yoko Shuppan, 1982, p.16. While the founder only referred to the Bible in rather general terms, it was Tebecis, a neurophysiologist and one of the main propagators of Mahikari in the West, who provided elaborate Biblical corroboration for the teachings of Mahikari.

18 The latter is believed to correspond to Sukuinushisama's revelation of 27 February 1959 at 5 p.m.: 'You will be made to reveal the innermost depths. The Holy Spirit of Divine Truth has entered you. . .Speak what you hear.' *Ibid.*, p.27. Among the revelations of 15 May 1959, in the *Goseigenshu*, the sacred scripture of Mahikari, is the following: 'I also let Jesus speak. When He, the Spirit of Truth comes, He will guide you into all the Truth' (p. 27).

19 *Ibid.*, p. 21. Tebecis here refers to Gen. 3:24, Job 38:24, Isaiah 41:2 and 46:11, Ez. 43:1-2 and 47:1, Hosea 13:15, Matt. 2:1-2 and 9-10.

20 This leads to an often rather odd and sometimes tasteless mixture of traditional Japanese and Western aesthetic expression in the rituals of the new Japanese religions.

21 This is done literally at the occasion of grand autumn- and spring-feasts at the World Shrine, or the Suza in Takayama. On the day before the feast, a big parade is organized through the streets of the city, with the members from foreign countries appearing prominently.

22 Quoted in the Mahikari record of its history in Europe.

23 It is included in the first pages of Tebecis' book *Mahikari: Thank God for the Answers at Last.*

24 The current leader of Mahikari, the adopted daughter of the founder, who is addressed as Oshie-nushisama, often herself appears to her disciples in the white papal robe.

25 This was started by the Theosophical movement and became popular in books such as that of A. Faber-Kaiser, *Jesus Died in Kashmir.* London: Gordon and Cremonesi, 1978.

26 *The Authentic History of the World Secreted Away in Japan.* Tokyo, 1964.

27 A.K.Tebecis, *Mahikari: Thank God for the Answers at Last*, p.358.

28 Tebecis refers to various sources: the discoveries of the journalist Rowland Gould, published in the article 'The Man from Isohara' in Y. Takenouchi, *Kamiyo no mukashi no hanashi.* Ibaragi: Koso Kotai Jingu, 1978; M. Nakazono, *Ancient World History.* Santa Fe: Nakazono, 1975; and the findings of a Frenchman, Michael Coquet, on Christ's death in Japan published in the February 1980 issue of *Le Monde Inconnu.*

29 To be allowed to follow the third course, a member must have been in the movement for at least four years, have followed the first and second courses a few times, and have brought seven members into the movement. Moreover, the advanced course is offered only in Japan, and thus requires of Westerners major financial and other sacrifices.

30 In *Mahikari: Thank God for the Answers at Last*, p. 351.

31 *Ibid.*, p. 362.

32 This is expressed in the symbol of Mahikari, where a horizontal blue line representing the former religions is crossed by a vertical red line representing Mahikari. In the Suza, or the main World Shrine in Takayama, a long horizontal aquarium with a number of big fish under the main podium represents the blue line. The golden shrine elevated beyond the podium then represents the beginning of a new era. The dawning of the fire epoch is also symbolised by a big red (fire-) bowl which is located on the top of the roof (itself a representation of the ark of Noah) of the Suza.

33 In *Dojo. Magic and Exorcism in Contemporary Japan.* Stanford: Stanford University Press, 1980, p. 83.

34 'Teachings given by Gautama, Jesus and Mohammed are surely teachings. . . The age shall

come when teachings alone can no longer be effective in any aspect. There is only one way left' (*Goseigenshu*, p. 206.)

35 It refers, in fact, to a pseudo-etymological 'word-science' in which new meanings are allotted to Japanese syllables, thus revealing new, and according to the followers, the true meaning of words and texts. The *Goseigenshú* is replete with *kotodama*. Okada Kótama, moreover, does not limit himself to Japanese words. The word 'Christ' or 'Ku-ri-su-to' is analyzed as 'suffering, tightening, an end, stop' (p. 251.)

36 *Mahikari, Thank God for the Answers at Last*, p. 395. This symbol consists of a star, within which there is a circle crossed by a red vertical and a blue horizontal line, and itself ringed by 16 dots.

37 Of the Belgian members I studied, about sixty per cent were Christians at the time of joining. Three-quarters of that group continued to consider themselves as such, and about half of them were still regular Church-goers.

38 *Mahikari: Thank God for the Answers at Last*, p. 376.

39 This form of syncretism has been rejected by representatives of the Catholic Church. In an area of Belgium where Mahikari had become popular among Catholics, the vicar published an article to be read by all priests in the diocese in which the incompatibility of adherence to the Catholic faith and the teaching of Mahikari was insisted upon.

8

Japanese Monotheism and New Religions

J.H. KAMSTRA

POLYTHEISM, the belief in myriads of deities, always has been one of the pillars of Shinto in particular and of Japanese religion in general. Even in the course of history when Shinto and Buddhism became intertwined the whole pantheon of Tantric Buddhism was added to Shinto polytheism and became moulded into principles such as the *honji-suijaku* theory and *Ryōbu-Shintō* in Buddhism and Shinto respectively. This pillar of polytheism is very narrowly connected with another pillar of Japanese religion: shamanism. This led to the thesis that shamanism, being based on relations with concrete gods dwelling in trees and mountains, is incompatible with monotheism.

Yet a furtive look at the *shinkō-shūkyō* and the *shin-shin-shūkyō* not always bears witness to this kind of shamanism based on polytheism. It is interesting that right from the beginning of Tenrikyō, Konkōkyō and other religions, their (shamanistic) founders testified of deities not with polytheistic but with monotheistic qualities. Where does this monotheism come from? To what degree is Harry Thomsen's remark right that it originated in the monotheism of *inter alia* the Kakure-kirishitan (Hidden Christians)? In this paper I will try to analyze the impact of Christian theistic ideas on Japanese religion and on the new religions in particular.

MONOTHEISM IN JAPAN'S NEW RELIGIONS

It is a striking fact that it is precisely the oldest *shinkō-shūkyō* such as Tenrikyō, Konkōkyō and Ōmotokyō which believe in deities with monotheistic qualities.

In the Tenrikyō, Tenri-Ō-no-Mikoto (the Lord of Divine Wisdom) is 'the sole deity of all, the creator of all things, and the gracious sustainer of life. He is also referred to as Oya-gami (God the Parent)... God first revealed Himself as Kami, which here means the creator of this world and all human beings, or the original, true God. Later God revealed himself as Tsuki-hi (Moon-sun God)'.[1]

In the *Tenrikyo kyoten* (3) God reveals himself as follows: '*Ware wa moto no kami, jitsu no kami de aru*', I am the god of origin, I am the true god.[2] Amano Muhendojin in his book *Tettsui Ichimei Tenrikyo Bemmo*, a Hammerblow on or refutation of Tenrikyo, written in 1896 and in some other booklets reports that Miki had been instructed in the Christian religion by a Christian *ronin*, and that she has borrowed from him several Christian elements. Who was this *ronin*? Was he a follower of Hirata Atsutane?[3] Van Straelen prefers to connect him with the '*Hanare-Kirishitan*'.

Is this remark also right if we take into account the 'functions' of this god Tenri o no mikoto. In *Die Lehre der Tenrikyo* and in the *ofudesaki* we read:[4]

> When God was creating man he provided him with his protection. In order to clarify his protection he gave special names to any of his functions (Wirkungen):
>
> *kunitokotachi no mikoto*: the function of the eyes and of moisture;
>
> *omotari no mikoto*: fire in the world and body-warmth;
>
> *kunisazuchi no mikoto*: the first organ of the woman, the skin and the union of the world;
>
> *tsukiyomi no mikoto*: the first organ of the males, the function of support in particular of the skeleton and supporting in general in the world;
>
> *kumoyomi no mikoto*: the functions of absorption and of rejection, of eating and drinking, and in the world of ascending and descending of vapour, mist;
>
> *kashikome no mikoto*: the functions of breathing and speaking and in the outside world the wind;
>
> *taishokuten no mokoto*: in the human body the cutting of the umbilical cord from the placenta during birth, and also of cutting the life cord at death, and in the outside world the phenomena concerning separation;
>
> *otonobe no mikoto*: during birth the pulling of the child out of the womb and in the outside world the function of pulling out;
>
> *izanagi no mikoto*: the archetype of man, the seed of man;
>
> *iznami no mikoto*: the archetype of woman, the location of the human seed.

In the *ofudesaki* we read:[5]

Das Weltall ist der Korper Gottes. Überdenkt diese Wahrheit, bis sie genügend erfasst wird.

God is also '*der liebevolle Eltern Gott: Mioya no kami*'.

In spite of the polytheistic atmosphere which also qualifies Tenri o no mikoto the monotheistic character of Tenri o-no-mikoto is obvious. It can be defined as what van Baaren calls pluriform monotheism.

The Kurozumikyó was founded by the Shinto-priest Munetada Kurozumi (1780-1850). In his Kurozumikyó the sun-goddess is looked at as the supreme deity: Amaterasu-o-mikami, who according to Thomsen – 'is regarded as the absolute deity of the universe, the creator of heaven and earth'.

'One God is embodied in a million gods, and a million gods are found in one God. All is ascribed to One God.' The word *kami* should be derived from the word *kakuremi*, the hidden and first cause of the universe. Here also the one and the same god appears in many gods as Tenri o no mikoto did.

Where did this Kurozumi idea come from? In the Konkokyo founded by Kawate Bunjiro, Tenchi kane no kami, the great golden god of the universe (1859) has also monotheistic qualities. The name of this god in unknown in Shinto. The Meiji government urged the sect to add three other gods who henceforth were considered as manifestations of Tenchi-kane-no-kami.[6] After world war II the Konkokyo abandoned these three additional deities in order to return to its original monotheism. All these different forms of Japanese monotheism, however, are not limited to these three shinkoshukyo only.

The concept of god of Konkokyo is also maintained in the Omotokyó, the P.L.Kyódan and in Seichó no Ie, which considers God to be the: 'Creator of the whole Universe' and in other further ramifications of these religions such as Sekai kyuseikyo and many more recent new religions. Here I have in mind in particular the Mahikari movement.[7]

Mahikari from 1959 onwards believed in a Japanese type of monotheism based on more Christian information than the founders of Tenrikyo and Konkoyo had at their disposal. Mioya Motosu Mahikari no O-kami (who originated from Omoto's Ushitora no Konjin)[8] or Su-god, is a deity of yang-like attributes, whose essence is fire. He bathes the world in a hi no senrei, a baptism of fire.[9] The *mahikari no waza* is the method of reviving the *sumei-godo*: the unification of the five major religions (Buddhism, Taoism, Confucianism, Islam and Christianity),[10] under the supremacy of this mighty god preached by Moses and Jesus who were Japanese Jews (*nikkeijin*) and died in Japan.[11]

WHERE DID THESE MONOTHEISTIC IDEAS COME FROM?

It is out of the question that these developments were due to modern Christian denominations which have been in Japan only since the 1860s. At that time, however, the older *shinkó shúkyó* were already established and promoted a special kind of monotheism. In those days Japanese society already contained various monotheistic trends reflecting specific Japanese features. It is not difficult to trace these back to Kirishitan influences since Japan's religious traditions are polytheistic rather than monotheistic. It is, however, necessary to investigate further the opinion of Thomsen and the church-historian Drummond that the Kakure-kiristan followers who had been living and hiding in remote areas of Nagasaki prefecture would have necessarily influenced the ideas of the oldest *shinkō shūkyō*.[12] Thomsen does not substantiate his assertion with Kirishitan facts. Yet we should keep in mind that in Japan during the Edo period Christian ideas became rather modified due to neo-Confucian Shinto influences and to Buddhist ideas. Thus we can point at two roots: one being influenced by Christian literature translated in China which challenged Shinto-neo-Confucian tendencies; the other consisted of the traditions of the Kakure-kirishitan which were greatly influenced by Buddhism.

It is a well known fact that at the beginning of the Edo period (1603) Christianity was preached in Japan by Portuguese and Spanish missionaries (and had been for nearly 50 years earlier), and that after a short period Christianity and its literature were prohibited. Even the Dutch had to keep their bibles locked up in a '*bijbeltonnetje*', a bible barrel. But this does not mean necessarily that during the Edo period no spiritual literature of any kind entered Japan. In this context the Chinese played an important part. In spite of the general edict of 1630 which forbade the importing of Christian books written by Jesuits in China, there was a regular flow of imported Christian literature from China, as well as books on arithmetic, astronomy and other sciences.[13] In 1658, by special decree, a Chinese merchant was condemned to death for importing such books. In the same year the trafficking in foreign missionaries and Chinese books on Christianity into Japan was explicitly forbidden to the Chinese merchants. In 1685 the Japanese authorities discovered that some Chinese had been trying to sell Christian books smuggled by them into Japan. From then on the annual total of Chinese ships allowed into Nagasaki was restricted to 70. Even so, Chinese tradesmen continued to secretly import into Japan Chinese translations of many Jesuit books on Christianity: books of Matteo Ricci, Giulio Aleni, Alphonse Vagnoni and Didaco de Pantoja. Their writings circulated in secret and were read all over Japan by famous Japanese scholars such as Honda Toshiaki (1744-1821), Hirata Atsutane (1776-1843), Koga Toan (1788-1847), Sato Nobuhiro (1769-1850), and Mitsukuri Gempo (1799-1863).[14] Hirata Atsutane, the last of the 'great men' of *fukko shintō*, 'restoration Shinto', and populariser of this Shinto used Christian arguments in defence of this particular form of Shinto. He did not mention, however, the Chinese sources of his knowledge.[15]

Here I have to point out that there is a big difference between the Christianity introduced into China from that which was introduced into Japan. The nature of the Chinese form of Christianity was more acceptable to many Japanese intellectuals than was its Japanese form. The Portuguese and Spanish missionaries introduced Christianity into Japan via Portuguese colonies such as Goa and Macao and not by way of other Chinese cities. In doing so they did not take into account the fact that until then all foreign religions that had been accepted into Japan had undergone a centuries-old incubation process in China. The missionaries even bragged about their Portuguese descent and the support of the Portuguese government and preached Christianity disguised behind a cloak of Portuguese and Latin words. Unlike their confreres in China they refrained from any Chinese translations and ideas. The advantage of their method was that the religion they preached did not become identified with any Japanese religion. The disadvantage was, however, that many Portuguese and Latin words remained obscure. In other words, in Japan Christianity was preached as something new and completely different.

In China, on the other hand, Italian Jesuits like Ruggieri, Pasio and Ricci maintained that they and their religion came from Tianzhuguo, i.e. India. Why did they say this? Is it because their motherland, Italy, did not yet have any identity and consisted of a great number of small states and cities? The Jesuit Valignano who had been active in China as well as in Japan, explained this with the argument that what is known of India also goes for Europe: both being countries with water fit for the ablution of sins. Thus they stood out from the Portuguese and the Spaniards in China who stated that they originated in Folangji (France).

The Italian Jesuits in China originally presented themselves to the Chinese as *heshang*, Buddhist monks; however, in 1592 they replaced this term with that of *daoren*, a man of learning, and in 1600 with *shenfu*, spiritual father, which is still in use today. They gave God the Chinese name of *tianzhu*, lord of heaven, written by a Chinese Christian on a wooden tablet and placed on the altar erected by the fathers Ruggieri and Pasio. In naming God *Tianzhu* they intended to promote him to the status of the first divinity of the Chinese. Ricci named God also *Tiandi*, heavenly sovereign. He justified his choice of *Tianzhu* and *Tiandi* in saying that the Chinese considered *tian* as the highest divine being. Hence *Tianzhu*, lord of heaven, should indicate the superiority of God to heaven.[16] They called Mary *Tianzhu shengmu niangniang*: i.e. 'the holy lady and mother of the lord of heaven'. After having discovered that the Chinese identified Mary with the bodhisattva quanyin, they replaced the picture of Mary with that of Jesus Christ. Thus they tried to prevent the Chinese from seeing in Mary the main divinity of Christianity.[17] In Japan, on the other hand, Portuguese and Spanish Jesuits guided by the same Valignano confined themselves to transliterations from Latin and Portuguese. To that end they introduced a new style of writing: *romaji*. In the first books printed at the Christian press of Amakusa they used words such as: *Deusu Patere* (Deus Pater), *Deusu Hiiryo* (Deus Filius), *Ekerijia* (Ecclesia), *Hiidesu* (fides), *orashio* (oratio) etc, but with one exception: the devil being identified with *tengu*: 'the long-nosed goblin of Japanese legends'.[18]

In Japan God became known as *Deusu*, since Xavier did not succeed in replacing the Latin Deus with Japanese equivalents such as Dainichi (Mahavairocana), the principal buddha in esoteric Buddhism.[19] Even the Latin word Deus had its problems being understood as *dai-uso*: big lie.[20] Yet the Christians until 1868 and the Kakure-kirishitan until now maintain the word Deus for God. Since Xavier became convinced that in Japan the twin concepts of creator/creation were completely absent, the essence of God and his quality as creator was emphasised in the *Dochirina Kirishitan*. Hence the *Dochirina Kirishitan* introduced the idea of God as creator of the universe by refuting the concept of God found in some Buddhist sects and rectifying it with Aristotelean arguments.

SHINTO NEO-CONFUCIAN TENDENCIES: HIRATA ATSUTANE AND AME-NO-MINAKA-NUSHI

It is a well-known fact that the disciple of Motoori Norinaga, Hirata Atsutane (1776-1843), propagated Motoori's nationalistic ideas through Shinto priests at the Imperial Court and that 45 years after his death his ideas became generally accepted as the official state religion.[21] Yet – as Devine points out – he was much better acquainted with other developments than was his master:

'Hirata's intellectual pursuits were extremely wide-reaching – Chinese literature and medicine, *yomeigaku*, neo-Confucianism, Buddhism, Shinto, Western astronomy and physics, and more.'[22]

To that 'more' we should include Christianity and its literature. His first encounter with Christian writings dated from the first years of his career as appears in his writing *Honkyo Gaihen*. In his arguments against Confucianism and in favour of Shinto he was guided by the Chinese translations of Ricci, Aleni (*San Shan Lun*) and Pantoja.[23] In his *Honkyo Gaihen* he summarised several Jesuit works.[24] Even his style of argument: presentation of the argument of the opponent preceding his refutation (sed contra) seems to be derived from Jesuit writings and Thomas Aquina's *Summa Theologica*.[25] It is a debatable question whether he plagiarized the writings of Pantoja, Ricci and Aleni,[26] yet it is an established fact that he introduced Christian ideas into his form of Shinto. It would be wrong to approach him in an apologetic manner and dismiss his concept of God which is unique within Japan and which is akin to that of Nakae Tōju: an ancestor god without beginning and without end.

'God, Taigen Kōsoshin, that is, the first ancestral god, is in all creation. This god's name is Ame-no-minakanushi no kami. This god has no beginning and no end. He is in heaven, and possesses sufficient virtue to give birth to all creation. But though he permeates all, he rules creation in silence.'[27]

Takami-musubi and Kami-musubi should have emanated from this god and further have shaped the earth and their offspring. The name of Ame no miankanushi, the lord of the centre of heaven, has much in common with the name which the God of the Christians obtained in China: *tenshu*, the lord of heaven. Thus he applied and copied Giulio Aleni's *San shan lun hsüeh chi* of 1625 in favour of *Ame no minaka nushi no mikoto* in writing:

'For example, if you look about, it is as if the heavens and the earth are a palace, and this palace certainly has a ruler who made it. All the more so, if this earth does not have a ruling god, how could nature have come about? For this reason it can be understood that the ruler of heaven and earth existed prior to creation. From the beginning there was a god who had no beginning, and of course it was under these circumstances that all creation was made; he is the ruler of all creation and, so to speak, the founder of the country. If god had not existed before the heavens and the earth, if god is said to have appeared after the creation of the world, then how was this world made? And if he came later, where did he come from? and what is more, who made him the ruler? This just can't be explained.'[28]

His choice of Ame-no-minaka-nushi to be that preexistent deity is clear, the figure of this deity in Japan's oldest writings, however, does not confirm his theistic thesis at all. Who is Ame-no-minaka-nushi? In the *Kojiki* (712) and the *Kogo-shū* (807/8) mention is made of him being together with Taka-mi-musubi and Kami-musubi as one of the gods who came into existence 'when heaven and earth became separated'.[29] Together with these two *musubi*, who are believed to realise the creative intentions of the lord of heaven he can be considered as the focus of a Japanese trinity.[30] In the *gobusho* (twelfth century) Ame no minaka nushi became amalgamated with two other gods: Kuni-Tokotachi-no-Mikoto and Toyouke-Daijin into one deity: Daigenshin: the deity of the great origin.[31] In the collective god Inari he became amalgamated as the principal of four other gods.[32] Even now in many shrines he reveals himself in other gods. In the *honden* (main shrine) of the Kono-jinja e.g. Toyo-uke and Amaterasu are considered to be two manifestations of Ame-no-minaka-nushi-no-kami.[33] Hayashi Razan believed that this god dwells in everyone:

> 'The Deity is the Spirit of Heaven and Earth. The human mind partaking of divinity is a sacred abode of the Deity, which is the spiritual essence. there is no Ame-no-Minakanusi-no-kami (the Divine Lord of the Very Centre of Heaven) apart from the human mind.'[34]

Deguchi Nobuyoshi (1616-1693), another contemporary of Razan taught in his own Tokai Shinto that Ame-no-minaka-nushi, Kuni-toko-tachi and Toyo-uke-no-kami were three aspects of one and the same god.[35] After the Meiji Restauration Ame-no-minaka-nushi became under Chinese and Buddhist influence identified with the Pole star (Jap. Myōken, skt. Sudarsani).[36]

Hirata Atsutane in spite of these polytheistic developments turned Ame-no-minaka-nushi into a monotheistic god by ascribing to him the creative qualities which are peculiar to the Christian *tenshu*. He pointed at the existence of this – as the apostle Paul calls it – unknown god in the Japanese sources. It is beyond any doubt that Hirata was very influential. His ideas modified Shinto and determined other religious developments in Japan: they were familiar to the inner circles of the Imperial Court being propagated there by his disciple Mutobe Setsuka and his son Yoshika. His 533 disciples and his son-in-law Hirata Tetsutane with as many as 1330 followers disseminated his ideas all over the country. In the so-called Hirata Shinto the mythical parents Izanagi and Izanami were made equal to Adam and Eve.

AME-NO-MINAKA-NUSHI IN SHINTO STUDIES AND THE NEW RELIGIONS

That Japanese monotheism concentrated on Ame-no-minaka-nushi is also apparent in more recent Shinto-studies. Genchi Kato for instance must have delighted father Wilhelm Schmidt, the supporter of Andrew Lang's idea of primitive monotheism, in writing in 1926:

> 'We have good reasons to believe from the standpoint of a

comparative study of religion that Ame-no-Minakanushi-no-Kami is really the Deity of Japanese primitive monotheism, and I made public my own view on this point in detail in a paper published in the *Transactions of the Asiatic Society of Japan* nearly two decades ago, which the reader may well wish to consult.'[37]

He enumerates several arguments in favour of his opinion. So he points out that in the *Engishiki* (976), Japan's oldest register of gods and shrines, no shrine is mentioned relating to this god. So it is appropriate to argue that Ame-no-Minakanusi was an 'unknown god'. Kato also tries to refute the opinion that this god could have been a recent fabrication or Chinese import. Therefore, this god could be evidence of Japan's own peculiar expression of monotheism.[38]

It goes without saying that Hirata's ideas also had considerable influence on the ideas of many new religions. In 1947 the Shinto-shinkyo was founded by Mrs Unigame Itoko (*1876). It worships Ame-no-minaka-nushi as its chief divinity.[39] Omotokyo founded in 1892 considered Tenchi-kane-no-kami to be the creator of the universe. Afterwards other names of this god came into use. shortly after 1952 the third foundress, the Sandaisama, Naohi said:

> 'Nous, adeptes de l'ômoto, nous croyons en un seul vrai Dieu, Créateur de l'univers. Et si l'on insiste pour que nous disons que Il est, nous ne pouvons répondre que ceci: il est à peu près impossible d'exprimer en langage humain le juste concept de Dieu, car sa Divinité ne connaît pas de bornes, et elle est plus merveilleuse qu'on ne peut le dire. "Ce Dieu 'unique' a cependant, pour en dire le moins, plusieur aspects différents. "Le Dieu qui a créé le monde est un. Il s'appelle Ame-no-minaka-nushi-no-mikoto".'[40]

It is obvious that the creative qualities of Ame-no-minaka-nushi also became ascribed to other divinities. It is out of the question that these developments were due to the existence of modern Christian denominations in Japan.

THE PLURIFORM MONOTHEISM OF THE KAKURE KIRISHITAN

We have met already the Kakure-Kirishitan. As this name indicates they are Christians who kept their secret, in order not to be detected by the (Tokugawa) authorities. Since 1872 when the Tokugawa ban on Christianity was lifted many of them became united with the Roman Catholic Church. In 1877 their numbers were calculated at 15,397 and in 1953 of the 185,000 Catholics about 100,000 were descendants of the Kakure-Kirishitan. In spite of the return of many to the R.C. Church, there still are some 30,000 Kakure-Kirishitan who do not comply with the Roman Catholic teachings and continue their practice of faith in hiding. The Roman Catholics named them 'Separated', *Hanare Kirishitan*, though they were separated from the Roman Church by the Tokugawa laws only and not by any separatist movement within their own ranks.

What does the theism of the Kakure-Kirishitan look like? The best description of it is presented by the late professor Tagita Koya in his *Showajidai no Senpuku Kirishitan*. They fixed their concepts of God in a secret oral tradition which was put in writing about 150 years ago. This secret text is called: *Tenchi no hajimari no koto*, the beginning of heaven and earth. Tagita received this manuscript in the village of Kurosaki. About eight manuscripts of it were handed down to him on the peninsula of Nishisonogi and on the Gotō islands. In 1865 this text was also discovered by Petitjean, the first missionary who met Kakure-Kirishitan. The text was considered to be very significant to the Kakure-Kirishitan of Nishisonogi and the Gotō islands. It was put in hiragana writing in 1822-23 but went missing in 1874.[41] The theme of hiding the faith is manifest in this book.[42] In 1938 the text was translated into German by A. Bohner.[43] I quote here some details of Tagita's translation:

> To begin with (somo somo) Deusu, there were no heaven and earth, human beings or other things to worship him. God had 200 forms (comparable with the 12 laksana's of Buddha and the 33 forms of Kannon) which were dark and with the aid of 42 forms, he in the beginning with one beam of light separated these forms. This beam of light was named *nitten*: the *sundeva* (Amaterasu). Deusu in his one body is the origin of wisdom, disposes of everything, creates everything. Evenmore he created the twelve *ten* (deva's) and the *bembo* (limbo). (Of the twelve *ten* one is named *nitten*, the other eleven have Portuguese names). He named *inuheru* (inferno) *jigoku*, and *mambo* (mundo) the world.[44]

The creation of man is described as follows:

> Deusu while creating all things, put earth, water, fire, wind, salt, and oil (salt and oil being Catholic ritual elements: compare it with the moulding of the Nara daibutsu) in his own bones and flesh during the second (*shikuta*), the third (*terushiya*), the fourth (*kuwaruta*), the fifth (*kinta*), the sixth day (*sesuta*), sabbath (*sabato*) successively and all this became the body of man.[45] Thereupon Deusu himself brought his breath into it. He gave him the name of Atan in 33 forms. Subsequently he made the seventh day into a feast day. Next he made a woman and he called her by the name of Ewa. He made them into man and wife, build yourself a house and give birth to boys and girls . . . .'.[46]

The book 'The beginning of heaven and earth' describes many

biblical beings in a Japanese fashion.[47] Lucifer with his hundred forms is the guardian of the house of Deusu in his absence. It mentions the god of thunder in ten different forms. What are these forms of Deusu, Atan, Lucifer and the god of thunder?

Form is written as *sō*. Three characters are used for this *sō* meaning: X, two, a pair, or X, tadashi, however, or X, assist.[48] In this book Christianity also received a Buddhist cloak. Jesus discusses with the scribes the disputes of Saicho, Kukai and other Buddhist scholars. Jesus was informed that in Jerusalem a scribe of the Shaka-school (Sakyamuni) studied many books and read also the *Issaikyo*, the complete compilation of Buddhist literature. Jesus when entering the temple is told by the scribe that in invoking *Namu Amida Butsu*, he would undoubtedly obtain Buddhahood in paradise. Jesus answered that Deusu, the Lord of Heaven, who is worshipped as Buddha, is none other than the Buddha who accomplishes salvation in the world to come.

Deusu himself is depicted as an independent, free and living Buddha or *ikibotoke*. He creates ten thousand angels. The angels appear in 33 forms just like Kannon (Avalokitesvara). In his Buddha-power he creates man. After the Fall of Adam and Eve Deusu cannot admit anymore the children of Adam and Eve in heaven, but he promises them to show them heaven if they atone for their sins and adore the moon and the stars (do they have to become shintoists first?).

The last page of this book reads as follows:

> In the chapter called *kirinto no koto* (Credo) it describes the Ascension of Jesus Christ. On the *sesuta no hi* (the sixth day) the lofty body descended under the *Daichi* (great earth) and stayed there until the day of *sabato* (Sabbath). Many (*amato no*) disciples adored him laying in state on the coffin. Hereafter he ascended to heaven (*ten ni noborasetamae*). On the third day he was endowed with a place to the right of Mioya Deseu (written as: *tentei*: the emperor of heaven), Godfather.[49] Then he descended from heaven (*ama kudarasaretmai*) in order to rescue live and dead people (*ikitaru hito shishitaru hito tasuketamawan ga tame*) and he stays in the 'santa ikirenja no tera' the temple of the holy church. . . On the fiftieth day his lofty body in front of Santa Maruya, disciples and a great meeting of many listeners went up to heaven. His mother Santa Maruya received from heaven a message, had a meal on the third day of July, and on the 22nd day from the mountain called Oribete she went up to heaven. She appeared in front of Mioya Deusu. Thereupon she received the office of intermediary. The lofty body received the office of saviour. *Mioya Deusu* became *hateru* (pater) the lofty body *onko hiryo*, the holy mother (*seibō*) became *suheruto santō* (the Holy Ghost). *Mioya Deusu* as *pa-teru*, *hiryo* and *suberu* became *Tenteisantai*: the

heaven emperor in three bodies. Even if God is called three bodies, santai, yet there is one body only.[50]

The Jesuits who during the sixteenth and seventeenth centuries preached God as Deusu or Tenshu never expected their ideas to develop into specific Shinto concepts of pluriform monotheism such as Ame no minaka nushi no mikito or to Buddhist manifestations of God in many forms akin to the 33 forms of Kannon. Since then a special brand of Japanese theism contributed also to the reduction of myriads of gods to one monotheistic god in Tenrikyō, Konkokyō and Omotokyō. There still is a lot of research to be done in order to bridge the gap between these religions on the one hand and the ideas of Hirata Atsutane and of the Kakure-Kirishitan on the other. It is clear that Japan's monotheism, though differing from Christian monotheism, became established in more than a third of Japan's population, a figure forty times larger than the total number of Christians in Japan.

FOOTNOTES

1 Thomsen, 1963: 49.
2 van Straelen, 1954,7.
3 van Straelen, 1954,7.
4 Tenrikyo, 1960: 36.
5 Tenrikyo, 1960: 40.
6 See Thomsen, 1963: 73.
7 Thomsen, 1963: 134, 158, 181 and J.H. Kamstra, 1990: 99, note 25.
8 Young, 1990,40.
9 Young, 1990: 35.
10 Young, 1990: 43.
11 Young, 1990: 44.
12 Drummond, 1971: 122: 'Mention has been made that popular memories of Christianity, or perhaps accounts from even more direct sources, possibly influenced the leaders of the three most prominent new religions of the common people founded during the nineteenth century, Tenrikyō, Konkōkyō and Omotokyō. It is impossible to prove or to disprove this thesis, but the virtual monotheism, or at least strongly theistic position, which emerged in the case of each of these religious movements, suggests some such influence. Theistic faith had been known in Japan before the advent of Christian missionaries, most notably in the Pure Land sects of Japanese Buddhism, but the national experience with Christianity had created a new religious climate. Furthermore, the home district of Kawate Bunjirō, who founded Konkōkyō in 1859, had contained numerous *Kirishitan* during the Catholic period. In general, the ethical level of these religions was high. They emphasised purification from ethical failure and social responsibility and had universalist perspectives far beyond those of the much older Shintō religion.'
13 This so-called edict of Kan'ei issued by Shogun Iemitsu forbade all Western books on Christianity, including 32 works of Matteo Ricci and other Europeans. Descriptions of Christian habits, however, were allowed. Yet some inspectors interpreted this prohibition very strictly. So in 1685 the inspector Mukai Gensei banned all books which used words such as Catholic, Jesus, Western, Europe, Ricci and Nestorian Christianity. See G.K. Goodman, 1986: 34,35.
14 The economist Honda Toshiaki (1744-1821) was a warm promoter of foreign trade and even advocated the removal of the Japanese capital to Kamchatka; Koga Toan (1788-1847) was a famous economist, the *rangakusha* Sato Nobuhiro (1769-1850) took lively interest in all

sciences, those related to agriculture and medicine in particular, and the *rangakusha* Mitsukuri Gempo (1799-1863) translated Dutch books, but was also very competent at Chinese. See G.K. Goodman, 1986: 218,219; Jennes, 1973: 187-188.

15 See Jennes, 1973: 188.

16 Here I have to refer to the excellent analysis of Ricci by Dudink in cooperation with E. Zürcher (Leyden university). Dudink, 1979: note 42 (p. iv). Contemporary Buddhist monks as Sanhuai and Zhuhong, saw in *Tianzhu* only an inferior god under an immense multitude of higher Buddhist divinities. Dudink, 1979: 12.

17 Dudink, 1979: 12.

18 For more details see: Jennes, 1973: 81, 82.

19 See J.H. Kamstra, 1988: 67 ff.

20 Jennes, 1973: 12.

21 See Magarey Earl, 1964: 77, n.20.

22 R. Devine, 1981: 40.

23 See J.M. Kitagawa, 1988: 239 and Jennes, 1973: 188. See for a verbal translation of the text of his argument: Devine, 1981: 43.

24 Devine, 1981: 41, 42.

25 Devine, 1981: 44.

26 See Devine, 1981: 44 ff.

27 Devine, 1981: 42.

28 Devine, 1981: 43.

29 This formulation is taken from the *Kogo-shûi*. The opening words of the *Kojiki* are:

'Die Namen der zu Beginn von Himmel und Erde im Gefilde des Hohen Himmels entstandenen Gottheiten waren Ame no Mi-naka-nushi no Kami, ferner Taka-mi-musubi no Kami, ferner Kami-musubi no Kami. Diese drei Gottheiten waren sämtlich als Einzel-Gottheiten entstanden und verbargen ihre Leiber [in Unsichbarkeit].'

See Florenz, 1919: 10. Florenz translates his name as: 'Herr der hehren Mitte des Himmels'. For the text of the *Kago-shûi* see: K. Florenz, 1919: 416. In the *Nihonshoki* (735), however, Kuni no Toko-tachi no Mikoto takes this first place. See K. Florenz, 1919: 124. A similar text to that of the *Kojiki* is also mentioned in the *Nihonshoki*. See K. Florenz: 125 under IV.

30 See Kamstra, 1967: 41 ff. Genchi Kato points out that in Shinto several triads of gods are well known such as the triad of Uwazutsu-no-o, Nakazutsu-no-o and Sokuzutsu-no-o. Kato, 1971: 70.

31 Kato G.: 131, 132.

32 According to J. Herbert, 1967: 97. Others have a different opinion about the development of Inari. In 908 Uka no mitama, Sada hiko no kami, and Omiya no me no mikoto and in 1266 six more gods were added to the collective deity Inari. See J.H. Kamstra, 1989, 185.

33 See J. Herbert, 1967: 89.

34 See Kato G., 1971: 182.

35 J. Herbert, 1967: 130.

36 Prior to this the god Ame-no-kagase-wo or Ama-tsu-mika-hoshi (the god 'star of heaven') became identified with the polar star. See J. Herbert, 1967: 15, 16. See also G. Kato, 1971: 15.

37 Genchi Kato, 1971: 63.

38 See G. Kato, 1971: 64 ff.

39 The sect counts 6,500 members. Herbert names this sect Tensha-tsuchimikado-shintô-hombu. It worships Ame-no-minaka-nushi-no-kami in his Taoist name of Taïzan-fukun. The sect appears to have been founded in 1954 by Yoshio Fujita (* 1898) and claims 57,000 members. It is, in fact, a much older sect. It was outlawed by the Meiji government between 1870 and 1873 for being opposed to its policy of the 'separation of Shinto and Buddhism'. It even dates back to 1680. The sect was revived in 1954.

40 Herbert, 1967: 173.

41 See also Jennes, 1971: 204, note 181.

42 See Tagita, 1955: 76 and ff.

43 Alfred Bohner, Tenchi Hajimari no Koto. Wie Himmel und Erde entstanden, in M.N., vol. I (1938): 465-514.

44 See Tagita, 1955: 83.

45 In another edition the moulding of man is depicted as follows: 'He made men in great numbers. He had to create only good things. With his own hands he descended from heaven to earth, he took several pounds of earth, he moistened it with water, flavoured it with salt

and oil. . ., and he kneaded it with the power of Buddha, and on the second day he created *kofube*, and on the third day he created the hands, in his body he created bones, and to the left he created the ribs (*abarabone*) just by joining them together. That was *kuwaruta*, the fourth day. He made gold that was the *kinday*: quinta. He made his feet. That was the sixth day. On *sabato* he made the heart of man, he took the moon and put it inside the soul, he took the stars and set them into the eyes. From his *kofube* Deususama changed his own breath, and nine sticks gave light (*kokonotsu no hogeta ga akari* should be: *kokonotsu no ana ga hiraite* meaning: he opened nine holes). And what was finished he named Adan. He received 33 forms (Just as the bodhisattva Kannon). On this clear day millions of *anjō* (angels) came together and this became the day of rest, *rakusei*. On this day he created many women, by turning ribs into big bones. He named her Ewa and they became man and wife. Tagita, 1955: 87, 88.

46 See Tagita, 1955: 86, 87.
47 The details mentioned here are derived from the summary of Piryns (1971: 160).
48 See Tagita, 1955: 83 note 3.
49 See Tagita, 1955: 151.
50 Tagita, 1955: 152.

REFERENCES

Bonner A., 'Tenchi Hajimari no Koto. Wie Himmel und Erde entstanden' in: M.N., vol. 1 (1938): 465-514.
Devine R., 'Hirate Atsutane and Christian Sources', in M.N., 36 (1981): 37-54.
Drummond R.H., A History of Christianity in Japan, Michigan 1971.
Dudink A., Een westerse Godsdienst oostwaarts, Amsterdam 1979.
Florenz K., Die Historischen Quellen der Shinto Religion. Göttingen 1919.
Goodman G.K., Japan: The Dutch Experience, London 1986.
Herbert J., Dieux et sectes populaires du Japan, Paris 1967.
Jennes J., A History of the Catholic Church in Japan, Tokyo 1973.
Kamstra J.H., Encounter or Syncretism, Leiden 1967.
Kamstra J.H., De Japanse Religie, een fenomenale godsdienst, Hilversum 1988.
Kamstra J.H., 'The goddess who grew into a bodhisattva fox: Inari', in: I. Hijiya-Kirschnereit e.a., (red.); Bruno Lewin zu Ehren: Festschrift aus Anlass seines 65. Geburtstages. Band II, Bochum 1989: 179-214.
Kato G., A Study of Shinto, London 1971.
Kitagawa J.M., 'Some remarks on Shinto', in H.o.R, 27 (1988): 227-245.
Magarey Earl D., Emperor and Nation in Japan: Political Thinkers in the Tokugawa Period, Washington 1964.
Piryns E., Japan en het Christendom: naar de overstijging van een dilemma, Lannoo 1971.
Straelen H. van, The Religion of Divine Wisdom, Tokyo 1954.
Tagita K., Showajidai no sempuku kirishitan, Tokyo 1955.
Tenrikyo, Die Lehre der Tenrikyo, Tenri 1960.
Thomsen H., The New Religions of Japan, Tokyo 1963.
Young R.F., 'Magic and Morality in Modern Japanese Exorcist Technologies - A Study of Mahikari', in: Japanese Journal of Religious Studies, vol. 17 (1990): 29-49.

9

Of Priests, Protests and Protestant Buddhists: the Case of Soka Gakkai International

BRIAN BOCKING

THIS PAPER discusses Soka Gakkai International, which is well known as the largest and most successful of the post-war Japanese lay religious movements, both in Japan and overseas. It considers the direction of development of Soka Gakkai International in Japan and abroad, following the well-publicized split in November 1991, between the Soka Gakkai organizations and the Nichiren Shōshū sect of which it was a lay movement. Since the split took place between a priestly hierarchy and a lay Buddhist movement the discussion brings into focus the issues of the role of the priesthood and the nature of lay religiosity in contemporary Buddhism.

Sōka Gakkai's origins and development over the last 50 years represent a classic example of a 'new' movement formed by religious syncretism, involving:

> '. . . the coexistence of elements foreign to each other within a specific religion. . . (elements which) need not necessarily themselves be all of a religious origin but may include political, philosophical and other secular elements of all kinds.'[1]

Two elements brought together by Sōka Gakkai's first founder, Makiguchi, which have remained most obviously in tension, are Makiguchi's own secular educational 'Theory of Value', and the medieval Buddhist tradition of chanting the title of the Lotus Sutra preached by the thirteenth-century monk Nichiren, a tradition transmitted through the Nichiren Shōshū priestly lineage. Makiguchi, a schoolteacher whose progressive ideas on education found no favour with the pre-war Japanese authorities, founded the lay movement which is now known as Sōka Gakkai after developing independently his theory of value. Late in life Makiguchi came to believe that the practice of chanting the *daimoku* '*namu-myōhō-renge-kyō*' – the powerful title of the Lotus Sutra – provided the key to practical realization of the values which he had identified as important for individual and social development.

The tensions between these two elements – the thirteenth-century chant and the twentieth-century humanistic theory of education – reflect broader cultural tensions in Japan and throughout the modern world: between traditionalism and modernism, hierarchy and egalitarianism, objective knowledge traditions and subjective understanding, mysticism and rationalism, collective authority and individualism, sacredness and secularism, faith and scepticism, and so on.

Syncretic tension eventually seeks resolution through assimilation or separation,[2] and in November 1991 the Nichiren Shōshū high priest 'excommunicated'[3] all Sōka Gakkai followers in Japan and abroad.[4] The breakdown of the relationship between Nichiren Shōshū and Sōka Gakkai took place at that point for a number of reasons. One important underlying factor contributing to the break was the long-standing challenge to the authority of the Nichiren Shōshū priesthood posed by the Sōka Gakkai and its leadership. The split was triggered by various incidents and excesses, each party blaming the other for the breakdown of trust.[5] As a result of the split, Soka Gakkai International, headed by its long-time leader, Daisaku Ikeda, now exists as a separate and self-contained lay Buddhist movement, cut off from the priestly lineage which until 1991 provided it with sacerdotal authority by virtue of priestly succession based on the concept of 'blood inheritance' from Nichiren himself.[6] Under the pre-1991 system, members of Sōka Gakkai depended spiritually on Nichiren Shōshū, but not vice-versa. The head priest of Nichiren Shōshū, for example, is the only person authorized to issue, through local priests, a *Nichiren Shōshū gohonzon* (sacred Lotus Sutra mandala inscribed by Nichiren or successive high priests) to a new member of Sōka Gakkai.

The Nichiren Shōshū/Sōka Gakkai split could be described as an unprecedented 'protestant reformation' or long-overdue 'modernization' within Japanese Buddhism; an interpretation which Sōka Gakkai International is energetically canvassing,[7] although this begs the question of whether it is helpful to liken the relationship between priestly hierarchy and laity in Japan to the relationship of priest and people in Western Christianity. Since the rate of cultural change in any given context is normally glacial, we would expect many Sōka Gakkai followers in Japan to find the split from their priests disturbing, and many will be looking for a way, despite their excommunication, to regroup fairly swiftly in a culturally satisfying configuration of lay-clerical relationships. It is inevitable, for example, that most Japanese members will continue to feel the need to have a 'proper' priest involved in funeral and ancestral rites, if only for the sake of the deceased.[8]

The implications of the excommunication of Soka Gakkai International for its future development as a religious movement outside Japan need also to be considered. Amongst British adherents, for example, there is little if any culturally-felt need for a priest to be involved in ancestral rites, which are the major preoccupation of Buddhist priests in Japan, even supposing there are British members who believe that ancestors are amongst those who benefit from their Buddhist practice. Indifference to the spiritual welfare of ancestors follows on naturally from the fact that British official and popular religion since the sixteenth century has been largely protestant in character, so that death rituals, for example, are popularly conceived of as rites of passage or rituals of grief, marking the change of status from life to death. This contrasts with the Japanese view of funerary rites as a long-term process involving merit-producing activities by the surviving family members which are designed to help the dead achieve transformation into spiritual entities. The bereaved thereby both discharge the obligations of filial piety and (despite *tatari*[9] being no part of official Sōka Gakkai belief) avoid the potential problems caused by unhappy ancestral spirits.

Even drawing attention to ancestral or funeral rites as if they were central to religious practice is nonsensical in a British context. If there are British adherents of Sōka Gakkai who feel that priests are necessary to their religious life, this will not be in connection with funerals and ancestral rites, but because a member believes that priests are required in order for the technicalities of the religious practice of the living to be effective. The sole right of the high priest of Nichiren Shōshū to issue the *gohonzon* in fact falls into this category of actions reserved for the priesthood. Its closest analogy – particularly in the minds of British converts to Sōka Gakkai from Anglican or Catholic backgrounds – would be the assumption that an ordained priest, a recipient of the apostolic succession, is necessary in order for the Christian Eucharist to 'work'. But is it legitimate to draw a parallel between the role of a Japanese Buddhist priest and a British Christian one?

The priest, or monk, in a Buddhist context, may play a number of roles. Despite the popular Western image of the Buddhist monk as an individual separated from worldly concerns it was and is normal, even within the most conservative Theravadin traditions of Sri Lanka and despite the restrictions of the vinaya, for the majority of monks to be involved in local communal religion, education, the arts, landowning, and politics; the forest-dwelling 'supramundane' calling was (and is) reserved for the very few.[10]

In Japanese Buddhism, influenced from the beginning by the Mahayana belief in the potential for enlightenment in all living beings, and by Confucian respect for fulfilment of social obligations as a sacred value, the lay/monastic distinction was always viewed as somewhat provisional. The medieval Pure Land monk Shinran is thought to have married partly in order to demonstrate the vacuity of priestly status in this degenerate age of *mappō*,[11] and it has been normal for Japanese Buddhist priests since at least the nineteenth century to marry and carry on secular occupations as well as fulfilling priestly functions. Nevertheless, the notion that a monk-as-priest has special powers, and fulfils a special spiritual role which only an ordained priest – regardless of his moral conduct – can fulfil, remains powerful within Japanese Buddhism. In his account of Buddhism in Sri Lanka, Carrithers refers, in addition to 'the monk as forest-dweller', to 'the monk as teacher, preacher and priest', 'the monk as landlord' and 'the monk in politics'.[12] In the case of Sōka Gakkai in Japan, in his customary function as officiant at funeral and memorial services, the Nichiren Shōshū Buddhist priest plays the role of 'monk as undertaker', and on behalf of the high priest, the role of 'monk as tantric initiator'.[13] Only the high priest (or his proxy), by virtue of his blood-succession from Nichiren himself, can bestow upon devotees of the Lotus an inscribed mandala, the *gohonzon*, the empowered visual text of the *daimoku* which in sound and appearance is the focus of the Nichiren Shōshū tantric practice and the very means by which this world can be transformed into a Buddha-land. The copy of the *gohonzon* which is issued to new members is not a picture of the Buddha or a purely symbolic diagram, but includes the *daimoku* in written form, surrounded by the representations by the name of various bodhisattvas and deities of China, India and Japan. The fact that the *gohonzon* is itself an 'utterance' or text of the sacred title of the Lotus Sutra underlines the importance Nichiren attached to propagation and remembrance of the *daimoku* as the quintessential Buddhist practice, but according to orthodox Nichiren Shōshū teaching a copy of the *gohonzon* must be empowered by the high priest – a 'counterfeit' *gohonzon* has no value.

Even in the case of the sacred *gohonzon*, however, the high priest's role seems somewhat compromised in Sōka Gakkai by the ready accessibility of the means to practice Nichiren's Buddhism. Often in mantra traditions the words of the empowering phrase to be repeated are secret, or at least are regarded as ineffective if they have been received without the authority of their 'owner', for example a guru. Bestowal of a mantra sometimes involves payment (as in the case of Transcendental Meditation) or more often some other kind of reciprocal undertaking by the neophyte in exchange for the mantra, such as a vow to follow the practice or keep the mantra secret. In the case of Sōka Gakkai there is nothing secret about the *daimoku*, although the inscribed *gohonzon* is of course an object to be treated with profound reverence. On the contrary, it is well known that potential converts are encouraged to chant '*namu-myōhō-renge-kyō*' even without the *gohonzon*, to see for themselves the effect *daimoku* practice has, 'proof' being one of the signs of the true teaching. It could reasonably be argued, therefore, that the *gohonzon*, while important, is not absolutely essential for Buddhist practice in the tradition of Nichiren. This view is reinforced by the interpretation of the *gohonzon* as something which exists within the heart of the worshipper. A quotation from Nichiren reproduced in a Soka Gakkai International publication runs 'Never seek this *gohonzon* outside yourself. The *gohonzon* exists only within the mortal flesh of us ordinary people who embrace the Lotus Sutra and chant *namu-myōhō-renge-kyō*'.[14]

The recent separation of Sōka Gakkai from Nichiren Shōshū might, therefore, be seen by many members, particularly members from 'protestant' cultures overseas such as the UK, to be less a tragic division in a religious body than a positive opportunity to cleanse the movement of elements deriving from traditional Japanese Buddhist culture; elements whose relevance to modern life (and 'true Buddhism') may not be apparent, particularly to foreigners.[15] The institution of the Japanese Buddhist priesthood, I would suggest, falls firmly into this category. We can already see, for example, Soka Gakkai International writings which claim that Nichiren himself rejected, or would have rejected an authoritarian priestly hierarchy, and had faith in a democracy of the laity in the matters of religion.[16]

Unusually amongst the multitude of new (or indeed old) Japanese religions, Sōka Gakkai has a well-developed doctrinal dimension.[17] While Sōka Gakkai members may not routinely study Makiguchi's 'Theory of Value' as part of their training, the emphasis on studying and passing examinations in Sōka Gakkai doctrine does reflect the fact that the first two founders, Makiguchi and Toda, were teachers. The unusual emphasis on rational explanations of Buddhism and the study of systematic doctrine (unusual that is, for Japanese religions) underlines the point that Sōka Gakkai is not simply a religious sect, but a modern lay movement founded on an essentially secular education theory. It also means that both ordinary members and leaders of Sōka Gakkai have a potential means of access, through their religion's positive attitude to education of the whole person, to the wider world of secular and religious meaning that exists beyond Nichiren Shōshū Buddhism and even beyond Buddhism, embracing secular, cultural and socio-political activities. This is in contrast to many other new Japanese movements which, though they cannot accurately be described as anti-intellectual, have little or no interest in educating their followers beyond the narrow confines of the world-view whose typical features are shared by most Japanese new religions.[18]

A point of departure in my own analysis of Sōka Gakkai's current situation, at what must be recognised as a crossroads in its history, is the notion of 'protestant Buddhism' a concept first used to describe nineteenth-century Ceylonese Buddhism and recently examined in relation to two British Buddhist groups, Friends of the Western Buddhist Order and the English Sangha, by Philip Mellor in his article 'Protestant Buddhism? The cultural translation of Buddhism in England'.[19]

'Protestant' is a term with a wide range of historical meanings, none of which need necessarily be applicable to Buddhism in Japan, although Religious Studies scholars in Japan currently debating the Sōka Gakkai/Nichiren Shōshū issue readily use the analogy of Catholicism and Protestantism to unravel some of the implications.[20] My concern is with the direction of development of Sōka Gakkai, an issue which involves, above all, the questions of how decisions are made and priorities established within the movement.

In an earlier paper, I resorted to Niehbuhr's typology of Institutional, Calvinist and Sectarian protestantism to categorize phases in the developing self-definition of Nichiren Shōshū/Sōka Gakkai. Niehbuhr's typology is almost as old as Sōka Gakkai itself, but still has its heuristic uses, despite theoretical advances in the Sociology of Religion.[21] According to this typology, I would identify Nichiren himself as broadly comparable to an 'institutional' Protestant, who sought in the thirteenth century to replace the established but corrupting 'church' of Shingon, and what he saw as the theological errors of Zen and the vile populism of Pure Land, with a cleansed and revitalized version of Tendai Buddhism, of which the Emperor, Shogun and all the people of Japan would be devout sponsors and adherents. Indeed, the conversion of the Emperor was vital to Nichiren's plan to establish a *honmon no kaidan* or national ordination platform as a centre for the propagation of true Buddhism. Elements of an 'institutional Protestant' approach – one which seeks to replace a corrupt, single, established national church with a purified and revitalised, single, established national church – were evident in Japan in the 1950s and early 60s when Sōka Gakkai had aspirations to convert the whole of Japan to

Nichiren Shōshū and established their own political party, Kōmeitō, precisely to assist in bringing about the total unity of Buddhism and state (*ōbutsu myōgō*) within a constitutional democracy.

As Sōka Gakkai grew rapidly in the 1950s and '60s, it moderated its political ambitions and developed into a kind of 'Calvinist' protestantism, in which religious and political authority are conceived of as remaining different and unequal for the foreseeable future, though it is assumed that their aims will eventually harmonize. It was felt no longer necessary (though it remained of course desirable) for the Emperor to become a Nichiren Buddhist in order for Nichiren's aim of *ōbutsu myōgō* or union of government and religion to be achieved. Sōka Gakkai was apparently succeeding, even without government approval or patronage, in creating an alternative society in Japan based on the principles, aims and practices of *ningen kakumei* or 'human revolution', a governing principle which it saw as objectively superior to the confusion, compromise and directionlessness of conventional politics and everyday life. The principles and aims of Sōka Gakkai's 'human revolution' included, for example, the establishment of world peace by dialogue, persuasion and the beneficial influence of religious practice; opposition to weapons of mass destruction, Buddhist ethics in science and the promotion of educational opportunity.

Within Sōka Gakkai in Japan, and regardless of the formal subordination of all members of Sōka Gakkai to the Nichiren Shōshū priesthood, a two-tier system of religious authority had also developed which resembled the internal hierarchical structure of Niehbuhr's 'Calvinist' model of protestantism, where an upper layer of believers, the clergy, exercise considerable authority over the ordinary lay members, though they are spiritually equal. (This differs from Niehbuhr's third type, 'sectarian' protestantism in which decisions are made at a grass-roots, communal level.) Although there was a certain amount of grass-roots involvement in decision making, all important doctrinal and policy decisions in Sōka Gakkai were made from above, by a quasi-clerical hierarchy epitomized by the charismatic figure of Daisaku Ikeda, whom a proportion of followers came to see as a 'living Buddha' (Ikeda's perceived status has always been one of the main points of friction with the priesthood). Officially, however, the lay hierarchy headed by Ikeda derived its authority to govern the affairs of Sōka Gakkai not upwards, from a democratic process within Sōka Gakkai, but solely downwards from the Nichiren Shōshū priesthood.

The relationship between Nichiren Shōshū and Sōka Gakkai throughout the post-war decades theoretically conformed to the typical Japanese model of 'parent-child', with the Nichiren Shōshū priesthood providing spiritual guidance for Sōka Gakkai's leaders and members, and Sōka Gakkai obediently receiving such guidance and supporting the Shōshū in its aims. In reality, because of the enormous human and financial resources available to the Sōka Gakkai leadership for purposes largely determined by that leadership, Sōka Gakkai's relationship with the Nichiren Shōshū priesthood has never actually resembled that of 'parent and child'. One of the first acts of Sōka Gakkai members when Sōka Gakkai was revived after the war by Jōsei Toda was publicly to confront, indeed attack, a former Nichiren Shōshū priest and force him to apologise for compromising the exclusivist claims of Nichiren Shōshū Buddhism by endorsing government directives on religion during the war.[22]

As a result of its obvious success in winning, motivating and organizing members in a constructive way in the cause of spreading Nichiren Shōshū Buddhism, Sōka Gakkai has maintained the view that it occupies the moral or even spiritual high ground within the priest/laity relationship. This is despite regular publicity in the Japanese tabloids about 'scandals' involving Ikeda and others in Sōka Gakkai. The status of Buddhist priests being low in Japan and the distinction between priest and lay follower weak, priests tend to be respected, if at all, for their ritual capacities and spiritual functions rather than as moral exemplars. Moreover, even outsiders hostile to Sōka Gakkai in Japan are conscious that Sōka Gakkai, whatever they think of it as a religion, is a Japanese success story, whereas Nichiren Shōshū is just another denomination of Buddhist priests. All of this reflects the fact that Sōka Gakkai has in practice been led and inspired by its upper tier of full and part-time lay leaders, who constitute a kind of protestant 'clergy', rather than by the ordained priests. It should be added that Japanese society is itself minutely hierarchical, and as Robert Bellah famously pointed out, dominated by 'political values'.[23] This means that a charismatic leader like Ikeda, lay person as he is, can nevertheless count on a degree of unquestioning loyalty and vigorous corporate effort among Sōka Gakkai members undreamed of in even the most hierarchical of Western religious organizations.

The third type of Protestantism identified by Niehbuhr is 'sectarian Protestantism', which is represented in the UK by nonconformist groups such as Congregationalists or Quakers; voluntarist and usually minority groups who organize their affairs communally at a local level, recognise only one tier of spiritual authority (i.e. the local congregation including its pastor) and form regional, national or international networks or adopt centralised administrative structures only for convenience, without ever yielding control to the centre. Nichiren Shoshu in America (NSA) experienced a taste of sectarian Protestant attitudes a few years ago when local American members started to resist directives from Tokyo and began to make decisions on their own authority. American membership began to decline at this point (not necessarily for this reason), and Sōka Gakkai headquarters in Tokyo reasserted its own control. This, so far as I know, is the only documented example of an overseas branch of Sōka Gakkai acting in a way which could be described as 'sectarian Protestant' – but that was before the changes of 1991.[24]

The Nichiren Shōshū sect has publicly accepted financial and other kinds of support from Sōka Gakkai over the years – support which has transformed Nichiren Shōshū from a tiny and marginal religious denomination to a prestigious sect with impressive headquarters and regional temple buildings and a prosperous priesthood. Yet, judging from the bitter attacks on Nichiren Shōshū mounted by Sōka Gakkai since the split became public, many members and certainly the leaders of Sōka Gakkai hold very little respect for the Nichiren Shōshū priests as exemplars of the religious life. Why, then, has Sōka Gakkai persisted with this difficult relationship?

The relationship between Sōka Gakkai and Nichiren Shōshū has been through difficult patches on several occasions, but the strenuous efforts made to repair the relationship (including at one point the resignation of Ikeda as President of Sōka Gakkai) demonstrate that it was always judged to be in Soka Gakkai's best interests to maintain the relationship. Clearly, this was because the lay leadership of Sōka Gakkai derived its authority from the priestly succession, and any rupture with the Nichiren Shōshū lineage could have diminished the authority of the lay leadership, and hence the power of that leadership to govern Sōka Gakkai.

From this point of view, the 1991 split could be seen as disastrous for Sōka Gakkai's leaders, because it removed at a stroke the main constitutional support for their authority to run the lay movement 'from above'. Indeed, the first drastic step which eventually led to the excommunication of the entire membership of Sōka Gakkai was the announcement on 27 December 1990 that Ikeda and his close colleagues were being stripped of their posts as 'lay representatives' of Nichiren Shōshū. Bearing in mind the crucial role played by 'blood' lineage in the establishment and preservation of religious authority in Japanese Buddhism, what guarantee is there, without the mystical transmission of sacerdotal authority through the head priest, that Sōka Gakkai's leaders can maintain their position as undisputed spiritual guides for the mass of the membership?

Trying to chart the future direction of Sōka Gakkai – in Japan as well as overseas – following the split with Nichiren Shōshū, is far from easy. Sōka Gakkai's leaders and scholars are sophisticated and well-informed, and they have made it their business to study and try to learn from the experience of other religious movements faced with leadership crises, changing state-church relationships, different cultural expectations and generational changes in membership of religious sects. Information is change, and whatever happens to Sōka Gakkai will be affected to a significant degree – except in the view of the most zealous social determinist – by what Sōka Gakkai leaders and members *think* should be the future direction of Sōka Gakkai. There seem at present to be three broad options for the future of Sōka Gakkai.

1. Sōka Gakkai can retain its current character, religious beliefs etc. and organizational structure, but remain divorced from the priesthood.

2. It can reunite with the priesthood (possibly by aligning itself with dissident priests in place of the high priest, possibly by achieving a reconciliation with the next high priest).

3. It can adapt to the new situation and change into something it has not been before – perhaps a less centralized movement, developing differently in different countries.

Several constraints which might shape Sōka Gakkai's future can be identified. The first is institutional self-preservation. Sōka Gakkai will survive. Institutions tend to work for their own preservation, and there is in any case no question of Sōka Gakkai simply evaporating as a result of recent events. Whatever the actual and much-debated figures are for membership, Soka Gakkai International is a very large and very well-funded organization engaged in a wide range of international activities. It could afford to lose even large numbers of disaffected or disillusioned members and it would still remain a massive movement; in fact its current stand against the Nichiren Shōshū priesthood could gain it new admirers in Japan and abroad. This being the case, resources on the scale needed to administer a movement which sees itself as 'on the verge of becoming a world religion',[25] can surely only be guaranteed if the religion maintains a strongly centralized, quasi-hierarchical structure, with its headquarters in Japan. I have no information about the flow of resources to and from overseas communities, but it seems obvious that there is still a net outflow of funds from Japan to support commitments to overseas missionary work and projects such as the purchase of buildings. This implies a strong element of cross-subsidy from local Japanese groups to overseas missions which could not be sustained at its present level if Sōka Gakkai in Japan, or overseas, became decentralized – in other words, followed something like the model of sectarian protestantism with decisions made by local groups on their own behalf. Soka Gakkai International has a strong incentive to retain the power of decision-making within the central lay hierarchy, notwithstanding recent arguments that priests and lay believers are all equal.

A second factor is the Lotus Sutra, and Nichiren's interpretation of it. The Lotus Sutra warns that true preachers of the Lotus should expect persecution; indeed, obstacles and hindrances can be seen as a sign that the true dharma is being propagated, while indifferent acceptance by outsiders is a sure sign that the teaching is being diluted. Sōka Gakkai's 'religion of protest' role in Japanese society was originally, and has remained, one of its main strengths and attractions; members have been motivated by the idea that they are helping to transform society for the better as well as benefitting themselves, and the social hostility Sōka Gakkai received in the early years was exactly what its members expected. Soka Gakkai International, however, runs the very real danger (from the sobering standpoint of the Lotus Sutra) of being found acceptable, both overseas and perhaps now in Japan. Overseas, Sōka Gakkai has kept a deliberately low profile with emphasis placed on harmonizing Sōka Gakkai aims and activities with values of the host culture.

There has been diligent evangelism but nothing like a *shakubuku*[26] campaign in the UK, for example. The vigilant spirit of Nichiren, however, sits rather uneasily with such adaptation to the mainstream culture of nations who do not worship Shakyamuni and the Lotus.[27] The Nichiren Shōshū priests, on the other hand, who appear to have handled relations with Sōka Gakkai with an almost endearing ineptness, may find that they have inadvertently retrieved credibility as heirs of the indomitable – and in his time heroically unsuccessful – Nichiren. They have, after all, tackled head-on, and in a completely unsubtle manner, the monolithic and superior might of today's Sōka Gakkai. Also, Nichiren Shōshū has the *gohonzon*. All religious movements must continually judge the extent to which accommodation to the aims and values of the wider society, other religions, etc. reduces or enhances their ability to achieve their own aims. The Nichiren Shōshū priesthood could, if it had wished, have saved the relationship with Sōka Gakkai. Would Nichiren have done so?

Thirdly, under the influence of all-pervading liberal individualism Soka Gakkai International might conceivably adapt to its new status by modernising and liberalising its religiosity – particularly outside Japan, where the traditional Nichirenite denunciation of 'other

Buddhisms' means very little, and where the perceived enemy is much more likely to be the Christian church or secular materialism – to the point where it starts to talk to other Buddhist and non-Buddhist religious groups. By acknowledging the existence of the contemporary 'supermarket of religions' as an authentic manifestation of religiosity, relaxing its claims to exclusive possession of the truth and focusing on the under-exploited contribution made by Makiguchi to the holistic founding educational philosophy of the movement, Sōka Gakkai could become a liberal, even ecumenically-minded religious movement within a few years, something which it has arguably only been prevented from doing in the last decade by the restraining influence of the Nichiren Shōshū traditionalists.[28]

In the light of the above few considerations – for many more could be added – what will Sōka Gakkai become?

In Japan, it is extremely unlikely that Sōka Gakkai can maintain itself independently of a Buddhist priesthood. As Helen Hardacre has pointed out, '. . . many [Japanese] new religions find it difficult to overcome the attachment to established Buddhist funeral and ancestral rites, producing the incongruous situation of religions able to provide doctrine, ritual and an organization perfectly adequate for a human life span but forced at death to return their believers to Buddhist temples for final disposition'.[29] Hardacre's remarks refer to new religions which have grown out of, but may not acknowledge the connection with, Buddhist denominations. Since Sōka Gakkai sees itself not as a new religion but as the most orthodox form of Nichiren's Buddhism, it is utterly inconceivable that the funerary and memorial rites so central to the family-centred religiosity of the Japanese could be abandoned to 'heterodox' Buddhist (or indeed Christian) priests. Moreover, just as the Buddhist priest-as-undertaker is considered essential for funeral rites because he has special spiritual powers derived from the sacerdotal succession, so it is unlikely, too, that ordinary Sōka Gakkai members in Japan will accept 'unauthorized' copies of the *gohonzon* in place of a *gohonzon* received from the high priest; the priest as tantric initiator.

Overseas, however, particularly in predominantly 'Protestant' countries such as the UK, a reinterpretation of the priest's functions which sees them as symbolic rather than magical could be readily envisaged. Funeral rites, as we have seen, are not an issue, and a reinterpretation of the idea of the *gohonzon* as primarily an internal spiritual reality which is only secondarily symbolized and represented by the external *gohonzon* would, I suspect, be uncontroversial. It is doubtful whether followers of Sōka Gakkai in Protestant cultures are aware that priestly functions and religious actions and artifacts are ever more than symbolic. The favoured option for overseas Sōka Gakkai communities is likely to be a complete break with the preisthood, or at least a complete overhaul of the Nichiren priesthood which will establish a new model of 'priest as moral exemplar' – the only kind of 'priest' that Protestantism will tolerate.

In conclusion, therefore, Sōka Gakkai's interests in Japan will be best served by achieving some kind of reconciliation with the priesthood. In turn, Sōka Gakkai's interests as a world-wide movement will be best served if its centre remains strong, and in Japan. But if a reconciliation with the priests is to be achieved, it is important that Sōka Gakkai as a whole makes no radical moves in the direction of an extreme, anti-hierarchical Protestantism, within which the magical authority of priests in spiritual matters such as death and initiation is denied – an option which would be the natural choice for some of Sōka Gakkai's influential overseas followers.

Sōka Gakkai is currently poised between two worlds; not between the world of traditional hierarchical authority and the world of modern egalitarian individualism, as those who seek to discredit priests by discrediting the idea of priesthood might like us to think, but between the very different worlds of Japanese and Western religiosity.

FOOTNOTES

1 Michael Pye, 'Syncretism and Ambiguity.' *Numen* (1971) 18,2:83 & 92-3. See also my discussion of this point in relation to earlier troubles between Sōka Gakkai and Nichiren Shōshū in 'Reflections on Sōka Gakkai.' *The Scottish Journal of Religious Studies* (1981) 2,1:38-54, reprinted in *Proceedings of the British Association for Japanese Studies* (1981) 6,2:58-73.

2 One of the problems to be resolved in developing a useful notion of syncretism is that of time: how long can a 'syncretistic' situation persist and still be called syncretistic (especially since all religion can be said to involve a degree of syncretism)? I would tentatively suggest that a syncretistic religion that persists without substantial change beyond the third generation of believers should no longer be regarded as syncretistic, otherwise the term lose its explanatory power.

3 The Japanese term is *hamon* meaning 'expulsion from the sect'.

4 The break resolves in one sense the question of authority for Nichiren Shōshū, but it is not strictly speaking a resolution of the syncretic tension within Sōka Gakkai; indeed the break was a symptom of this tension. Soka Gakkai International still represents a syncretism of Nichiren's Buddhism with the theory of Creation of Value.

5 Causality is always hard to demonstrate. Different metaphors have been employed to dramatise the nature and causes of the breakdown of the relationship between Sōka Gakkai and Nichiren Shōshū (see Astley,T. 'A Matter of Principles.' *Japanese Religions* (1992) 17,2:167-175 for several examples). From the standpoint of the study of religions there is nothing remarkable about the split, if only one can resist being drawn into the religious discourse of the participants. We can identify long-term underlying factors, e.g. the inherent tensions within a relatively new syncretistic religious movement, and the immediate precipitating factors such as provocative words said or songs sung, power, money, *amour propre*, cumulative frustrations, etc., all of which contributed to the split *at this point*, but such underlying and precipitating 'causes' had existed for a long time in Nichiren Shōshū/Sōka Gakkai without the break occurring (see note 1).

6 In Japanese *kechimyaku sōjō*. See Murata, K. *Japan's New Buddhism: an objective account of Sōka Gakkai*. (1969) Weatherhill New York & Tokyo, p.44. In the Nichiren sect this is not, of course, a reference to biological heredity. For an interesting autobiographical account of a Japanese Buddhist succession (and disputes surrounding it) based on 'blood' (in this case, in Pure Land Buddhism) see Kosho Ko-nyo Otani *The Successor – My Life* (1985), Buddhist Books International.

7 See for example the collection of papers on 'The Traditional and the Contemporary in Religion' and particularly the lead discussion on this topic between Fujio Ikado, Noriyoshi Tamaru and Tsuyoshi Nakano published in the (Sōka Gakkai sponsored) *The Journal of Oriental Studies* (1992) 4:1-22.

8 Trevor Astley 'A Matter of Principles' p.173 (see note 5) reports 'untold distress' among adherents on this point and believes, as is suggested here, that Sōka Gakkai's policy of encouraging members to perform their own funeral and memorial ceremonies is unlikely to suffice.

9 *Tatari* is retribution by psychic means, often the result of neglect of memorial services for ancestors (implying also of course a moral failure of filial piety). In the recent disputes between Sōka Gakkai and Nichiren Shōshū priests the issue of the number and significance of *tōba* offerings (a *tōba* is a wooden Buddhist memorial tablet offered for the repose of the deceased person) has been prominent. Sōka Gakkai's position is that offering *tōba* does not contradict the teachings of Nichiren, if done properly. If, however, the offering of an excessive number of *tōba* is induced, on the grounds that failure to offer *tōba* will result in retribution from the unhappy ancestor, and especially where this is done by priests to make money, Sōka Gakkai strongly disapproves. See *Issues between the Nichiren Shōshū Priesthood and the Sōka Gakkai*, (1991) Soka Gakkai International, Vol. 3, pp.69-102, esp. p.99.

10 See Michael B Carrithers ' "They will be Lords upon the Island": Buddhism in Sri Lanka.' in H Bechert & R Gombrich (eds.) *The World of Buddhism*. (1984) London: Thames and Hudson. pp.133-146. Census figures show no more than 600 'forest dwellers' among ca.20,000 monks in Sri Lanka (p.144).

11 See James C. Dobbins *Jōdo Shinshū: Shin Buddhism in Medieval Japan* (1989) Indiana University Press. pp.24-27.

12 See note 10.

13 Nichiren Shōshū Buddhism is essentially a tantric form of Buddhism, with its roots in both exoteric and esoteric Tendai (the tradition which Nichiren set out to reform from within). The main features of esoteric Buddhism are the mantra and the mandala (*daimoku* and *gohonzon*), the notion of a special text and special transmission which supersedes all other forms of Buddhism, and the belief in enlightenment in the present lifetime.

14 The *gohonzon* distributed by Nichiren Shōshū, unlike other *gohonzon* issued by Nichiren groups, includes a warning (top right-hand corner) that a person who criticises the *gohonzon* will have their head broken into seven pieces. This is an obvious deterrent to any suggestion that the *gohonzon* as a physical object is unnecessary for practice. The Nichiren Shōshū *gohonzon* is reproduced as a frontispiece to Laurel Rasplica Rodd *Nichiren: Selected Writings* (1980) Hawaii.

15 Ian Reader in 'The Institutionalisation of Buddhism in Japan.' *The Journal of Oriental Studies* (1992) 4:91-105 (a paper presented at Sōka Gakkai headquarters in the UK) writes: 'Since Buddhism in the West is relatively young it has not yet had time to gather the sorts of social and cultural baggage that it has accumulated and that are weighing it down in Japan' (p.104). While this contrast between Buddhism and the 'baggage' it attracts is appealing, particularly to the protestant mind, there are to date no examples of Buddhism existing outside particular societies and cultures, and little prospect of anyone recognizing such an example if it occurred!

16 See for example comments by Richard Causton, head of Sōka Gakkai in the UK, who argues that 'a religion with an authoritarian hierarchy would never be tolerated by the British people . . . we cannot believe this was the intention of Nichiren Daishonin'. *Issues Between the Nichiren Shōshū Priesthood and the Sōka Gakkai* Vol. 1, (1991) Tokyo: Soka Gakkai International. p.68.

17 Reiyūkai, for example, is a successful Japanese New Religion also deriving from Nichirenism. Describing a Reiyūkai Youth Group meeting Helen Hardacre writes: 'Another participant asked what the meaning of the sutra was, and the leaders were unable to respond. The situation was the same when they were asked what its main points are, or why it is important in life. . . . Here we see the price Reiyūkai pays for having disavowed any form of doctrinal study'. Helen Hardacre, *Lay Buddhism in Contemporary Japan*, (1984) Princeton, p.72.

18 For an excellent analysis of what might be called the 'common language' of Japanese (new) religions see the chapter 'The world view of the new religions' esp pp.7-28 in Helen Hardacre *Kurozumikyo and the New Religions of Japan* Princeton, 1986.

19 Philip Mellor. 'Protestant Buddhism? The Cultural Translation of Buddhism in England'. *Religion* (1991), no.21, pp.73-92.

20 See, for example, the discussion on 'The Traditional and Contemporary in Religion' between Fujio Ikado, Noriyoshi Tamaru and Tsuyoshi Nakano in *The Journal of Oriental Studies*, (1992) Vol. 4, pp.1-22.

21 See my 'Is nothing sacred? The Protestant ethos and the spirit of Buddhism' *Journal of Oriental Studies* (1993) Vol. 5. The main drawback of Niehbuhr's typology is that it refers to the historical developments of Western European protestantism, and Japanese Buddhism does not fall so neatly into the same categories. The extreme view that Japanese religion is *sui generis* however creates another set of problems, especially when Japanese religions such as Sōka Gakkai spread beyond Japan to countries where the followers think like Western protestants. The limits of all such scholarly adventures into the realms of typology are lucidly explained by Bryan Wilson in *Magic and the Millennium* (Heinemann, 1973) esp pp.17-18. I have not, in this paper, attempted to locate Sōka Gakkai within Wilson's seven types of 'response to the world' (ibid. pp.18-27), although I can recommend the attempt as a useful exercise.

22 This and other issues involving confrontations between Sōka Gakkai and Nichiren Shōshū over the years are dealt with in my 'Reflections on Sōka Gakkai' (see note 1). Nichiren Shōshū is now claiming that Sōka Gakkai is deviating from the path of orthodoxy.

23 Robert Bellah in *Tokugawa Religion* 1985 (1957) wrote: 'Japan is characterised by a primacy of political values, the polity takes precedence over the economy. . . . The central concern is with collective goals (rather than with productivity) and loyalty is a primary virtue. Controlling and being controlled are more important than 'doing' and power is more important than wealth.' (p.5) These comments are applicable to Japan (and to Soka Gakkai in Japan) today. It is relevant, in the context of this discussion of the 'protestant' character of Sōka Gakkai, to note that Bellah's objective in *Tokugawa Religion* was to identify a functional analogue to the Weberian 'Protestant ethic'. To the extent that this analogue can be discerned, it is rooted in a Japanese/Confucian world-view in which loyalty to one's superior is a primary value, '. . . giving one's full devotion to one's particularistic superiors, and expressing this devotion in vigorous and continuous performance with respect to the collective goal, was seen as the best means to acquire the approval and protection of divine beings or to attain some form of harmony with ultimate reality.' (pp.39-40) Since Western Protestantism has developed, via European Enlightenment thought, into an infinite post-modernist unravelling of traditional values (particularly personal loyalty, which is sacrificed to universal/individual values), the complexity of the situation in which Sōka Gakkai currently finds itself, as a Japanese organization spanning a number of different Asian and Western cultures, cannot be overstated.

24 See Susumu Shimazono 'The expansion of Japan's new religions into foreign cultures' in *Japanese Journal of Religious Studies* (1991) Vol. 18, nos.2-3 pp.105-132. '. . . but the new leadership stratum made up principally of non-Japanese did not like the central-administrative, organization-mobilizing nature of the group and attempted to adopt policies that set a value on the autonomous activities of regional groups and on democratic procedures for running NSA as a whole.' This led to a secession; Shimazono notes in passing that a large-scale secession also occurred in Indonesia.

25 *Issues Between the Nichiren Shōshū Priesthood and Sōka Gakkai*, Vol. 3 (1991) Tokyo: Soka Gakkai International. p.xxxiv.

26 Shakubuku (literally 'break and subdue') refers to the methods of persuasion and attacks on other teachings employed to convert new members (modelled on Nichiren's own forceful example), especially in the early years of Sōka Gakkai's post-war growth in Japan.

27 Which is presumably why the priesthood made an issue of Ikeda singing Beethoven's 'Ode to Joy' at a Sōka Gakkai meeting. See *Issues between the Nichiren Shōshū Priesthood and Sōka Gakkai* Vol. 1. pp.129-132 for the Shikoku women's division response, which includes the following: 'Now that the priesthood tells us not to sing this song in German, we will sing this song proudly in Japanese because Shikoku is the first place in Japan where Beethoven's symphony No.9 was played'.

28 I should perhaps make it clear that I am not suggesting Sōka Gakkai *should* do this, only that it might.

29 Hardacre: *Kurozumikyo and the New Religions of Japan*, p.6.

10

Sōtō Zen Buddhism in Britain

REVEREND DAISHIN MORGAN

THIS PAPER is an account of how Sōtō Zen has become established in Britain and how it has begun to acclimatize to a different culture. I will focus on the largest Sōtō Zen organization, which centres around Throssel Hole Priory, and its related congregation. Throssel Hole Priory is a Sōtō Zen training monastery situated in Northumberland, that was established in 1972. I have been the Abbott of Throssel Hole Priory since 1982.

ORIGINS

The Zen tradition has its origins in India. It is a transmission of the Truth from Master to disciple in an unbroken lineage from Shakyamuni Buddha to the present day. The essence of this transmission is enlightenment itself. The purpose of meditation and Zen training is, 'to find within oneself the certainty of that which is unborn, undying, unchanging, uncreated. This certainty is brought about by meditation, the study of the Precepts, and doing that which leads to becoming one with the unborn, undying, unchanging, uncreated so that at the time of death, we enter into eternal meditation without fear and, during our life, we may live in certainty beyond fear.'[1]

The word Zen means meditation, it derives from the Sanskrit word *dhyāna* which in Chinese became *ch'an* and in Japanese became *zen*. Meditation is the central practice of all the Zen schools. Gradually, different schools of Zen began to emerge, the main ones were Lin-chi, Wei-yang, Yún-mén, Fa-yen and Ts'ao-tung (known in Japan as Rinzai, Igyó, Unmon, Hógen and Sōtó). The Lin-chi and Wei-yang schools later developed the *kôan*[2] system of teaching while the others continued with the emphasis on serene reflective meditation. In Japan today, there are three schools, Sōtō, Rinzai and Ōbaku. At first differences between the schools were merely the result of different approaches adopted by individual Zen Masters.

There was no great division between schools and monks passed from one to another quite freely. As time went by these differences became more pronounced as teaching methods began to be systematized.

The teaching style of Zen Masters, at least until the ninth century, was very flexible without being confined to any system. It has always been the ideal of the Sōtō School to preserve this flexibility.

It was in the thirteenth century that the Japanese monk Dōgen (1200-1253) journeyed to China to find the Truth. He eventually studied under Ju-ching (*Jap.* Tendō Nyojō) of the Ts'ao-tung lineage, and after two years intensive practice became Ju-ching's Dharma successor, having realized the liberation of body and mind. In 1227 he returned to Japan where he matured his understanding and eventually founded Eiheiji, one of the two head temples of the Sōtō school. Between the years 1231 and his death in 1253 he wrote the *Shōbōgenzō*, a work that establishes him as one of the most profound and original religious writers in Japanese history. Dōgen had a strict attitude towards monastic practice and keeping the Precepts, he had a deep religious fervour which sometimes appeared to be puritanical, but his deep spiritual insight helped to transform Japanese Buddhism.

It was three generations after Dōgen that Sōtō Zen began to make a wide impact in Japan under the guidance of Keizan Jōkin (1267-1325). However, this was at the cost of a difference of opinion within the school between those who felt that attempts to adapt Dōgen's teachings were wrong, and the more flexible approach of Keizan's Master, Tettsū Gikai. Eventually, the more flexible branch proved the stronger and the two streams were reunited with both Keizan and Dōgen recognized as joint founders. Keizan's great contribution was to make the teachings of Sōtō Zen far more accessible to ordinary people through the medium of ceremonial, particularly funeral services and the ceremonies of *jūkai* that encouraged the laity to receive and practice the Buddhist Precepts. Keizan's most important written work is the *Denkōroku* which is the story of the Transmission of Light from Shakyamuni Buddha through all the lineage of Masters down to Dōgen. Dōgen is regarded as the strict father of Sōtō Zen in Japan and Keizan as the compassionate mother.

The form of the Sōtō School in Japan today has been shaped by a history of tight government control. During the Tokugawa era (1600-1868), following a long period of social upheaval in which religion had taken a significant part, the government regulated the practice of religion in a quite draconian way. Its aim was to make religion into an arm of government through the introduction of the *danka seido* system of temple registration. Every family was required to register with a local temple, that temple then had the right and the legal duty to carry out funeral services for all the members of its registered families. Even Shinto priests had to be buried as Buddhists. The temples charged fees for their services and thus had a source of guaranteed income. Any attempt at proselytisation was forbidden as it would upset the religious *status quo*. The result was that religious initiative was stifled. Carrying out funerals became the main activity of temple priests, and more emphasis came to be placed upon funeral and memorial services than meditation.

The Meiji government that came to power in 1868 marked a resurgence of Shinto Nationalism that was unfriendly towards Buddhism. In 1871 the *danka seido* system of temple affiliation was abolished. Although this threatened the income of the main Buddhist Schools, it also stimulated a revival of religious activity. However, the government also introduced legislation that enabled monks to get married, even though this had been contrary to Buddhist monastic practice since the time of the Buddha. Today, 80% of Sōtō Zen priests in Japan are married and most of the 15,000 Sōtō temples are passed from father to son.[3]

Traditional Sōtō support was in the rural areas of Japan, and the process of industrialization and the consequent move to the cities has eroded its traditional support. It remains, however, the largest Zen school. The figure of 6.8 million members that is often quoted is somewhat misleading, as are the figures for all the traditional Buddhist schools in Japan, since they are compiled by counting the number of affiliated households and multiplying by the average family size. A 1985 survey carried out by the Sōtō School administration (Shūmuchō) found that 287,135 of the nominal figure of 6.8 million were active believers or participants in temple activities.[4]

The ideal of the monastic life is still preserved in the training temples. There are two main training temples, Eiheiji and Sōjiji, founded by Dōgen and Keizan respectively. These are the centres where young novice monks go for their basic training before taking up their responsibilities in a local temple. The training is strict; it follows the methods established by Dōgen, with much emphasis on serene reflection meditation, working meditation and training in ceremonial.

ESSENTIAL TEACHINGS

The essence of the teachings of Sōtō Zen can be found in the earliest Buddhist Scriptures. The School has grown from the basic teachings

135

of the Four Noble Truths, the Three Signs of Being, the law of karma (moral causation) and rebirth. Sōtō Zen has evolved its particular practice, teachings and emphasis, while continuing to share a common heritage with all other schools of Buddhism.

Zazen, or serene reflection meditation, is regarded as the essential practice. In order to know the Three Refuges one must study them directly. Since the foundation of our being is the Buddha Nature, we study the Buddha Refuge by being still within the heart. When we let go of our attachment to the illusion of a separate self, the Buddha nature is revealed, like the sun coming from behind a cloud. Similarly the Dharma is discovered through meditation. There are the outward teachings expressed through their intellectual formulations in Scriptures etc., but these are not enough; we must also open the Dharma eye, the ability to know the Buddha's teaching by living in oneness with the Buddha nature. Zazen is not just a means to enlightenment, it is enlightenment itself, for training and enlightenment are one. The meaning of taking refuge in the Sangha is revealed in meditation when we recognize that the Buddha Nature in ourselves and others is one and undivided. We can then take refuge in others without subservience or pride, thus the harmony of the Sangha becomes a reality.

Followers of Sōtō Zen are encouraged to practise serene reflection meditation every day. This consists of sitting still with the back straight, the eyes lowered and the hands placed in the lap so the thumbs and fingers form an oval. Thoughts and feelings are neither suppressed nor indulged, but allowed to fall away naturally. 'Neither trying to think nor trying not to think. Just sitting with no deliberate thought is the important aspect of serene reflection meditation.'[5] Serene reflection meditation is seen as the true practice of the Buddha and, as such, it is not limited to any one school of Buddhism.

Dōgen taught that the Buddha Nature is one and undivided; it embraces all of existence; nothing is outside of it, and it is simultaneously within everything. He viewed the direct Transmission of the Truth of Buddhism from Master to disciple without interruption as essential. The Truth of the Transmission of the Unborn cannot be known in the abstract, one must know it within oneself and within the Master with absolute certainty. When the Master experiences the disciple's certainty within him or herself then the Transmission takes place.

Training under the guidance of a Master is essential, for that is the best way of coming to know the true expression of Buddhism in the day-to-day reality of life. Although one can learn the outer doctrine and the initial practice outside of such a relationship, it is through the contact with a Master that one can gradually gain an intuitive sense of the depth of the teaching, and at the same time, see that the realization of that depth is humanly possible. The Master's job is to puncture the balloon of theory and bring the disciple to the practical application of the Precepts and meditation in every detail of daily life. All pride and ambition must be relinquished if enlightenment is to be genuine. It is easy to interpret the teaching to one's own liking, avoiding those aspects that cause the ego to feel insecure, and so it is the Master's function to guide the disciple towards cleansing those aspects that might otherwise be ignored.

Because of this emphasis on learning directly from a Master the monastic life is at the core of Zen training. This has never been to the exclusion of lay practice, but with only a handful of exceptions, all the great Zen Masters were male or female monks.[6] The ability to pass on the Dharma from generation to generation is sustained by the monastic framework that supports both Master and disciple. A Master should not be seen in terms of an idealized perfection. They are still human; they can still make mistakes; they have further to go in their training, but they have reached a point at which they can help others without getting themselves in the way. All sincere monks take refuge in the Sangha; they are willing to be guided by the wisdom of their colleagues. If something does go wrong then the monastic framework provides some important safeguards. From the point of view of the lay congregation the monastery provides a source of teaching, a place of retreat and a spiritual anchor.

COMING TO THE WEST

The first significant impact made by Sōtō Zen Buddhism in Britain was a three-month teaching tour of this country in 1970 by Rev. Master Jiyu-Kennett, an English woman who had spent nearly eight years as a monk in Japan as the disciple of the Chief Abbot of Daihouzan Sōjiji, one of the two head training temples of Sōtō Zen. Her efforts at spreading the Dharma were sufficiently successful to enable her to return in 1972 to launch Throssel Hole Priory as the first Sōtō Zen Buddhist monastery in Britain. She returned again in the summer of 1973 to support the newly-established community and congregation.

Buddhism had begun to be known in Britain since the latter part of the nineteenth century, when translations of Buddhist texts began to be published. But it was the publication in 1879 of Sir Edwin Arnold's *The Light of Asia* that first made an impact with the British public. This was an account of the life and teaching of Gautama the Buddha told in the form of an epic poem. Its appeal has endured and it is still in print today. In 1881 the Pali Text Society was established by T.W. Rhys Davids, and eventually a full translation of the Buddhist canon in its Pali recension was published. However, within all this activity the focus was upon the Theravada branch of the Buddhist tradition and the other main branch, that of the Mahayana, to which all the Zen schools belong, remained largely unknown.

This situation began to be remedied through the work of Dr D.T. Suzuki. In 1927 he published his first series of *Essays in Zen Buddhism* and went on to publish many more works in English that not only brought the Zen tradition to the attention of the West, but other Mahayana traditions as well. Suzuki was a Japanese scholar of Mahayana Buddhism and a follower of Rinzai Zen. He lived for many years in the USA lecturing and publishing books on Zen Buddhism and other Mahayana traditions. Until the early 1970s, his interpretation of Zen Buddhism was the only accepted version in Britain. Although others wrote about Zen, their work was largely based upon Dr Suzuki's interpretation. Of the two principle surviving Zen schools, Rinzai and Sōtō, Suzuki wrote almost entirely about Rinzai and in consequence Sōtō remained largely unknown.

In 1924, Travers Christmas Humphreys and his wife, Aileen Faulkener, founded the Buddhist Lodge as a branch of the Theosophical Society of Great Britain. Madame Helena Petrovna Blavatski (1831-1891), the founder of Theosophy, claimed that Theosophy was the heart of all religions and that the world religions were merely outward manifestations of an esoteric or secret doctrine that was reserved for the highly initiated. Theosophy, however, was a very poor bedfellow for Buddhism; Madame Blavatski's dangerous ideas about the occult history of human life were to find fertile ground in Germany where others developed her notions. By 1943 formal connections between Theosophy and Buddhism had come to an end and the Buddhist Lodge was renamed the Buddhist Society. Christmas Humphreys remained the President of the Buddhist Society until his death in 1983.

In 1936 D.T. Suzuki travelled to London to attend the World Congress of Faiths. Here he made a deep impression on Christmas Humphreys and the two of them became friends with Mr Humphreys organizing publication of many of Suzuki's works. Christmas Humphreys went on to publish many of his own books on Zen which included, *Zen Buddhism*; *Zen, A Way of Life*; *Zen Comes West* and *Zen, A Manual for Westerners*. Humphreys was a Queen's Counsel and served as First Treasury Counsel. In 1946 he travelled to Japan to sit on the International War Crimes Tribunal;

he remained for seven months, visiting D.T. Suzuki whenever he could. Back in Britain, he led a Zen class at the Buddhist Society, in which he offered what he felt to be an adaptation of Rinzai Zen suitable for Western minds.[7] I attended this class in the early 1970s and found that his approach was largely intellectual with little emphasis on the practice of meditation.

PEGGY KENNETT

The Buddhist Society was not averse to meditation, and it was while I was attending one of their regular meditation classes in 1972 that I met Rev. Jiyu-Kennett Rōshi, who had agreed to visit the Society and give a talk on Sōtō Zen Buddhism. The first thing I remember her doing was offering incense before the Buddha statue in the lecture hall, something I had not seen anyone else at the Society do before. She gave a very down-to-earth talk on Sōtō Zen that focused on the need to cleanse oneself of greed, anger and delusion; to follow the Buddhist Precepts; and to meditate, not just as the means to enlightenment, but as the expression of enlightenment itself. She had just opened Throssel Hole Priory as a Sōtō Zen monastery in Northumberland and so I was keen to visit.

The story of how Peggy Kennett became a Buddhist monk and a Zen Master or Rōshi[8] goes back to 1960. In that year, the Very Reverend Kōhō Keidō Chisan Zenji, the Chief Abbot of Sōjiji, one of the two head temples of the Sōtō Zen School, embarked on a world tour. Mindful of the need for Japan and the West to rebuild bridges after the war, he visited many countries, including America where he met President Eisenhower at the White House, and the Vatican for a meeting with Pope John II. He also visited London where Peggy Kennett met him, and during their time together he invited her to come to Japan to become a monk.

In her adult life, disillusioned with the Church of England, for whom she had worked as an organizt for many years, she had sought out Buddhism and studied under the guidance of Ven Saddhatissa, an eminent monk of the Theravada School. She attended some of the lectures given by Dr Suzuki in London and was a member of, and lecturer at, the Buddhist Society. When Kōhō Zenji's invitation came, she seized the opportunity to pursue her vocation with gratitude.

On her way to Japan she stopped off in Malaysia where she had been invited to give some lectures. Here she was ordained as a Buddhist monk by Rev. Seck Kim Seng, Abbot of Cheng Hoon Teng temple in Melaka. After three months in Malaysia, Rev. Kennett went on to Japan where she was warmly received by Kōhō

Zenji, who performed a special ceremony accepting her as his personal disciple.

Once in Japan the situation was far from straightforward. In fact, throughout the eight years she spent in Japan, she had to overcome a great deal of prejudice and opposition as a woman and a foreigner. Memories of the war still rankled and Japan is a culture not exactly feminist in outlook. However, Kōhō Zenji prevailed, and she was able to stay in the monastery and eventually receive the Transmission. Then, as the Foreign Guestmaster, she developed a regular programme for the many foreign guests, especially Americans, who were beginning to take an interest in Zen. She was also installed as Abbess of Unpuku Temple in Mie Prefecture, where she was given permission to train disciples. She was recognized by Kōhō Zenji as a Rōshi, probably the first Western woman to receive such certification.

It was Kōhō Zenji's wish that she eventually return to the West to teach. He felt that if the basic Truth could be carried to the West it would find its own cultural setting in just the same way that Chinese Cha'an had become Japanese Zen. 'Like the Buddhist at rebirth, the new Zen will neither be completely new, being the same stream of Truth, nor completely old, having new forms, ways, customs and culture.'[9] In 1967 Kōhō Zenji died and soon it became clear that the time had come for her to return to the West.

Rev. Kennett had made many American friends in her role of Foreign Guestmaster at Sōjiji and while living at Unpuku Temple. Many of these friends invited her to come to America and so, accompanied by two Western disciples, she went there on a lecture tour in 1969. In the spring of 1970 she established Shasta Abbey in Northern California, and before long there were over 20 monks in residence.

The publication in Britain in 1973 of her *Selling Water by the River*, since revised and republished as *Zen is Eternal Life*,[10] helped to swell the congregation considerably. This book is a manual of Zen training that includes important translations from the work of Dōgen and Keizan.

In 1972 Throssel Hole Priory was established when someone bought the property and offered it for use as a monastery. Not owning the property caused some difficulties. In addition, some elements of the Buddhist establishment in Britain were less than welcoming. With regret she decided to make her permanent base in the USA where she experienced no such problems.

After her visit to Britain in 1973, her health began to deteriorate and further visits to Britain were postponed. A community of four monks remained behind at Throssel Hole Priory and did their best to run retreats for the congregation and continue their monastic training. In 1976 she began to undergo another *kenshō*[11] or enlightenment experience which she has since described in her book *How to Grow a Lotus Blossom or How A Zen Buddhist Prepares for Death.*[12] This *kenshō* was of profound depth and her teaching developed very significantly as a result, a process that has continued to the present. Other monks and some congregation members began to experience *kenshō* as well, not yet on the same level that Rev. Kennett had experienced, but nevertheless sufficient to contribute to the spiritual deepening of the whole Order.

In 1976 an American trained monk, Rev. Jishō Perry, was appointed Prior. He had trained with Rev. Kennett at Shasta Abbey for five years. He guided the community and congregation spiritually while also raising the funds to buy the Priory property. He also managed to reorganize the legal structure of the Priory so that it was able to become a registered charity.

By the end of 1976, it was obvious to all concerned that the monastic community needed more thorough training than could be managed without the direct guidance of a sufficiently experienced teacher. The decision was made to move the monks to Shasta Abbey, where a group of five remained between 1977 and 1982. During this period the Priory was kept functioning by American monks who came over in turn to run it for a year or so at a time.

In September of 1982, the group of British monks returned to Throssel Hole Priory and a new period of development began. It was again possible for those with a monastic vocation to receive ordination in Britain, and a slow but steady growth in the monastic population took place. Since 1982, 23 men and women have been ordained at the Priory. In addition, a further six senior monks, trained at Shasta Abbey, have joined the community. The community has so far remained fairly stable with only three monks leaving since 1982, so the current total is 31 monks plus one postulant. Monks regularly return to Shasta Abbey for further training under the guidance of Rev. Kennett. In 1990 a small branch community was established in Reading where two of the community now live serving an active congregation in the South of England. In addition, there are 26 meditation groups meeting in Britain, the Netherlands and Germany that are affiliated to Throssel Hole Priory.

As well as the two centres in Britain and the Headquarters at Shasta Abbey in California, Rev. Kennett has established a further five centres in the USA and one in Canada. The original parent organization was called *The Zen Mission Society* and was an outgrowth of the Foreign Guest Department of Sōjiji. By 1980 the movement required a new structure to embrace the communities that were developing in different countries with a variety of legal requirements. To answer this need, the Order of Buddhist Contemplatives (OBC) was formed through which all communities and their members could be unified and regulated in one Sangha.

Currently, there are two other organizations active in Britain who have their roots in the Sōtō Zen tradition. The International Zen Association UK, founded by Deshimaru Taisen Rōshi, which first became active in Britain in 1986. This organization is most active in France and Italy but it has six meditation groups in Britain organized from a centre in Bristol. There is also the Kanzeon Sangha, founded by Maezumi Taizan Rōshi in Britain in 1982. Although these two organizations and Throssel Hole Priory follow the Sōtō Zen School, they are not affiliated with each other in any way.

PRACTICE OF SŌTŌ ZEN IN BRITAIN

What follows is a description of the practice within the Order of Buddhist Contemplatives and its related congregation. In accordance with Zen tradition, Throssel Hole Priory was established as a monastic training monastery and a retreat centre for a lay congregation. In many respects it is similar to a Japanese training monastery, but since the cultural and social climate is very different there are some variations.

A typical schedule at Throssel Hole Priory runs as follows:

6.00   Rising
6.15   Meditation
6.55   Morning service (chanting scriptures)
7.50   Temple cleaning
8.30   Breakfast
9.00   Spiritual reading
9.30   Working meditation
10.30 Community tea, questions and discussion
       Working meditation
12.30 Lunch
       Cleaning, rest and reflection
2.30   Working meditation
5.00   Service and meditation
6.00   Medicine meal
7.30   Meditation
8.45   Tea
10.00 Lights out

During *sesshin* (intensive retreats) and on certain other days there is more meditation, while during the summer months there tends to be less formal meditation and more working meditation. Allowance is made for members of the community who are older and/or suffer from ill health. While far from being indulgent, the schedule and temper of the monastery has a gentle rather than an ascetic quality. Over the last 10 years in particular, a marked softening has taken place as a result of a maturing of the practice. As community members have increased their faith in the Teaching, and in themselves and their practice, the need for external measures of sincerity, such as how many hours a day are spent in formal meditation, how ascetic are the physical conditions, how little you eat or sleep – all take second place to truly following the path that lies beyond forms, but which leads through the deepest cleansing of the heart and mind. Outer forms of practice retain their deep significance, but they are no longer relied upon as authenticators. A much freer and more relaxed atmosphere results, one that is much more deeply committed than ever before.

On the first and fifteenth of every month a 'Spiritual Examination Ceremony' (*shōsan*) takes place after morning service. On this occasion the Abbot stands in front of the altar and each monk comes up to ask a question that reflects their state of training. All novice monks must ask a question, older monks may ask if they wish. Questions must be short and to the point. They can be challenging or a cry for help, either way, the question must be direct from the heart. For the younger monks, it can be quite disquieting to have to come up with a question and ask it publicly, but it does focus the mind on what one's purpose is, and having to give that expression helps to clarify it. These ceremonies can be moving and on occasion humorous, and they reflect the level of meditation of the community.

Twice a year there is a monastic searching of the heart retreat (*sesshin*) when the monastery is closed to visitors, work projects are set aside and emphasis is placed on meditation. Most of the day and all of the evening are spent in the meditation hall. Meals are taken in the meditation hall, and there is usually a daily lecture by the Abbot. This period of intense practice helps to deepen the experience of meditation and bring up those aspects of oneself that need to be recognised and cleansed. On the last day of the retreat, sometimes at midnight, the Abbot's Dharma Ceremony (*jōdō*) takes place. Like the twice a month Spiritual Examination Ceremony, questions and answers between the Abbot and the monks lie at the heart of it, but on this occasion the Abbot stands upon the altar where the statue of the Buddha has been removed.

The whole tone of the ceremony is more intense, especially as it is taking place at the end of a week of reflection and meditation. It is an awe-inspiring ceremony, even for the more experienced monks. A full calendar of festivals is celebrated throughout the year. Festivals for the Buddha's Birth (*Wesak*), Renunciation, Enlightenment (*Jōdō*) and Death (*Parinirvāna*) are celebrated on the traditional dates as are festivals commemorating the death of major figures such as Dōgen, Keizan and others. There are festivals for Bodhisattvas, the personifications of attributes of enlightenment, such as Compassion (*Avalokitesvara*), Love (*Samantabhadra*) and Wisdom (*Mañjuśrī*). Some of the festivals include special vigil ceremonies that take place the night before. Festivals are celebrated with a special ceremony during which scriptures are chanted and sung. All the scriptures are translated into English and generally sung in plainsong.

The traditional way of chanting in Japan does not fit the language structure of English. It is very fortunate that the Rev. Kennett, before becoming a monk, was an expert in early medieval music and so it was very easy for her to set the scriptures to plainsong. We also sing gathas or hymns appropriate to the particular ceremony, borrowing the best tunes from hymn books or wherever they are to be found. This has provoked the comment that we are somehow 'Christianizing' Zen. While we are obviously using musical forms and tunes that have been used by Christian churches, the content of the hymns and Scriptures is entirely Buddhist. There is a long history of the use of music within the Mahayana tradition and what we have done is to use those musical forms that are familiar and easy on the Western ear.

Festivals are often scheduled to coincide with times when lay people will be able to come – usually on the first Sunday of each month. A Dharma talk takes place after the ceremony and this is followed by a buffet lunch. Children are encouraged to come and there is a special class for them. (I will describe in more detail below how the lay and monastic communities interrelate.)

At the Priory, Sunday afternoons and Mondays are designated as renewal time; an opportunity to rest, reflect and relax. Rising time on Mondays is 7.45 followed by a short form of Morning Service. Time is spent in cleaning and meal preparation before a mid-morning meal. Monks then shave each other's heads in a short ceremony in the meditation hall. The rest of the day is free time, with a medicine meal in the evening as usual. On Monday evening the community usually watches television, often watching something recorded earlier in the week. A recorded digest of the week's news is also played for those monks who wish to watch on Sunday afternoon. Television, if programmes are chosen carefully, is regarded as something that can be used creatively in monastic training. The community can relax together and watch a comedy, or perhaps appreciate a drama. Without being didactic, what is watched can provoke questions; it can be a reminder of why one is in the monastery, it can sometimes teach by clarifying what not to do. Television tends to reflect current norms in society and it is important for monks to keep up to date.

THE LAY CONGREGATION

The lay congregation is a vital part of the Order. Although I have emphasized the monastic core of Sótó Zen, that core exists in order to serve the lay community. There is a mutual interdependence between the two. We emphasize that there are two broad vocations in Buddhism, monastic and lay, and each have their contribution to make. Lay people, through the example of their committed practice, are an inspiration to others. If the world is to move away from values based upon fear, greed and self-interest, then it will be through the efforts of those who are prepared to work within it.

Most people are introduced to Sótó Zen by attending a weekend introductory retreat at either Throssel Hole Priory or Reading Buddhist Priory. However, the network of 26 meditation groups spread throughout Britain, the Netherlands and Germany, are increasingly important points of first contact, especially for those unable to commit themselves to a weekend retreat.

A weekend introductory retreat is held approximately once a month at Throssel Hole Priory with an average attendance of 20. The main topics that are covered include how to meditate; the meaning of the Three Refuges and the Buddhist Precepts; the importance of gratitude and compassion; the workings of the law of karma (ie cause and effect); how to establish a practice at home. The aim is to help people establish a meditation practice and to begin to feel at ease with the forms that we use.

Among the most prominent of these is the practice of bowing which has always been an integral part of Buddhism. We bow to a Buddha statue placed upon an altar in recognition of the Buddhahood that is within all things and we bow to each other for the same reason. When we meet each other we make *gassho*, the gesture of reverence made by putting the palms together. A central aspect of the teaching is that all beings are Buddhas, whether they are currently exhibiting the attributes of a Buddha or not.

Committed lay people meditate once or twice a day at home, some also recite all or part of the scriptures used at Morning Service.

It is left up to the individual to organize how they do this. Home altars are encouraged, but here again, it is up to the individual. It frequently occurs that one member of a family, or one partner of a couple, is a practising Buddhist while the other is not. We encourage people not to thrust their belief and practice onto others, nor to feel they must take a hard line. Buddhist training should help one to live peacefully with others, rather than be a cause of conflict. There is a tradition that one must be asked three times before giving the teaching. This means that one only speaks of the Dharma when asked. There should be no attempt to convert those who are content with their beliefs.

FINANCES

The Priory is a registered charity. It is financed by donations made by the congregation. Retreat guests are encouraged to make a donation, but no check is kept to see who makes an offering and who does not; it is entirely voluntary. The trust placed in those who come is amply repaid by their generosity. When the Priory first started, fees were charged for accommodation etc. Allowances were made for the unemployed or otherwise impoverished and we tried to have reduced fees for longer stays. In the end the fee structure became so complex, we decided to simply abolish it altogether and return to the traditional basis of depending on donations. Needless to say, we monitored this change very carefully, but found our income actually increased. Many regular congregation members make covenants and we have regular fund-raising drives to raise money for building work, purchase of new property and other capital investments.

The monastery runs a small Buddhist supplies shop that brings in about £9,000 per annum net. The monastery costs over £1,000 a week to run, excluding capital investments in building or land purchases. It is very much a hand-to-mouth existence with very little in the way of cash reserves. Although we do not go on an alm's round in the traditional way, we believe we have found the nearest equivalent and try to live by the same ideals.

So far, all building work has been done by the community. This includes the construction of three substantial two-storey buildings, one of which is still in the finishing stages. Building work progresses slowly, as it has to be fitted into the monastic schedule and is dependent on the rate at which donations come in.

Monks who join the community retain ownership of their assets. If monks have any capital of their own, or if they inherit any, they are expected to regard it as personal property which they must use responsibly – part of their karmic inheritance. Those who have such resources, which is a small minority, usually make some kind of offering towards their upkeep. They can make a gift if they so wish after having been a monk for a number of years. In the last year, the community has accepted the offer of two interest-free loans from members of the community to help purchase a neighbouring property. Most monks have no income at all and are supported by the congregation.

THE ADMINISTRATIVE STRUCTURE

The Priory, as a registered charity, is administered by a board of three trustees, one of whom is myself. The day-to-day running of the Priory is my responsibility as the Abbot or Prior, together with the other resident senior monks. The traditional practice is for the Abbot to have the central role in spiritual teaching and in the conduct of temporal affairs; this is to ensure that temporal affairs are conducted as an expression of the teaching and that the temporal involvements of the Priory are not allowed to interfere excessively with the teaching. However, there is an important safeguard that requires the Abbot to 'take refuge' in the community. In practice, this means that I discuss all important decisions with the other senior monks. Regular meetings take place at which matters of concern can be raised. No vote is taken at these meetings as decisions are arrived at through consensus. If differing views cannot be reconciled at the meeting, the matter is postponed for further reflection and discussion. When necessary the Abbot has the power to draw the discussion to a close and take whatever decision he feels is appropriate within the scope of the Precepts.

The Abbot is regarded as the Buddha of the monastery and therefore has the final say. So far, we have always managed to reach agreement on important issues and this prerogative has remained unused. This is because it is understood by the monks that the harmony of the community is more important than individual opinions. If a monk feels that a decision is an infringement of the Precepts, he or she is not required to go along with it. In such an event the matter would be referred to the Head of the Order and the trustees.

The OBC has a clearly defined structure. It is incorporated as a non-profit corporation in California. The Priory community, as part of the OBC, are bound by its bye-laws and rules. These are reviewed once every ten years at a conclave attended by all senior monks. The purpose is to keep under review the rules that have been made and consider if new rules are required. Between conclaves, any new rules that become necessary can be made by the Head of the Order in consultation with senior monks. Rules are only created when circumstances have demonstrated a need, therefore there are many elements of Buddhist monastic practice that are not specifically mentioned in the OBC rules, even though those practices are followed within the Order.

Serious breaches of the rules require the convening of a special council at which the monk concerned is both present and fully represented. In Britain, any such council must arrive at a unanimous decision, and even then, the decision of the council can be appealed to the Head of the Order. Fortunately, such a council has not yet had to be convened in Britain, but the structures exist should it be needed. The most severe sanction that can be imposed is suspension or expulsion from the Order. The conduct of a disciplinary council must be in accordance with the principles of compassion, wisdom and the keeping of the Precepts; the good of the individual and of the Order are the primary considerations. All monks and lay ministers are issued with annual licences that prove that they are members in good standing. Much care is taken to regulate the Order so that congregation members and others do not have their faith damaged. The rules cover such matters as confidentiality, celibacy, good financial practice and much more. If the lay supporters of a Priory or group feel that the monks are not behaving as they should, then there are clear procedures for them to follow to get the matter resolved.

Throssel Hole Priory maintains friendly relations with other Buddhist traditions represented in Britain. Members occasionally join in celebrations and festivals organized by other groups, for example, the recent visit of the Dalai Lama to Britain. Monks and lay members participate in *Angulimala*, the Buddhist Prison Chaplaincy Service. This year, I have been involved, along with Buddhists from other organizations, with a consultation process organized by the National Curriculum Council concerning teaching RE in schools. As a result, the Priory is organizing a series of seminars for primary and secondary school teachers who wish to include Buddhism in their syllabus.

CONCLUSION

Sōtō Zen has now been established in Britain for over 20 years. This period has seen a deepening of practice and understanding both within the monastic community and the lay congregation, and this process is continuing. Within the monastic community the full Buddhist monastic office, which includes a series of monastic ceremonies not previously performed at the Priory, will soon be introduced. It naturally takes time for the full extent of Buddhist monastic practice to become established in a new country. In monastic terms, 20 years is a short time, but as the deeper aspects of monastic practice are introduced and appreciated, there is a corresponding increased understanding of what it means to live the monastic life. This is a lifetime's work.

Within the lay congregation, new meditation groups are being formed and it is hoped that a new Priory will shortly be established in the Midlands. The congregation is developing a greater sense of its own identity and of the validity of religious training outside of the monastic setting. Growth has been steady and sustained and there is still much work to be done. Western culture is becoming increasingly receptive to Buddhism and so there is a growing opportunity to make a contribution to the religious life of Britain.

FOOTNOTES

1. Rev. Jiyu-Kennett, unpublished source.
2. This system, which is the principle practice of the Rinzai School, involves meditating on one of the enlightenment stories or kōans of the old masters. It was developed into a system of set kōans that trainees are expected to meditate on and 'pass' in order. Dōgen was very critical of this system, regarding it as artificial.
3. Sōtōshū-shūmuchó (ed) *Sōtōshú shúsei sōgóchósa hókokusho*; Tokyo 1987 pp24-26. Quoted in Reader: *Images of Sōtō Zen: Buddhism as a Religion of the Family in Contemporary Japan*. Scottish Journal of Religious Studies, Spring 1989 p19.
4. Sōtóshú-shúmuchó (ed) *Sōtōshú shúsei sōgó hókokusho* pii. Quoted in Reader: *Images of Sōtó Zen: Buddhism as a Religion of the Family in Contemporary Japan*. Scottish Journal of Religious Studies, Spring 1989 p9.
5. Dōgen Zenji, *Fukanzazengi*. Trans: Rev. Rōshi Jiyu-Kennett, *The Liturgy of The Order of Buddhist Contemplatives For the Laity*, Shasta Abbey Press, 2nd Edition 1990, p97.
6. The term 'monk' is used for both men and women within the Order of Buddhist Contemplatives.
7. Christmas Humphreys, *A Western Approach to Zen*, Unwin 1971 p191. I attended Mr Humphrey's Zen Class for about a year or so in the early 1970s.
8. The title 'Rōshi' is translated into 'Reverend Master' within the Order of Buddhist Contemplatives.
9. Kōhō Keidō Chisan Zenji, Foreword to *Zen Is Eternal Life* Rōshi Jiyu-Kennett 2nd Edition, Dharma Publishing 1976 p xiv.
10. See note 9.
11. To see into one's own nature; the enlightenment experience. Rev. Kennett first experienced this during the early years of her training in Japan. An account of it appears in *The Wild White Goose* vol I. Shasta Abbey Press 1977 pp64-9.
12. Rōshi Jiyu-Kennett, *How to Grow a Lotus Blossom: Or How A Zen Buddhist Prepares For Death*. Shasta Abbey Press 1977.

11
Japanese 'Old', 'New' and 'New, New' Religious Movements in Brazil

PETER B. CLARKE

SINCE THE EARLY YEARS of the twentieth century numerous Japanese Shinto/Buddhist and Japanese Buddhist movements have been started in Brazil and the following offers some insights into the nature of the appeal and the impact of two of these movements: Seichô-no-Ie or House of Growth and Sekai Kyûsei Kyô (SKK) or World Salvation Teachings and/or the Church of World Messianity.

To date I have carried out a limited amount of research on the first of these movements and on Sôka Gakkai (Value Creation Society) in Salvador capital city of the northeastern state of Bahia and in the town of Suzano in the state of São Paulo in southern Brazil. The observations made here are based largely on my research on Seichô-no-Ie among its Brazilian adepts of European descent. I compare my findings with Derrett's study of SKK in Brazil.[1]

It is my intention to expand this present research to include two nineteenth-century movements – Tenrikyô (Heavenly Wisdom) and Ômotokyo (The Great Origin) founded in 1838 and 1899 respectively, Risshô-kôseikai (The Establishment of Righteousness and Friendly Intercourse) and Sekai Mahikari Bumei Kyôdan (World True Light Civilization). These are either 'new' or 'new, new' Japanese religions. This research will also be widened to cover the impact and appeal of these 'new' and 'new, new' movements to Brazilians of Japanese descent, a subject about which virtually nothing is known. Furthermore, some of the more historic Japanese Buddhist traditions will also be studied in this broader project and in particular the Amida or Pure Land and the True Words or Shingon traditions.

The preliminary part of my research concludes that the appeal of Seichô-no-Ie lies chiefly in the fact that it empowers individuals to take control of their own destiny. And one of its indirect and latent consequences is a certain 'secularisation' of the Brazilian mind. Ōmotokyo, Risshō-kōseikai, Seichō-no-Ie, Sōka Gakkai and Sekai Kyūsei Kyō belong to the category of the 'new' Japanese Religions rather than the 'new, new' Japanese religions. Tenrikyo was founded by Miki Nakayama, the daughter of a farmer, who received her first revelations in 1837. She taught that the Heavenly Kingdom was drawing near, bringing to an end a world of sickness and poverty. Her appeal was in the main to the farming communities that had lost their property and status during the period of the Meiji land reforms in the second half of the nineteenth century.

Tenrikyō has around one hundred and fifty thousand teachers and an estimated membership of two-and-a-half million who worship God the Parent, the creator and sustainer of all life. Miki Nakayama is both the shrine of God, the Parent, and the mediatrix between this god and humanity.

This movement, whose creation account places Japan at the centre of the universe and depicts the Japanese as the original and supreme race, is prototypical of many of the 'new' Japanese religions combining as it does elements of Shintoism and Buddhism while emphasizing the laws of karma and reincarnation. Tenrikyo, like Ōmotokyo, has had a seminal influence on a number of the other movements in this study including Seichō-no-Ie.

Ōmotokyo was established in 1899 by Nao Deguchi (1836-1918) and has served as a source of inspiration for, among other Japanese movements, SKK which was founded in 1934 by Mokichi Okada. Ōmotokyo's main object of worship is the Supreme God of the Great Origin and its two most important centres of worship are in Kyoto prefecture. Relatively speaking, the size of its membership is small, totalling around one hundred-and-fifty thousand adherents. SKK which, as just noted, has derived much by way of belief and practice from Ōmotokyo has a membership of around three-quarters of a million in Japan. This movement whose main temples are at Atami, Hakone and Kyoto addresses its worship to the True God of the Marvellous Light and like so many Japanese new religions lays great stress on healing. Its principal healing rite is *johrei*. Seichō-no-Ie likewise owes much to Ōmotokyo. It was begun in 1930 as a separate movement by Masaharu Taniguchi (b.1893) a former member of Ōmotokyo from where he derived some of his teachings and practices.

Another important source was the New Thought Movement. Taniguchi read among other things *The Law of Mind in Action* by Fenwicke Holmes, founder of Religious Science, a New Thought, Positive Thinking movement. Both inside and outside of new and old religions there is a growing tendency to believe that one's life and one's world are predicated on one's thought. Idealism is a very old philosophy, much older than New Thought which is essentially a popular manifestation of this philosophical tradition that took shape in the United States in the late nineteenth century. The essence of idealism is that the highest reality and the foundation of existence itself is mental: mind, consciousness, ideas, thoughts, constitute both the basis of reality and the causes of all that happens. There are clear links at the level of ideas between New Thought and the New Age Movement which came into its own as a 'new' movement in the early 1970s.

Seichō-no-Ie's principal object of worship is, as its name implies, the Great God of the House of Growth and its main temples are in Nagasaki prefecture and at Uji in Kyoto prefecture. The movement has an estimated 900,000 'members' in Japan, size of membership being calculated on the basis of the number who purchase its magazine *Truth of Life*. Believing sickness to be in essence an illusion or 'deceit of the mind' Seichō-no-Ie advocates that it can be overcome by the healing power of the Word.

Sekai Mahikari Bumei Kyōdan, (World True Light Civilization) was founded in 1959 by Okada Kotama (1901-1974). As already noted this is a 'new, new' religion, and is chiefly known for its practice of *okiyome* or purification which is believed to effect the eradication of misfortune and disease caused by the angry spirits of the ancestors and the rest of the dead. Pacification of ancestors occupies a prominent place in many of the Japanese 'new' and 'new, new' religions. Mahikari is also an interesting example of the primacy of action characteristic of both kinds of Japanese new religions. As Reader points out, there is no obligation to believe first and then practise. On the contrary; individuals are encouraged to experiment and prove for themselves that *okiyome* works before committing themselves to believing in the teachings and doctrines underlying the practice.[2] There is a splinter group from Mahikari, Sukyo Mahikari, Religion of True Light.

The Japanese religions just mentioned above, though eclectic, tend on the whole to be shaped as much by Shinto as by Buddhism. Risshō-kōseikai and Sōka Gakkai on the other hand clearly belong to the Nichiren Buddhist tradition, a tradition of Buddhism pioneered and fashioned in Japan. The Nichiren tradition is based on the teachings of the Japanese Buddhist monk of the Tendai sect, Nichiren Daishonin (1222-82) who regarded the Lotus Sutra of the Good Law as the final and supreme embodiment of Buddhist truth. The formula of worship known as the *Daimoku* or sacred name invocation consists in chanting '*Nam-myoho-renge-kyo*' (I take refuge in the glorious Lotus Sutra). Said to have been inscribed by Nichiren on the *Gohonzon* or sacred scroll, this mantra is believed to be the law of life and the principal means of attaining enlightenment. Sōka Gakkai, like so many other Japanese 'new' and 'new, new' religions is strongly millennarian and claims that Nichiren is the bodhisattva of the Last Days.

Nichiren Buddhism is defined as the Buddhism of the *True Cause* and is said to transcend the Buddhism of Guatama Buddha, the Buddhism of *True Effect*. Among the important elements of the Lotus Sutra stressed by Nichiren were the religious equality of all whatever their socio-economic background, the possibility for all to achieve Buddhahood and the duty to proselytise. There are several Nichiren traditions. Risshō-kōseikai formed in 1938 after splitting off from Reiyūkai belongs to the Nichiren Shu (sect) tradition. This movement claims the right to determine the theory of orthodoxy for the Nichiren tradition and has as its main object of worship the Universal Buddha, the Great Mandala and the Lotus scripture. Key elements in Risshō-kōseikai's system of belief and practice are ancestor worship and the concept of bodhisattva, the enlightened one, who delays entry into Nirvana in order to help suffering humanity. It also practises the *hoza* system – a form of group counselling which on the one hand is directed at fostering the bodhisattva spirit and on the other provides adherents with the opportunity to discuss in open forum their personal difficulties and anxieties. The holy centre of the movement is the Great Hall at its Tokyo headquarters.

Sōka Gakkai, started in 1930 by Tsuneburo Makiguchi, belongs to the Nichiren Shōshū (Orthodox Nichiren sect) tradition and is the largest of the 'new' Japanese religions with an estimated membership in Japan of around 10 million families. It is a lay organization with links, at present tenuous and strained (see chapter 9), with the priests of Nichiren Shōshū who claim to be the guardians of the original *Gohonzon* and provide the movement with its spiritual legitimacy. It holds that all people possess the Buddha nature and can attain enlightenment in this world by believing in the *Dai-Gohonzon*, the previously mentioned object of worship inscribed by Nichiren in 1279 and found in the temple at Taiseki-ji. The movement also teaches the practice 'for self and others' which aims at the attainment of personal enlightenment and the salvation of others and society through *kosen-rufu* or the widespread propagation of the Mystic Law that is the already referred to law of *nam-myoho-renge-kyo*. Sōka Gakkai emphasizes that because the self and the objective world are essentially one the individual in attaining Buddhahood simultaneously transforms the environment into Buddha Land.

This movement also teaches that chanting or *gongyo* can alter *karma* or the law of cause and effect and bring in its train benefits of a psychological, emotional and material kind. Moreover, it likewise makes use of a system of discussion/counselling groups, *zadakandai*, and its main objects of worship are, as already noted above, the Lotus Sutra and the mandala in the Taiseki temple in Shizuoka prefecture.

THE BRAZILIAN CONTEXT

It is estimated that there are between eight hundred thousand and one million Japanese and/or Brazilians of Japanese descent in Brazil and this presence is largely the result of immigration dating back to the early years of the twentieth century. It is commonly believed that the first group of 781 immigrants set sail for Brazil on the steamer *Kasato Maru* from Kobe in Japan on 28 April 1908 and arrived three weeks later on 18 June at the port of Santos in the state of São Paulo. Some of the first settlers are now in their nineties. Most were employed on the coffee plantations where they often came under the influence of the Catholic clergy. For many of the pre-World War II settlers in Brazil, Japanese remains their only language. Many second- and third-generation Brazilians of Japanese descent are bilingual, speaking both Japanese and Portuguese; they know virtually nothing about the religious beliefs and practices of their parents and grandparents. They were thoroughly 'Catholicized' and until relatively recently that meant the rejection of all that was 'non-Catholic'.

Often one finds that the younger generation of Brazilians of Japanese descent have never visited the temple frequented by their parents and the *butsudan* or household altar is usually in the parents' bedroom and it is only the parents who pray and place offerings there. On the other hand, Japanese influence pervades the entire household from furnishings to wall hangings to diet. Not all of the older generations of Japanese settlers have remained exclusively Buddhist. Some have joined Christian denominations and in particular the Pentecostal churches such as the Assemblies of God. In one of the larger Japanese-Brazilian Assemblies of God churches in São Paulo the congregation is in the main middle-aged or older. There is also a movement of Japanese towards Umbanda and once again the older generations of Brazilian Japanese are as involved in this new religious venture as are the younger ones. There is on the whole little interaction with official Catholicism apart from the occasional request to a priest to offer prayers in the case of serious sickness and misfortune. Where these matters are concerned there are no boundaries of a religious or spiritual kind dividing Japanese Brazilians from others.

Japanese temples in turn attract many from Umbanda and Catholicism. These temples are known locally as 'igrejas' or churches. Much of the terminology used in speaking about Japanese religion in Brazil is Catholic and/or Christian. Naming rites are referred to as baptism and the main temple ceremony is called the mass while the one who presides over the rituals is the padre or priest. The temples are sought out principally for the healing that they offer. There are numerous shrines to Jizó the bald-headed Buddhist figure who guards travellers, children and the souls of the dead. These 'santos' or saints as they are known do not always perform exactly the same role as in Japan or conform precisely to the image people have of them there. In Brazil both have been somewhat modified by the differing demands and requirements of life there. Similarly, the same process of domestication is marked in Afro-Brazilian religion, also known as Candomble or Umbanda, where the image and understanding of the role and function of certain gods of African origin have been changed almost beyond recognition.

Assimilation in terms of religious language and 'saintly' roles and functions notwithstanding, the Japanese Buddhist traditions in Brazil have retained much of their Japanese heritage in terms of beliefs, rituals, outlook, and architectural style among other things. There is often more than one Japanese Buddhist tradition in the same locality and where this situation exists there is generally very little direct contact of a religious or social kind between them. The tendency is for practitioners to frequent one temple only, an exclusivism which would not be strongly in evidence in Japan and which in the Brazilian context is, somewhat paradoxically, the product in part of differences of a religious, historical and political kind which have their origins in Japan.

SUZANO CITY

The city of Suzano, already mentioned as one of the foci of this study, is situated to the southwest of São Paulo, and is home to numerous Japanese 'new' and 'new, new' religions and to several 'old' Japanese Buddhist traditions. Among the 'new' religions are Sóka Gakkai which has a membership of around one thousand families, Risshó-kóseikai, Ōmotokyo, Tenrikyó, Seichó-no-Ie, Buts-Ryu-Shu (Followers of Buddha), all of which have far fewer members. The most active and the largest of the 'new, new' movements in Suzano is Mahikari.

Suzano has two main Japanese temples for a population of about one hundred and sixty thousand, fifty per cent of which is of Japanese descent. One, the Honpa Honganji temple, is of the Amida or Pure Land Buddhist tradition, and is affiliated to the Mother temple in Kyoto, the Jōdō Shinshū Honganji-ha – often referred to as Nishi (western)-Honganji. There is also the Shinshū Ōtaniha or Higashi (eastern) Honganjiha tradition of Pure Land Buddhism, which is not as strong in Suzano as the Nishi Honganji.

The tradition of Pure Land Buddhism has a Chinese prototype and owes its origins in Japan to Hōnen (1133-1212) who divided Buddhism into two types: one in which people attempted to gain enlightenment through disciplined self-effort and one in which people seek to be born in the Pure Land, the spiritual state of oneness with ultimate reality, through reliance on the mercy of Amida Buddha. Hōnen himself followed the second type giving as his reasons his belief that the saving power of Amida Buddha was so absolute and his conviction that people were so deeply enmeshed in sin as to be incapable of achieving enlightenment through their own efforts. Hōnen was convinced that in this final period of history (mappō) in which Buddhisn had degenerated into little more than an empty shell, the only way to salvation was through reliance on the merciful compassion of Amida Buddha. All forms of ritual and meditation were left to one side in favour of the *nembutsu* practice that is the chanting of the invocation *Namu-amida-butsu*, meaning devotion to the Amida Buddha.

One of Hōnen's best known disciples is Shinran (1173-1262) founder of the True Sect of the Pure Land and/or Jōdo Shinshū, basing himself on the Larger Sutra of Immeasurable Life and went further than his master in rejecting the possibility that individuals could save themselves by their own efforts. Instead, he insisted that the compassion and saving power of Amida were absolute. More precisely, Shinran's doctrine of predestination asserted that the compassion and saving power of Amida had already in fact been effective in that all had already in principle been saved by these means although many perhaps were unaware of this.

Shinran also brought Buddhism closer to ordinary life by teaching that although secular, worldly values and aspirations do not constitute an authentic basis for living, nevertheless people should not break off their ties with the world. He rejected the idea of a religious elite and attempted to abolish the distinction between religious virtuosi and lay people claiming that it was not necessary to lead a monastic, celibate life in order to be a devout Buddhist and live up to its highest ideals. Rather it was perfectly possible to live in the world, marry and bring up a family and achieve the same goals as a monk. His teachings had wide appeal and his movement is one of the largest Buddhist movements in present-day Japan.

The other main Japanese temple in Suzano, the Igreja Buddhista Nambei Yugazam Jyomiyoji, possibly the largest Japanese Buddhist temple in Brazil, belongs to Shingon (True Words) Buddhism, the oldest tantric Buddhist sect in Japan founded in 815 by Kukai or posthumously Kobo Daishi (774-835) who brought the teachings from China. More precisely, the temple is a branch of the Shingon movement known as Shingon Shugendo, reportedly founded by En-no-ozunu (posthumously honoured as Jinpen Daibotsatsu), the seventh-century shamanistic mountain ascetic. The sect features the climbing of sacred mountains, mountain worship and magic rituals and the temple in Suzano is appropriately situated in elevated woodlands outside the town.

A great deal of the activity in the Suzano temples revolves round the statue of the previously mentioned Buddhist figure Jizó who according to one of its four monks is '*mais para as mulheres, para as pessoas que querem bebe* (more for women, for people who want children)'.

The Shingon movement bases its teachings on the *Dainichi* and *kongocho* sutras and one of its main practices for the attainment of Buddhahood is the chanting of the secret words of the Mahávairochana Buddha. It claims that its esoteric teachings were transmitted from Mahávairochana Buddha to Vajrasattva and on down through Nágárjuna, Nágabodhi, to Vajrabodhi and Amo-ghavajra, who brought the teachings from India to China in the eighth century. It was in Ch'ang-an in China that the Japanese priest Kóbó Daishi studied these teachings from 804-06 under the master Hui-Kuo before returning to Japan and founding a temple on Mount Koya in 816 and another at To-ji in 823. The sect divided on Kóbó Daishi's death into the Ono and the Hirosawa schools and today there are numerous branches of Shingon. Both the Pure Land (Jódo Shinshú) and the True Word (Shingon) traditions of Buddhism were brought to Brazil in the first instance by immigrants from Japan.

THE APPEAL AND IMPACT OF SEICHÓ-NO-IE

Not surprisingly, Japanese 'new' and 'new, new' religions – among them Seichó-no-Ie, Sóka Gakkai, Sekai Kyúsei Kyó and Mahikari – are strongest in the south of Brazil for it is there that the vast majority of Japanese-Brazilians are to be found, and especially in São Paulo and Rio. However, these movements are moving north to towns such as Salvador da Bahia De Todos Os Santos and Recife, the capital cities of the states of Bahia and Pernambuco respectively, as Japanese-Brazilians move north on account of work or business. They have even penetrated the interior of these states and are established in towns such as Feira de Santanna in Bahia. As previously pointed out, the main focus here is on the appeal of these movements and of Seichō-no-Ie in particular to Brazilians of European descent. As already mentioned some comparisons will be made with Derrett's study of SKK.

Derrett studied the progress of Sekai Kyūsei Kyō (SKK) in Brazil and Thailand and here we will confine our comments to Brazil.[3] The majority of SKK's growing membership in Brazil – its following is estimated at about one hundred and twenty thousand[4] – is urban, middle-class, middle-aged, female and of European descent. Although the number of male and younger members – under 35s – is said to be increasing. The social composition of SKK also seems to differ from that of Sōka Gakkai where there appears to be a much higher number of young male members. One reason for this may be that Sōka Gakkai places less direct emphasis on healing and more on active engagement in the world.

SKK is millennarian and its ultimate goal is the creation of an earthly paradise. In the case of certain other new Japanese movements this will be effected by the deity alone while SKK preaches that it will come about through a partnership between the deity and human beings. The teachings of SKK's founder, Okada, are believed to be perfectly in keeping with this goal. These are seen as the final, ultimate guidance on this matter, incorporating and at the same time transcending the teachings of Christianity, Hinduism, Buddhism and other religious traditions. However, certain of its concepts are distinctly Japanese in terms of their form and expression and require considerable reinterpretation if they are to be understood in another cultural context.

Sōka Gakkai whose beliefs and practices are even more firmly grounded on one single Japanese tradition of Buddhism may experience even greater difficulties in communicating its ideas to Brazilians of non-Japanese descent than SKK. Moreover, the absence of a notion of a deity or supreme being constitutes an obstacle in a culture such as that of Brazil where, while religious practice may be low, belief in God is almost universal. Seichō-no-Ie with its more loosely constructed and eclectic belief system which, as already indicated, contains a large element of New Thought and therefore indirectly of New Age, appears to be less tied to its Japanese heritage than either SKK or Sōka Gakkai.

SKK is not exclusivist and while it will not guarantee entry to the earthly paradise to its members, it does maintain that it offers the best way of attaining this goal. A reformist sect of the kind described by Wilson),[5] SKK looks to a gradual process of change that will result in the advent of a perfect world. The process will take the form of a change in the individual effected by divine power and proof of this is the healing that comes about through *johrei* or ritual purification.

Although the emphasis is on human participation in the creation of the earthly paradise according to Derrett, SKK members are inclined to be passive, to expect things to happen to them. All they need be is responsive. She provides a description of the typical Brazilian understanding of the origins of experience and the 'causes' of suffering and relief. Brazilians believe, Derrett informs us, that the source of all experience is external to the individual. They do not, therefore, initiate action to change the course of their lives but adopt 'a responsive role'; in other words they 'open themselves up to the influence of either good or evil forces'.[6]

Derrett explains that it was chiefly although not exclusively through *johrei* – miraculous healing consequent on spiritual purification – that Brazilian SKK members became convinced of the movement's claims.

Seichō-no-Ie is one of the largest Japanese new religions in Brazil and maintains over two hundred shrines and around one thousand places of worship. Its membership is close to one million, a large percentage of whom are Brazilians of European descent. This makes it a much larger concern than Tenrikyō, for example, which has no more than fifty shrines, one hundred and fifty mission stations and an estimated Brazilian membership of only ten thousand.

The appeal of Seichō-no-Ie when it began in Japan was primarily about healing. However, its appeal in Brazil is somewhat different. In Suzano where, as we have seen, the membership consists mainly of Brazilians of Japanese descent healing in terms of offering a remedy for psychosomatic and physical illnesses is important to its appeal. However, the questions of self-identity and a readily accessible, reliable and 'incorrupt' enabling power that can change the individual and society as a whole are equally important.

Seichō-no-Ie's belief in the imminent advent of a world of peace and justice and that every living creature possesses the soul of the 'divine' are among its most appealing ideas. Moreover, in Seichō-no-Ie there is a concern with purification of the body, soul or mind or all three before healing and progress towards wholeness can begin and the purpose of *shinkosan* or meditation to visualize God are: to purify and regulate the rhythm of the mind in order to be able to communicate with the spirits of the various realms of the spirit world and receive their guidance and also to enable individuals to recognize and experience their own nature as divine so that they may live in a state of absolute freedom.[7] Like the 'Self-Religions'[8] Seichō-no-Ie is a modern form of Pelagianism. Although it stresses the need for purification its overriding emphasis is on the unflawed nature of the real self. Its founder writes:

'When we say "I am good" we refer to our true image, the self that is one with heaven and earth, the self which is a child of God. When we say "I am bad" we point to the "false self", the phenomenal self.' (Ibid).

A majority of the Brazilian Seichō-no-Ie members interviewed for this research described it as a philosophy rather than a religion while the SKK and Sōka Gakkai movements seem to be regarded by their members as their religion. This may have much to do with the origins of my informants: while the SKK and Sōka Gakkai members interviewed were either Japanese or of Japanese descent most of the Seichō-no-Ie adepts were of Spanish and Italian origin and gave their religion as Catholicism. It has to be borne in mind that in Brazil it is not uncommon for a Catholic who may not even be practising, to be an active participant in another religion, quasi-religion or secular alternative to religion but who nevertheless continues to profess to be a loyal Catholic.This, for example, is the position adopted by most members of Candomble.

Seichō-no-Ie informants found no reason to abandon their Catholicism and this was one of the attractions of the movement. Another was the absence of long, time-consuming ceremonies and rituals. Early evening meetings in the homes of members for readings of the writings of the founder Taniguchi or for *shinsokan* were practical, posed few problems for family life and provided a setting for mutual support and community in a highly urbanized and increasingly impersonal world. What also drew members to the movement was the feeling and sense of stability that it gave them in what they regarded as a world that was not only changing at an unprecedented rate but also in a seemingly arbitrary and directionless manner. I was presented at one meeting with an extract of a frequently used meditation text which read:

'Reality is eternal, Reality does not perish,
Reality does not grow old, Reality does not die,
The fact of knowing this truth is to know the way.'
(Taniguchi, 1985)

For its members, Seichō-no-Ie ideas seem to have considerable explanatory power where the changing world of Brazil is concerned. Moreover, they are seen to empower individuals to take control over their own destiny in a world where all forms of authority and power appear to have failed. This enabling notion of the self as divine and in control of one's own destiny and all that affects it would seem to be one of the movement's chief attractions.

These ideas do, however, tend to relativize and marginalize faith in and reliance on the supernatural order and in this respect Seichō-no-Ie can be said to facilitate a move away from a faith in divine intervention from above, in an external source of supernatural power upon which humans depend for salvation and from faith in the miraculous, to belief in the enabling, energising, dynamic power of the god within. It also suggests that Seichō-no-Ie in facilitating the change from belief in divine intervention in human affairs towards a faith in the idea of 'self' as god or divine and totally responsible for all that happens acts as a 'secularising' agency and is similar in this respect to other 'Self-Religions'.[9]

BIBLIOGRAPHY

1. 3. 4. 6. Derrett, E. 'Signs along a better way: The Methods of Evangelization of a Japanese New Religion in Brazil and Thailand', in Peter Clarke (ed) *The New Evangelists. Recruitment, Methods and Aims of New Religious Movements*. London. Ethnographica. 1987. pp. 95–112.
2. Reader, I. *Religion in Contemporary Japan*. London. Macmillan. 1991.
5. Wilson, B. *Religious Sects*, London/New York. Weidenfeld and Nicolson and McGraw-Hill, 1971.
7. Taniguchi, M. Sutra Sagrada. *Chuva De Nectar da Verdade*, (Kanro No Hoou) S. Paulo. Seichō-no-Ie do Brasil. 1985.
8. 9. Heelas, P. 'Western Europe: the Self Religions' in S.R. Sutherland and P.B. Clarke (eds) *The Study of Religion, Traditional and New Religion*. London. Routledge. 1991. pp. 167–73.

Glossary

(Page numbers refer to first-time use of the term.)

Ágama sutras (p.6): in the Chinese Tripitika there are four of these which roughly correspont to the Pali Nikayas.

Bodhisattva (p.93): in Mahayana someone who has achieved enlightenment but renounces Nirvana in order to lead all humanity to the same goal.

Bodhisattva Maitreya (p.93): the bodhisattva who will come at the end of time.

Butsudan (p.59): a household Buddhist altar.

Chuon (p.68): a symbol rather like a comma which represents creator God, Su.

Daimoku (p.61): the invocation of Namu-myóhó-renge-kyó.

Daoren (p.107): Chinese for a man of learning.

Dharma (Chapter 11): the law or ultimate truth, the Buddha's teaching.

Dóshi (p.68): trained leaders.

Dójóchó (p.68): head of training centre.

Dójó (p.68): training centre.

Fudó Myóó (p.26): the immovable one. A Buddha guardian.

Gohonzon (p.11): object of worship.

Gongyó (p.61): 'assiduous' practice or chanting recitation before an object of worship.

Goshintai (p.68): an object of worship.

Heshang (p.107): Buddhist monk.

Ikigami (p.56): living god.

Jóbutsu (p.6): Buddhahood.

Johrei (p.63): a purification ritual used in Sekai kyúsei kyó and believed to bring sbout physical and spiritual healing.

Kakusha (p.82): an enlightened person.

Kami (p.29): the deities of the Shinto tradition.

Kamidana (p.55): a shelf for the household Shinto gods.

Karma (p.19): the law of cause and effect.

Kenshó (p.140): enlightenment experience in Zen.

Kóan (p.132): Zen riddle.

Kojiki (p.26): one of the oldest Japanese books and one of the two basic books of Shinto.

Kotodama (p.97): the language of the gods.

Mappó (p.120): the final or last age.

Miteshiro ritual (p.90): a purification ritual used in Ómotokyó for the purpose of spiritual and physical healing.

Óbutsu myógó (p.123): union of government and religion.

Okiyome (p.90): purification ritual used in Mahikari and believed to bring spiritual and physical healing.

Omitama (p.67): divine jewel.

Reisa (p.27): spirit investigation.

Rónin (p.104): masterless samurai.

Ryóbu-shintó (p.103): an amalgam of Buddhism and Shinto.

Satori (p.8): enlightenment.

Shakubuku (p.42): coercive persuasion.

Shenfu (p.107): spiritual father.

Shinsókan (p.58): a form of prayerful meditation.

Shinkóshúkyó (p.1): 'new' religion.

Shinshinshúkyó (p.6): 'new new' religion.

Theravada (p.17): early Buddhism which continues to be practised in Ceylon, Burma, Siam and Cambodia and sometimes referred to as 'Hinayana'.

Tianzhu (p.107): Lord of the heavens.

Tsuki-hi (p.103): moon-sun God.

Zadakandai (p.61): system of counselling groups.

Zen (p.8): Buddhist sect with three main divisions in Japan, **Sótó**, **Rinzai** and **Óbaku**. The most important practice is meditation.

Select Bibliography

Blacker, C., 'Millenarian Aspects of New Religions in Japan' in D.H. Shively (ed) *Tradition and Modernization in Japanese Culture*, Princeton: Princeton University Press, 1971.

———, *Catalpa Bow: A Study of Shamanistic Practices in Japan*, London: George Allen &Unwin, 1975.

Davis, W., *Dojo: Magic and Exorcism in Modern Japan*, Stanford, Cal: Stanford University Press, 1980.

Davis, Winston, *Japanese Religion and Society: Paradigms of Structure and Change*. New York. State University of New York Press, 1993.

Dore, R.P., *City Life in Japan: A Study of a Tokyo Ward*. Berkeley, Cal.: University of California Press, 1958.

Earhart, H.B., *The New Religions of Japan: A Bibliography of Western Language Materials*, Ann Arbor, Michigan: Centre for Japanese Studies, 1983.

———, *Gedatsukai and Religion in Contemporary Japan*, Bloomington, Ind.: University of Indiana Press, 1989.

Ellwood Jr., R.S., *The Eagle and the Rising Sun*, Philadelphia: Westminster Press, 1974.

Fields, R., *When the Swans Came to the Lake*, Boulder, CO: Shambala, 1986.

Hardacre, H., *Kurozumikyo and the New Religions of Japan*, Princeton, NJ: Princeton University Press, 1986.

Kitano, H.H.L., *The Japanese Americans: the Evolution of a Subculture*, Englewood Cliffs, NJ: Prentice Hall, 1976.

McFarland, H.N., *The Rush Hour of the Gods*, New York: Macmillan, 1967.

Gordon Melton, J., *Encyclopedia of American Religions*, Detroit: Gale Research Company, 4th edition, 1993.

Nabutaka, I. (ed), *New Religions. Contemporary Papers in Japanese Religion (2)*, Tokyo: Kokogaguin University, 1991.

Offner, C.B. and Straelen, H. van, *Modern Japanese Religions*, Tokyo: Enderle, 1963.

Picone, M., Buddhist Popular Manuals and the Contemporary Commercialization of Religion in Japan in J. Henry and J. Webber (eds) *Interpreting Japanese Society: Anthropological Approaches*. Oxford: JASO, 1986.

Reader, I., *Religion in Contemporary Japan*, Houndsmill, Basingstoke

and London: Macmillan, 1991.
—— et al, *Japanese Religions, Past & Present*, Folkestone: Japan Library, 1993.
Smith, R.J., Ancestor Worship in Contemporary Japan. Stanford, Cal.: Stanford University Press, 1974.
Sutherland, S.R. and Clarke, Peter (eds), *The Study of Religion, Traditional and New Religions*, London: Routledge, 1991.
Thomsen, H., *The New Religions of Japan*, Rutland, Vermont: Charles E. Tuttle Company, 1963.
Wilson, B.R., *A Time to Chant*, Sōka Gakkai. *Buddhists in Britain*, Oxford: Oxford University Press, 1994.
Wilson, B.R., *Religious Sects*. London/New York. Weidenfeld and Nicolson and McGraw-Hill. 1971.

Index